Faith
In All
Its
Splendor

Faith
In All
It's
Splendor

Charles Spurgeon

Sovereign Grace Publishers, Inc.
P.O. Box 4998
Lafayette, IN 47903
2001

*Printed In the United States of America
By Lightning Source, Inc.*

CONTENTS

A LECTURE FOR LITTLE-FAITH

"We are bound to thank God always for you, brethren, as it is meet, because that your faith groweth exceedingly, and the charity of every one of you all toward each other aboundeth."–2 Thessalonians i. 3.

"We are bound to thank God always for you, brethren, as it is meet." Whether we shall praise God or not, is not left to our opinion. Although the commandment saith not, "Thou shalt praise the Lord," yet praise is God's most righteous due; and every man, as a partaker of God's bounty, and especially every Christian, is bound to praise God, as it is meet. It is true, we have no authoritative rubric for daily praise; we have no commandment left on record specially prescribing certain hours of song and thanksgiving; but still the law written upon the heart, teacheth us with divine authority that it is right to praise God; and this unwritten mandate hath as much power and authority about it, as if it had been recorded on the tables of stone, or handed to us from the top of thundering Sinai. The Christian's duty is to praise God. Think not ye who are always mourning that ye are guiltless in that respect; imagine not that ye can discharge your duty to your God without songs of praise. It is your duty to praise Him. You are bound by the bonds of His love as long as you live to bless His name. It is meet and comely that you should do so. It is not only a pleasurable exercise, but it is the absolute duty of the Christian life to praise God. This is taught us in the text,–"We are bound to thank God always for you, brethren, as it is meet." Let not your harps then hang upon the willows, ye mourning children of the Lord. It is your duty to strike them and bring forth their loudest music. It is sinful in you to cease from praising God; you are blessed in order that you may bless Him; and if you do not praise God you are not bringing forth the fruit, which He as the divine husbandman, may well expect at your hands. Go forth then, ye sons of God, and chant His praise. With every morning's dawn lift up your notes of thanksgiving; and every evening let the setting sun be followed with your song. Girdle the earth with your praises; surround it with an atmosphere of melody, so shall God Himself look down from heaven and accept your praises as like in kind, though not equal in degree, to the praises of cherubim and seraphim.

It seems, however, that the apostle Paul in this instance exercised praise not for himself but for others, for the church at Thessalonica. If any of you should in ignorance ask the question why it was that Paul should take so deep an interest in the salvation of these saints, and in their growth in faith, I would remind you, that this is a secret known only to the men who have brought forth and nourished children, and therefore love them. The apostle Paul had founded the church at Thessalonica; most of these people were his spiritual offsprings; by the words of his mouth, attended by the power of the Spirit, they had been brought out of the darkness into marvellous light; and they who have had spiritual children, who have brought many sons unto God, can tell you that there is an interest felt by a spiritual father, that is not to be equalled even by the tender affection of a mother towards her babe. "Aye," said the apostle, "I have been tender over you as a nursing father;" and in another place he says he had "travailed in birth," for their souls. This is a secret not known to the hireling minister. Only he whom God hath Himself ordained and thrust forth into the work, only he who has had his tongue touched with a live coal from off the altar, can tell you what it is to agonize for men's souls before they are converted, and what it is to rejoice with joy unspeakable, and full of glory, when the travail of their souls is seen in the salvation of God's elect.

7

And now, beloved, having thus given you two thoughts which seemed to me to arise naturally from the text, I shall repair at once to the object of this morning's discourse. The apostle thanks God that the faith of the Thessalonians had grown exceedingly. Leaving out the rest of the text, I shall direct your attention this morning to the subject of growing in faith. Faith hath degrees.

In the first place, I shall endeavour to notice the inconveniences of little faith; secondly, the means of promoting its growth; and thirdly, a certain high attainment, unto which faith will assuredly grow, if we diligently water and cultivate it.

I. In the first place, THE INCONVENIENCES OF LITTLE FAITH. When faith first commences in the soul, it is like a grain of mustard seed, of which the Saviour said it was the least of all seeds; but as God the Holy Spirit is pleased to bedew it with the sacred moisture of His grace, it germinates and grows and begins to spread, until at last it becomes a great tree. To use another figure: when faith commences in the soul it is simply looking unto Jesus, and perhaps even then there are so many clouds of doubts, and so much dimness of the eye, that we have need for the light of the Spirit to shine upon the cross before we are able even so much as to see it. When faith grows a little, it rises from looking to Christ to coming to Christ. He who stood afar off and looked to the cross by-and-bye plucks up courage, and getting heart to himself, he runneth up to the cross; or perhaps he doth not run, but hath to be drawn before he can so much as creep thither, and even then it is with a limping gait that he draweth nigh to Christ the Saviour. But that done, faith goeth a little farther: it layeth hold on Christ; it begins to see Him in His excellency, and appropriates Him, in some degree conceives Him to be a real Christ and a real Saviour, and is convinced of His suitability. And when it hath done as much as that, it goeth further; it leaneth on Christ; it leaneth on its beloved; casteth all the burden of its cares, sorrows, and griefs upon that blessed shoulder, and permitteth all its sins to be swallowed up in the great red sea of the Saviour's blood. And faith can then go further still; for having seen and ran towards Him, and laid hold upon Him, and having leaned upon Him, faith in the next place puts in a humble, but a sure and certain claim to all that Christ is and to all that He has wrought; and then, trusting alone in this, appropriating all this to itself, faith mounteth to full assurance; and out of heaven there is no state more rapturous and blessed. But, as I have observed at the beginning, faith is but very small, and there are some Christians who never get out of little faith all the while they are here. You notice in John Bunyan's *Pilgrim's Progress,* how many Little-faith's he mentions. There is our old friend Ready-to-halt, who went all the way to the celestial city on crutches, but left them when he went into the river Jordan. Then there is little Feeble-mind, who carried his feeble mind with him all the way to the banks of the river and then left it, and ordered it to be buried in a dunghill that none might inherit it. Then there is Mr. Fearing, too, who used to stumble over a straw, and was always frightened if he saw a drop of rain, because he thought the floods of heaven were let loose upon him. And you remember Mr. Despondency and Miss Much-afraid, who were so long locked up in the dungeon of Giant Despair, that they were almost starved to death, and there was little left of them but skin and bone; and poor Mr. Feeble-mind, who had been taken into the cave of Giant Slay-good who was about to eat him, when Great-heart came to his deliverance. John Bunyan was a very wise man. He has put a great many of those characters, in his book, because there are a great many of them. He has not left us with one Mr. Ready-to-halt, but he has given us seven or eight graphic characters because he himself in his own time has been one of them, and he had known many others who had walked in the same path. I doubt not I have a very large congregation this morning of this very class of persons. Now let me notice the inconveniences of little faith.

The first inconvenience of little faith is that while it is very sure of heaven it very seldom thinks so. Little-faith is quite as sure of heaven as Great-faith. When Jesus Christ counts up His jewels at the last day he will take to Himself the little pearls as well as the great ones. If a diamond be never so small yet it is precious because it is a diamond. So will faith, be it never so little, if it be true faith, Christ will never lose even the smallest jewel of his crown. Little-faith is always sure of heaven, because the name of Little-faith is in the book of eternal life. Little-faith was chosen of God before the foundation of the world. Little-faith was bought with the blood of Christ; aye, and he cost as much as Great-faith. "For every man a shekel" was the price of redemption. Every man, whether great or small, prince or peasant, had to redeem himself with a shekel. Christ has bought all, both little and great, with the same most precious blood. Little-faith is always sure of heaven, for God has begun the good work in him and He will carry it on. God loves him and He will love him unto the end. God has provided a crown for him, and He will not allow the crown to hang there without a head; He has erected for him a mansion in heaven, and He will not allow the mansion to stand untenanted for ever. Little-faith is always safe, but he very seldom knows it. If you meet him he is sometimes afraid of hell; very often that the wrath of God abideth on him. He will tell you that the country on the other side the flood can never belong to a worm so base as he. Sometimes it is because he feels himself so unworthy, another time it is because the things of God are too good to be true, he says, or he cannot think they can be true to such an one as he. Sometimes he is afraid he is not elect; another time he fears that he has not been called aright, that he has not come to Christ aright. Another time his fears are that he will not hold on to the end, that he shall not be able to persevere; and if you kill a thousand of his fears he is sure to have another host by to-morrow; for unbelief is one of those things that you cannot destroy. "It hath," saith Bunyan, "as many lives as a cat"; you may kill it over and over again, but it still lives. It is only one of those ill weeds that sleep in the soil even after it has been burned, and it only needs a little encouragement to grow again. Now Great-faith is sure of heaven, and he knows it. He climbs Pisgah's top, and views the landscape o'er; he drinks in the mysteries of paradise even before he enters within the pearly gates. He sees the streets that are paved with gold; he beholds the wall of the city, the foundations whereof are precious stones; he hears the mystic music of the glorified, and begins to smell on earth the perfumes of heaven. But poor Little-faith can scarcely look at the sun; he very seldom sees the light; he gropes in the valley, and while all is safe he always thinks himself unsafe. That is one of the disadvantages of Little-faith.

Another disadvantage is that Little-faith, while always having grace enough (for that is Little-faith's promise, "My grace shall be sufficient for thee") yet never thinks he has grace enough. He will have quite enough grace to carry him to heaven; and Great-heart won't have any more. The greatest saint, when he entered heaven, found that he went in with an empty wallet: he had eaten his last crust of bread when he got there. The manna ceased when the children of Israel entered into Canaan; they had none to carry with them there: they began to eat the corn of the land when the manna of the wilderness had ceased. But Little-faith is always afraid that he has not grace enough. You see him in trouble. "Oh!" says he, "I shall never be able to hold my head above water." Blessed be God he never can sink. If you see him in prosperity, he is afraid he shall be intoxicated with pride; that he shall turn aside like Balaam. If you meet him attacked by an enemy, he is scarcely able to say three words for himself, and he lets the enemy exact upon him. If you find him fighting the battle of the Lord Jesus Christ he holds his sword tight enough, good man, but he has not much strength in his arm to bring his sword down with might. He can do but little, for he is afraid that God's grace will not be sufficient for him. Great-faith, on the other hand, can shake the world. What cares he about trouble, trial, or duty?

"He that helped him bears him through,
And makes him more than conqueror too."

He would face an army single-handed, if God commanded him; and "with the jawbone of an ass, he would slay heaps upon heaps, and thousands of men." There is no fear of his lacking strength. He can do all things, or can bear all sufferings, for his Lord is there. Come what may, his arm is always sufficient for him; he treads down his enemy, and his cry every day is like the shout of Deborah, "O! my soul, thou hast trodden down strength." Little-faith treads down strength too, but he does not know it. He kills his enemies, but has not eyesight enough to see the slain. He often hits so hard that his foemen retreat, but he thinks they are there still. He conjures up a thousand phantoms, and when he has routed his real enemies he makes others, and trembles at the phantoms which he has himself made. Little-faith will assuredly find that his garments will not wax old, that his shoes shall be iron and brass, and that as his day is so shall his strength be; but all the way he will be murmuring, because he thinks his garments will grow old, that his feet will be blistered and sore; and he is terrified lest the day should be too heavy for him, and that the evil of the day shall more than counterbalance his grace. Aye, it is an inconvenient thing to have little faith, for little faith perverts everything into sorrow and grief.

Again, there is a sad inconvenience about Little-faith, namely, that if Little-faith be sorely tempted to sin, he is apt to fall. Strong-faith can well contest with the enemy. Satan comes along, and says, "All these things will I give thee if thou wilt fall down and worship me." "Nay," we say, "thou canst not give us all these things, for they are ours already." "Nay," says he, "but ye are poor, naked and miserable." "Aye," say we to him, "but still these things are ours, and it is good for us to be poor, good for us to be without earthly goods, or else our Father would give them to us." "Oh," says Satan, "you deceive yourselves; you have no portion in these things; but if you will serve me, then I will make you rich and happy here." Strong-faith says, "Serve thee, thou fiend! Avaunt! Dost thou offer me silver?—behold God giveth me gold. Dost thou say to me, 'I will give thee this if thou disobey?'—fool that thou art! I have a thousand times as great wages for my obedience as thou canst offer for my disobedience." But when Satan meets Little-faith, he says to him, "If thou be the Son of God cast thyself down"; and poor Little-faith is so afraid that he is not a son of God that he is very apt to cast himself down upon the supposition. "There," says Satan, "I will give thee all this if thou wilt disobey." Little-faith says, "I am not quite sure that I am a child of God, that I have a portion among them that are sanctified"; and he is very apt to fall into sin by reason of the littleness of his faith. Yet at the same time I must observe that I have seen some Little-faiths who are far less apt to fall into sin than others. They have been so cautious that they dared not put one foot before the other, because they were afraid they should put it awry: they scarcely even dared to open their lips, but they prayed, "O Lord, open Thou my lips"; afraid that they should let a wrong word out, if they were to speak; always alarmed lest they should be falling into sin unconsciously, having a very tender conscience. Well, I like people of this sort. I have sometimes thought that Little-faith holds tighter by Christ than any other. For a man who is very near drowning is sure to clutch the plank all the tighter with the grasp of a drowning man, which tightens and becomes more clenched the more his hope is decreased. Well, beloved, Little-faith may be kept from falling, but this is the fruit of tender conscience and not of little faith. Careful walking is not the result of little faith; it may go with it, and so may keep Little-faith from perishing, but little faith is in itself a dangerous thing, laying us open to innumerable temptations, and taking away very much of our strength to resist them. "The joy of the Lord is your strength"; and if that joy ceases you become weak and very apt to turn aside. Beloved, you who are Little-faiths, I tell you it is inconvenient for you always to remain so; for you have many nights and few days. Your years are like Norwegian years—very long winters and very short summers. You have many howlings, but very little of shouting; you are often playing upon the pipe of mourning, but very seldom sounding the trump of exultation. I would to God you could change your notes a little. Why should the children of a King go mourning all their days? It is not the Lord's will that you should be always sorrowful. "Rejoice in the Lord always, and again I say rejoice." Oh, ye that have been fasting, anoint your heads and wash your faces, that ye appear not unto men to fast. Oh, ye that are sad in heart, "Light is sown for the righteous, and gladness for the upright in heart." Therefore, rejoice for ye shall praise Him. Say unto yourselves,

"Why art thou cast down, O my soul, and why art thou disquieted within me? Hope thou in God, for I shall yet praise Him, who is the light of my countenance and my God."

II. Having thus noticed the inconveniences and disadvantages of little faith, let me give you A FEW RULES WITH REGARD TO THE WAY OF STRENGTHENING IT. If you would have your little faith grow into great faith, you must feed it well. Faith is a feeding grace. It does not ask you to give it the things that are seen, but it does ask you to give it the promise of the things that are not seen, which are eternal. Thou tellest me thou hast little faith. I ask thee whether thou art given to the meditation of God's Word, whether thou hast studied the promises, whether thou art wont to carry one of those sacred things about with thee every day? Dost thou reply, "No?" Then, I tell thee, I do not wonder at thine unbelief. He who deals largely with the promises, will, under grace, very soon find that there is great room for believing them. Get a promise, beloved, every day, and take it with you wherever you go; mark it, learn it, and inwardly digest it. Don't do as some men do—who think it a Christian duty to read a chapter every morning, and they read one as long as your arm without understanding it at all; but take out some choice text, and pray the Lord during the day to break it up in your mind. Do as Luther says: "When I get hold of a promise," says he, "I look upon it as I would a fruit tree. I think—there hang the fruits above my head, and if I would get them I must shake the tree to and fro." So I take a promise and meditate upon it; I shake it to and fro, and sometimes the mellow fruit falls into my hand, at other times the fruit is less ready to fall, but I never leave off till I get it. I shake, shake all the day long; I turn the text over and over again, and at last the pomegranate droppeth down, and my soul is comforted with apples, for it was sick of love. Do that, Christian. Deal much with the promises; have much commerce with these powders of the merchant: there is a rich perfume in every promise of God; take it, it is an alabaster box, break it by meditation, and the sweet scent of faith shall be shed abroad in your house.

Again, prove the promise, and in that way you will get your faith strengthened. When you are at any time placed in distress, take a promise and see whether it is true. Suppose you are very near lacking bread; take this promise, "Thy bread shall be given thee, thy water shall be sure." Rise up in the morning when nothing is in the cupboard, and say, "I will see whether God will keep this promise"; and if He does, do not forget it; set it down in your book; make a mark in your Bible against it. Do as the old woman did, who put T and P against the promise, and told her minister that it meant "tried and proved"; so that when she was again in distress, she could not help believing. Have you been exercised by Satan? There is a promise that says, "Resist the devil, and he will flee from you." Take that and prove it, and when you have proved it, make a mark against it and say, "This I know is true, for I have proved it to be so." There is nothing in the world that can confirm faith like proof. "What I want," said one, "is facts." And so it is with the Christian. What he wants is a fact to make him believe. The older you grow the stronger your faith ought to become, for you have so many more facts with which to buttress your faith, and compel you to believe in God. Only think of a man who has come to be seventy years of age, what a pile of evidence he could accumulate if he kept a note of all God's providential goodness and all His loving kindness. You do not wonder when you hear a man, the hairs of whose head are white with the sunlight of heaven, get up and say, "These fifty years have I served God, and He has never forsaken me. I can bear willing testimony to His faithfulness; not one good thing hath failed of all that the Lord hath promised; all hath come to pass." Now we, who are young beginners, must not expect that our faith will be so strong as it will be in years to come. Every instance of God's love should make us believe Him more; and as each promise passes by, and we can see the fulfillment of it at the heels thereof, we must be compelled and constrained to say, that God has kept so many of these promises and will keep them unto the end. But the worst of it is that we forget them all, and so we begin to have grey hairs sprinkled on our heads, and we have no more faith than when we began, because we have forgotten God's repeated answers, and though He has fulfilled the promise we have suffered it to lie

11

buried in forgetfulness.

Another plan I would recommend for the strengthening of your faith, though not so excellent as the last, is to associate yourselves with godly and much-tried men. It is astonishing how young believers will get their faith refreshed by talking with old and advanced Christians. Perhaps you are in great doubt and distress; you run off to an old brother, and you say, "Oh my dear friend, I am afraid I am not a child of God at all, I am in such deep distress; I have had blasphemous thoughts cast into my heart; if I were a child of God I should never feel like that." The old man smiles, and says, "Ah! you have not gone very far on the road to heaven, or else you would know better. Why I am the subject of these thoughts very often. Old as I am, and though I hope I have enjoyed the full assurance for a long time, yet there are seasons when if I could have heaven for a grain of faith, I could not think heaven was mine, for I could not find so much as a grain in me, though it is there." And he will tell you what dangers he has passed, and of the sovereign love that kept him; of the temptations that threatened to ensnare him, and of the wisdom that guided his feet; and he will tell you of his own weakness and God's omnipotence; and of his own emptiness, and of God's fulness; of his own changeableness, and God's immutability; and if after talking with such a man you don't believe, surely you are sinful indeed; for "out of the mouth of two witnesses, the whole shall be established," but when there are many such who can bear testimony to God, it would be foul sin indeed if we were to doubt Him.

Another way whereby you may obtain increase of faith is to labour to get as much as possible free from self. I have striven with all my might to attain the position of perfect indifference of all men. I have found at times, if I have been much praised in company, and if my heart has given way a little, and I have taken notice of it, and felt pleased, that the very next time I was censured and abused I felt the censure and abuse very keenly, for the very fact that I took the praise rendered me liable to lay hold upon the censure. So that I have always tried, especially of late, to take no more notice of man's praise than of his censure, but to fix my heart simply upon this—I know that I have a right motive in what I attempt to do; I am conscious that I endeavour to serve God with a single eye to His glory, and therefore it is not for me to take praise from man nor censure, but to stand independently upon the one rock of right doing. Now the same thing will apply to you. Perhaps you find yourself full of virtue and grace one day, and the devil flatters you: "Ah! you are a bright Christian; you might join the church now, you would be quite an honour to it; see how well you are prospering." And unconsciously to yourself you believe the sound of that syren music, and you half believe that really you are growing rich in grace. Well, the next day you find yourself very low indeed in godly matters. Perhaps you fall into some sin, and now the devil says, "Ah! now you are no child of God; look at your sins." Beloved, the only way in which you can maintain your faith is to live above the praise of self and the censure of self; to live simply upon the blood and merits of our Lord Jesus Christ. He who can say in the midst of all his virtues "These are but dross and dung; my hope is fixed on nothing less than Jesus Christ's finished sacrifice"—such a man, when sins prevail, will find his faith remain constant, for he will say "I once was full of virtue and then I did not trust in myself, and now I have none still do I trust in my Saviour, for change as I may, He changeth not. If I had to depend on myself in the least degree then it would be up and down, up and down; but since I rely on what Christ has done, since He is the unbuttressed pillar of my hope, then come what may my soul doth rest secure, confident in faith. Faith will never be weak if self be weak, but when self is strong, faith cannot be strong; for self is very much like what the gardener calls the sucker at the bottom of the tree, which never bears fruit but only sucks away the nourishment from the tree itself. Now, self is that sucker which sucks away the nourishment from faith, and you must cut it up or else your faith will always be little faith, and you will have difficulty in maintaining any comfort in your soul.

But, perhaps the only way in which most men get their faith increased is by great trouble. We don't grow strong in faith on sunshiny days. It is only in strong weather that a man gets faith. Faith is not an attainment that droppeth like the gentle dew from heaven; it generally comes in the whirlwind and the storm. Look at the old oaks: how is it that they have become so deeply rooted in the earth? Ask the March winds and they will tell you. It was not the April shower that did it, or the sweet May sunshine, but it was March's rough wind, the blustering month of old Boreas shaking the tree to and fro and causing its roots to bind themselves around the rocks. So must it be with us. We don't make great soldiers in the barracks at home; they must be made amidst flying shot and thundering cannon. We cannot expect to make good sailors on the Serpentine; they must be made far away on the deep sea, where the wild winds howl, and the thunders roll like drums in the march of the God of armies. Storms and tempests are the things that make men tough and hardy mariners. They see the works of the Lord and His wonders in the deep. So with Christians. Great-faith must have great trials. Mr. Great-heart would never have been Mr. Great-heart if he had not once been Mr. Great-trouble. Valiant-for-truth would never have put to flight those foes, and have been so valiant, if the foes had not first attacked him. So with us: we must expect great troubles before we shall attain to much faith.

Then he who would have great faith, must exercise what he has. I should not like to-morrow to go and shoe horses, or to make horse shoes on an anvil. I am sure my arm would ache in the first hour with lifting the heavy hammer and banging it down so many times. Whatever the time might be, I should not be able to keep time. The reason why the blacksmith's arm does not tire is, because he is used to it. He has kept at it all day long these many years, till there's an arm for you! He turns up his sleeve and shows you the strong sinew that never tires, so strong has it become by use. Do you want to get your faith strong? Use it. You lazy lie-a bed Christians, that go up to your churches and chapels, and take your seats, and hear our sermons, and talk about getting good, but never think about doing good; ye that are letting hell fill beneath you, and yet are too idle to stretch out your hands to pluck brands from the eternal burning; ye that see sin running down your streets, yet can never put so much as your foot to turn or stem the current, I wonder not that you have to complain of the littleness of your faith. It ought to be little; you do but little, and why should God give you more strength than you mean to use. Strong faith must always be an exercised faith; and he that dares not exercise the faith he has shall not have more. "Take away from him the one talent and give it to him that hath, because he did not put it out to usury." In Mr. Whitefield's life, you do not often find him complaining of want of faith; or if he did, it was when he only preached nine times in a week; he never complained when he preached sixteen times. Read Grimshaw's life: you do not often find him troubled with despondency when he preached twenty-four times in seven days; it was only when he was growing a little idle and only preached twelve times. Keep always at it, and all at it, and there is not much fear of your faith becoming weak. It is with our faith as with boys in the winter time. There they go round the fire, rubbing and chafing their hands to keep the blood in circulation, and almost fighting each other to see which shall sit on the fire and get warm. At last the father comes, and says, "Boys, this won't do; you will never get warm by these artificial means; run out and do some work." Then they all go out, and they come in again with a ruddy hue in their cheeks, their hands no longer tingle, and they say, "Well, father, we didn't think it half so warm as it is." So must it be with you: you must set to work if you would have your faith grow strong and warm. True, your works won't save you; but faith without works is dead, frozen to death; but faith with works groweth to a red heat of fervency and to the strength of stability. Go and teach in the Sunday-school, or go and catch seven or eight poor ragged children; go and visit the poor old woman in her hovel; go and see some poor dying creatures in the back streets of our great city, and you will say, "Dear me! how wonderfully my faith is refreshed just by doing something." You have been watering yourself whilst you were watering others.

Now my last advice shall be this—the best way to get your full strength is to have communion with Christ. If you commune with Christ, you cannot be unbelieving. When

His left hand is under my head, and His right hand doth embrace me, I cannot doubt. When my Beloved sits at His table, and He brings me into His banqueting house, and His banner over me is His love, then indeed I do believe. When I feast with Him, my unbelief is abashed and hides its head. Speak, ye that have been led in the green pastures, and have been made to lie down by the still waters; ye who have seen His rod and His staff, and hope to see them even when you walk through the valley of the shadow of death; speak, ye that have sat at His feet with Mary, or laid your head upon His bosom with the well-beloved John; have you not found when you have been near to Christ your faith has grown strong, and when you have been far away, then your faith has become weak? It is impossible to look Christ in the face and then doubt Him. When you cannot see Him, then you doubt Him; but if you live in fellowship with Him, you are like the ewe lambs of Nathan's parable, for you lie in His bosom, and eat from His table, and drink from His cup. You must believe when your Beloved speaks unto you, and says, "Rise up My love, My fair one, and come away." There is no hesitation then; you must rise from the lowlands of your doubt up to the hills of assurance.

III. And now, in conclusion, there is A CERTAIN HIGH ATTAINMENT TO WHICH FAITH MAY, IF DILIGENTLY CULTIVATED, CERTAINLY ATTAIN. Can a man's faith grow so strong that he will never afterwards doubt at all? I reply, no. He who has the strongest faith will have sorrowful intervals of despondency. I suppose there has scarcely ever been a Christian who has not, at some time or other, had the most painful doubts concerning his acceptance in the Beloved. All God's children will have paroxysms of doubt even though they may be usually strong in faith. Again, may a man so cultivate his faith that he may be infallibly sure that he is a child of God—so sure that he has made no mistake—so sure that all the doubts and fears which may be thrust upon him may not be able at that time to get an advantage over him? I answer, yes, decidedly he may. A man may, in this life, be as sure of his acceptance in the Beloved as he is of his own existence. Nay, he not only may, but there are some of us who have enjoyed this precious state and privilege for years; we do not mean for years together—our peace has been interrupted, we have now and then been subjected to doubts; but I have known some—I knew one especially, who said that for thirty years he had enjoyed almost invariably a full sense of his acceptance in Christ. "I have had," he said, "very often a sense of sin, but I have had with that a sense of the power of the blood of Christ; I have now and then for a little time had a great despondency, but still I may say, taking it as a general rule, that for thirty years I have enjoyed the fullest assurance of my acceptance in the Beloved." I trust a large portion of God's people can say that for months and years they have not had to sing

"Tis a point I long to know."

But they can say, "I know whom I have believed, and am persuaded that He is able to keep that which I have committed to Him." I will try to depict the state of the Christian; he may be as poor as poverty can make him, but he is rich; he has no thought with regard to the morrow, for the morrow shall take thought for the things of itself. He casts himself upon the providence of God; he believes that He who clothes the lilies, and feeds the ravens, will not allow His children to go starving or barefooted. He has but little concern as to his temporal estate; he folds his arms and floats down the stream of providence singing all the way; whether he float by mud bank, dark, dreary, and noxious, or by palace fair and valley pleasant, he alters not his position; he neither moves nor struggles; he has no will nor wish which way to swim, his only desire being to "lie passive in God's hand, and know no will but His." When the storm flies over his head he finds Christ to be a shelter from the tempest; when the heat is hot he finds Christ to be the shadow of a great rock in a weary land. He just casts his anchor down deep into the sea, and when the wind blows, he sleeps; hurricanes may come about his ears, the masts creak, and every timber seems to be strained and every nail to start from its place, but there he sleeps;

Christ is at the helm; he says, "My anchor is within the vail, I know it will keep its hold." The earth shakes beneath his feet; but he says, "Though the earth be removed and mountains be cast into the sea, yet will not we fear, for God is our refuge and strength, and a very present help in time of trouble." Ask him about his eternal interests, and he tells you that his only confidence is in Christ, and that die when he may, he knows he shall stand boldly at the last great day clothed in his Saviour's righteousness. He speaks very confidently though never boastingly; though he has no time to dance the giddy dance of presumption, he stands firmly on the rock of confidence. Perhaps you think he is proud—ah! he is a humble man; he lies low before the cross, but not before you; he can look you boldly in the face, and tell you that Christ is able to keep that which he has committed to Him. He knows that —

"His honour is engaged to save
   The meanest of His sheep,
All that His heavenly Father gave,
   His hands securely keep."

And die when he may he can lay his head upon the pillow of promise, and breathe his life out on the Saviour's breast without a struggle or a murmur, crying—"Victory," in the arms of death; challenging Death to produce his sting, and demanding of the grave its victory. Such is the effect of strong faith; I repeat, the weakest in the world, by diligent cultivation may attain to it. Only seek the refreshing influence of the Divine Spirit, and walk in Christ's commandments, and live near to Him; and ye that are dwarfs, like Zaccheus, shall become as giants; the hyssop on the wall shall start up into the dignity of the cedar in Lebanon, and ye that fly before your enemies shall yet be able to chase a thousand, and two of you shall put ten thousand to flight. May the Lord so enable His poor little ones so to grow!

As for those of you who have no faith in Christ, let me remind you of one sad thing—namely, that "without faith it is impossible to please God." If thou hast not put thy trust in Christ, then God is angry with thee every day. "If thou turn not He will whet His sword, for He hath bent His Bow and made it ready." I beseech thee, cast thyself on Christ; He is worthy of thy trust; there is none other to trust to; He is willing to receive thee; He invites thee; He shed His blood for thee; He intercedes for thee. Believe on Him, for thus His promise runs, "He that believeth and is baptized shall be saved." Do both of these things. Believe on Him, and then profess thy faith in baptism; and the Lord bless thee, and hold thee to the end, and make thee to increase exceedingly in faith, to the glory of God. May the Lord add His blessing!

SEEING JESUS

"We see Jesus."—Hebrews ii. 9.

The apostle in this place does not claim to have seen the Lord in the flesh, although he boasts in another passage that he has done so, and asserts it as one of the proofs of his apostleship. He is not, indeed, in this text referring to any seeing of the Lord by mortal eyes at all; he is speaking of faith: he means a spiritual sight of the Lord Jesus Christ. The point to which I shall have to draw your attention this evening is, that sight is very frequently used in Scripture as a metaphor, an illustration, a symbol, to set forth what faith is. Faith is the eye of the soul. It is the act of looking unto Jesus. In that act, by which we are saved, we look unto Him and are saved from the very ends of the earth. We look to Him, and we find salvation.

15

So far as seeing with these natural eyes of ours is concerned, it is the very opposite of faith. We have heard people speak as though they wished they had lived in the Saviour's day, and could have seen Him. It must have been a great privilege to those who were spiritually-minded, but it was no privilege (as they know now, alas! to their cost), to those who were spiritually blind; for many of those who saw our Lord, and heard Him preach, rose up in wrath, to thrust Him out of the synagogue, and cast Him down the brow of the hill. Instead of being overawed by His sweet majesty, or won by that love which sat upon His brow, they scoffed at Him, said He was a Samaritan, and had a devil, and was mad. Even the sight of Jesus Christ upon the cross did not convert the men that stood there, but they thrust out the tongue, and called Him by ignominious titles, and increased the sorrows of His death by their scornful expressions. To see Jesus Christ with the natural eye is nothing, my brethren; for this shall be the lot of all men, and they shall look on Him whom they have pierced, and shall weep and wail because of Him. The sight of Him, when He shall come in the latter days to judge the earth in righteousness, will be the source of terror to the wicked, so that there can be no kind of benefit, certainly no saving blessing, from such a sight of Jesus Christ with the eyes as will be afforded even to lost spirits.

The apostle is speaking of the spiritual eye here. He is speaking of that mental vision which God affords to those who have had their eyes anointed with heavenly eye-salve by the Holy Spirit, that they may see, and our business to-night is, first of all, to show why faith is so frequently compared to the sense of sight.

1. Let us, in the first place, give our attention for a few minutes to THE REASON WHY FAITH IS COMPARED TO THE SIGHT.

Is not sight, in many respects, the noblest of all the senses? To be deprived of any of our senses is a great loss, but perhaps the greatest deprivation of all, is the loss of sight. Certainly, whatever may be the degree of pain that may follow the loss of any other sense, they who lose sight, lose the noblest of human faculties.

For observe, in the first place, that sight is marvellously quick. How wondrously fast and far it travels! It does not take you an hour to make a journey from one part of the country to another by your eye. You are on a mountain, and you can see fifty or a hundred miles, as the case may be, and you see it by the simplest opening of the eye. It is all there. Your thought is flashed away in an instant, in the twinkling of your eye. Standing on some of the Alpine summits, you look far and wide, and see lakes spread at a distance beneath your feet, and far away, there is a range of black mountains, or of hills clothed with snows; you know they are perhaps two hundred miles distant, but in a moment you are there. So quick does the sense of sight travel, that we go to the moon or to the sun without knowing that any space of time is taken up by our eyes travelling there; and those remote stars which the astronomers tell us are so distant that they can scarcely compute how far off they are, yet mine eye travels to them in a second of time, when I gaze upon the starry firmament—so quickly does sight travel—and equally rapid is the action of faith. Brethren, we know not where heaven may be—where the state, the place called "heaven" is, but faith takes us there in contemplation in a single moment. We cannot tell when the Lord may come; it may not be for centuries yet, but faith steps over the distance in a moment, and sees Him coming in the clouds of heaven, and hears the trump of resurrection. It would be very difficult, indeed it would be impossible for us to travel backward in any other chariot than that of faith, for it is faith which helps us to see the creation of the world, when the morning stars sang together, and the sons of God shouted for joy. Faith enables us to walk in the garden with our first parents, and to witness the scene when God promised that the seed of woman should bruise the serpent's head. Faith makes us familiar with patriarchs, and gives us to see the troubles and trials of kings. Faith takes us to Calvary's summit, and we stand and see our Saviour as plainly as His mother when she stood sorrowfully at the cross-foot. We this day can fly back to the solemn day of Pentecost, and feel as if we could hear the mighty rushing wind, and see the cloven tongues sitting upon the chosen company, so swiftly does faith travel. And, best of all, in one moment faith can take a sinner out of a state of death into a state of life, can lift him from damnation into salvation, can remove him from the land of the shadow of death, where he sat in affliction and irons, and give him the oil of joy for mourning, and the garments of praise for the spirit of heaviness. O sinner, you can get at Christ in a moment of time. No sooner has your heart trusted Jesus, than you are with Him, united to Him. You need not say, "Where is He? I would fly to heaven if I could but find Him, or dive under hell's profoundest wave if I could but embrace Him." He is nigh to thee, so nigh that the act of faith conveys thee at once into His bosom, plunges thee into His blood, clothes thee with His righteousness, adopts thee into the family of God, and makes thee co-heir with Jesus Christ, joint-heir with Him in all things. See, then, why faith is like sight, because of the rapidity of its operations, requiring no time; so that a dying sinner, believing in Jesus, is saved at the eleventh hour, needing not to go roundabout to do penances, and pass through probationary periods, and I know not what besides. He may come to Jesus, weary, and worn, and sad; and the road to Jesus, though it seems long to some, is so short that one step takes you there. You have but to leave self behind, and trust in Him, and you are with Him. "We see Jesus" then. Faith is like sight for its quickness.

Is not faith like sight too, in the second place, for its largeness? It is a wonderful faculty, that of sight. Your eyes and mine, take in at once the whole of this building, with all the assembled company. This eye will next, if it be placed at a point of vantage, take in the entire city of London with the whole of its populous streets. Give the eye but the opportunity, let the sun go down, and it will take in all the thousands of worlds that stud the brow of night. What is there which the eye cannot grasp, and mark you, not the eye of the great and mighty only, but of the poorest also? Yes, the little insignificant eye of the lark can take in as much, no doubt, as the big eye of the bullock; and the smallest eyes that God creates, he enables to compass greatest things. A marvellous thing is that eye, darting its shafts everywhere, sending its rays around, and embracing all things. Now, just such a power is faith. What a faculty faith has for grasping everything, for it layeth hold upon the past, the present, and the future. It pierceth through most intricate things, and seeth God producing good out of all the tortuous circumstances of providence. And what is more, faith does what the eye cannot do—it sees the infinite; it beholds the invisible; it looks upon that which eye hath not seen, which ear hath not heard; it seeth beneath the veil that parts us from the land of terror, and, moved with fear, it makes us fly to the Saviour. Faith sees through the pearly gate, and, beholding the glory of the better land, it makes us fly to Jesus, who bears the keys of paradise at His girdle. Faith seeth—I know now how to describe fully what faith seeth. What is there she doth not behold? She seeth even God Himself; for though in my finite conception I cannot grasp God, and my understanding can only perceive, as it were, His train and skirts, yet my faith, with awful comprehension, can take in the whole of God, and believe what she does not know, and accept what she cannot comprehend. Oh! wondrous faculty of faith! God give it to thee, my dear hearer. God give thee more and more of it, that so it may be to thee the substance of things hoped for, and the evidence of things not seen, and that all-comprehending faculty shall enable thee to say—

"All things are mine, the gift of God,
The purchase of a Saviour's blood;
This world is mine, and worlds to come;
Earth is my lodge, and heaven my home."

Again, sight is a most remarkable faculty, because, in the judgment of most men it is very sure. We believe that we are often deceived by hearing. We are inclined often, when we hear a story, to say, "I should believe that if I saw it, but I should not else; I have been so often deceived by hearing tales, that I cannot always credit what my ears tell me." We know how by feeling we are readily enough deceived, like Isaac, who would not have given his blessing to Jacob had not his eye waxed dim, but his touch deceived him. But "seeing is believing," according to the world's proverb. When a man sees a thing, then he says he knows it; though, indeed, of late years especially, we have learned that even sight itself is not always to be trusted, for the most extraordinary illusions have been practised upon persons for amusement, and have become a part of the apparatus of pleasure and philosophy. You cannot believe your own eyes nowadays. You see a great many things, or think you see them, which are there, and things which you could declare to be in such-and-such a position, turn out not to be there at all; it is merely some reflection, or some delusion, simple enough when explained, but most puzzling until it is opened up to you. However, sight is generally regarded by men to be the surest of all our faculties. If we see a thing, there it is, there is no questioning it. Now, faith has this certifying power in a much higher degree, for the faith which is of the operation of God, and which distinguishes His own elect, is infallible. The faith of God's people will not believe a lie. It is written, that "if it were possible," such-and-such "would deceive the very elect," but it is not possible. Where faith takes the word of God as her basis, and rests upon it, she becomes an infallible faculty, and we may depend upon that which she reveals to us. It is a glorious thing to know certainties, such as the existence of God, and the everlasting covenant, ordered in all things and sure; such blessed certainties as the effectual atonement which has put away the sin of the Lord's people; and such certainties as the enjoyment of the presence of the Holy Spirit in his indwelling power within our soul. May we have much of this faith whi.h is like to sight for its certifying power.

Once more, is not faith wondrously like sight, from its power to affect the mind, and enable a man to realize a thing? What I mean is this. That eminent preacher in America, Mr. Beecher, frequently used to address his audience upon negro slavery, and his touching eloquence never failed to move his people to an abhorrence of the thing, and to a sympathy with those who smarted under its power. But on one occasion, as I have been told, he wished to produce an extraordinary feeling in order to raise a large sum of money for a certain purpose. He therefore expatiated upon the sorrows of a beautiful girl, almost white, but still with sufficient African blood in her veins for her master to claim her for his slave, and she was about to be sold far south for the worst of purposes. Mr. Beecher wanted to touch the hearts of his people to purchase her liberty, that she, their sister, might be free. He had spoken earnestly, but to produce the required effect, he called her from her seat, and bade her stand up in the midst, and you may guess that that morning there was no difficulty in collecting all the needed funds to set her free. The sight of the slave-girl had moved their hearts as the preacher's words could not do. Now, it is so usually. We talk about poverty, but when do you feel your hands go into your pockets so freely as when you have been visiting a poor family where the little ones are crying for bread, and where the parents have no means for providing for them? You feel for orphans. Many of us do very sincerely, but we never felt for them so thoroughly as when we began to deal with them and to see them and their widowed mothers. In our newly-founded Orphanage—for which I would bespeak your help continually—we have had already to deal with many fatherless ones, and we have come more than ever into contact with them, and we begin to feel that the fatherless are indeed objects of pity, for the sight of them and of the widows has put the thing forcibly before us. We have heard one who, being cold in the streets, and seeing a poor shivering family, thought that winter was very hard, and that when he got home he would take care to put by some money to buy blankets; but when he had sat down by the fire, and thoroughly warmed himself, and had partaken of his cheerful meal, he thought the weather must be changed, and that it was not so bad a thing, after all, to have a little winter; and so the blankets were never bought, and the poor were never cared for. There is nothing like sight, my brethren, to convince, notwithstanding the moment when sight is over, feeling may depart. Now, faith has also this mighty reasoning power in even a higher degree. If it is real faith, it makes the Christian man in dealing with God feel towards God as though he saw Him; it gives him the same awe, and yet the same joyous confidence which he would have if he were capable of actually beholding the Lord. Faith, when it takes a stand at the foot of the cross, makes us hate sin and love the Saviour just as much as though we had seen our sins placed to Christ's account, and had seen the nails driven through His hands and feet, and seen the bloody scourges as they made the sacred drops of blood to fall.

"We were not with the faithful few
Who stood Thy bitter cross around;
Nor heard Thy prayer for those who slew,
Nor felt that earthquake rock the ground;
We saw no spear-wound pierce Thy side:
Yet we can feel that Thou hast died."

Faith realizes the thing, and thus becomes "the substance of things hoped for, the evidence of things not seen." Hence the glory and the beauty of faith. Now, many of you have heard about the wrath of God, but it has all been forgotten. You have heard about the judgment, and the wrath of God to come afterwards. You have heard of the atonement, and the power of Jesus to put away sin; but you have had no effect produced upon your minds, because, as the apostle puts it, "It was not mixed with faith in them that heard it." But if you had had faith in that which was proclaimed, and had come savingly to trust in the truth which was presented as the ground of your salvation, you would have been moved, and stirred, and excited, and led to hate sin and to fly to Jesus. God grant to us, then, that we may have more and more faith.

I have thus, I trust, at sufficient length, shown the parallel between faith and sight.

II. And now we shall spend a minute or two upon another thought, namely, that FAITH, THE SIGHT OF THE SOUL, IS HERE SPOKEN OF AS A CONTINUOUS THING.

"We see Jesus." It does not say, "We can see Jesus"—that is true enough: the spiritual eye can see the Saviour; nor does it say, "We have seen Him;" that also, glory be to God, is a delightful fact, we have seen the Lord, and we have rejoiced in seeing Him; nor does the text say, "We shall see Him," though this is our pride and our hope, that "when He shall appear, we shall be like Him, for we shall see Him as He is;" but the text says, "We see Jesus;" we do see Him now and continually. This is the common habit of the Christian; it is the element of his spiritual life; it is His most delightful occupation; it is his constant practice. "We see Jesus."

Dear brethren and sisters, I am afraid some of us forget this. For instance, we see Jesus Christ as our Saviour, we being sinners still. And is it not a delightful thing always to feel one's self a sinner, and always to stand looking to Christ as one's Saviour, thus beholding Him evermore? "As ye have received Christ Jesus the Lord, even so walk ye in Him"—not merely sometimes coming to Him as you came at first, but evermore abiding in Him. "To whom coming"—always coming, constantly coming—"as unto a living stone." I was present at a meeting of believers a short time ago, when a conversation of this kind occurred. A brother in the Lord, one of the most fervent men I know, said that sometimes when his piety flagged and his heart grew cold, he found it a very blessed thing to go and visit the sick and the dying; and he found this to be such a sweet restoration to his faith that he recommended us all, as often as we could, to frequent dying beds. Now, another brother who was present, who preaches the gospel, but who at the same time is a butcher, said he thanked God he did not need to go to a dying bed to see Jesus, and to get his heart set right: that he had had as sweet fellowship with God in Camden Town Market, as he ever had in the house of prayer, and that he found it best always to live, as his brother wished to live sometimes, namely, always conscious of sin, and always looking to the Sin-offering. Come to Jesus, then, as you came at first. Fly to the fountain always as needing constant cleansing—not as though you had not been washed, but still abiding, continuing in blessed recognition of your present cleansing that flows from the fountain filled with blood. It is very sweet to remember that the fountain we sing about as being

19

opened in Jerusalem, is opened "for the house of David and for the inhabitants of Jerusalem"—not so much for sinners, though it is opened for them, as for saints—"for the house of David and the inhabitants of Jerusalem." Let us always be coming to it; and each morning and each night, let this be the cry of our spirit, "Still guilty, still vile, still polluted, we see Jesus, and, seeing Him, we know that we are saved."

Should not this, also, be the mode of our life in another respect? We are now disciples. Being saved from our former conversation, we are now become the disciples of the Lord Jesus, and ought we not, as disciples, to be constantly with our Master? Ought not this to be the motto of our life, "We see Jesus"? We should not regard the commands of Jesus Christ as being a law left to us by a departed Master whom we cannot see, and to whom we cannot fly. Is it not better to believe that Christ is a living Christ, that He is in the midst of His church still, observing our order, noting our obedience or our disobedience, a Master absent in one sense, but still in another point of view ever present, according to His promise—"Lo, I am with you alway, even unto the end of the world"? We should

"Stay with Him near the tree,
　Stay with Him near the tomb;
Stay till the risen Lord we see,
　Stay watching 'till He come."

My brethren, should we be so frequently cold and careless if we could always see Jesus? Would our hearts be so hard towards perishing sinners if we always saw that face which was bedewed with tears for them? Do you think we could sit still, or grow worldly, or spend all our energies upon ourselves, if we could see the Crucified, who though "He saved others, Himself He could not save?" I wish I could always come here to preach Jesus seeing Him by my side, and feeling in my heart that I was preaching in my Master's presence. I would that you could always come into this place, both at prayer-meetings and at all other times, feeling "The Master is there; let us bow in His sight; let our worship be given—not to one who is blind, and who will not see us, but to one who beholds us all, and sees our inmost thoughts." As disciples we should be more punctual in our obedience, more consistent in our imitation of Jesus, if we had Him always before us. The Romanist puts up the crucifix before his eyes; well, let us put up Christ in our spirits. He wears the cross on his bosom: let us carry Christ on our heart, still thinking of Jesus, seeing Him at all times.

Would it not also, dear friends, be very much for our comfort if we were to see Jesus always as our Friend in our sojourn here? "Henceforth," saith He, "I call you not servants, but I have called you friends." You are very poor, my dear brother; do you see Jesus? He was poorer than you. You have somewhere to go to sleep in to-night, but He could say, "The foxes have holes, and the birds of the air have nests, but the Son of Man hath not where to lay His head." Are you racked with pain to-night? Let it help you to see Jesus. You are not "exceeding sorrowful even unto death," nor are your griefs to be compared with His. Have you been deserted and betrayed? See Jesus kissed by Judas! Have you been denied by some friend who promised to be faithful? Look into the face of Jesus as He turns upon Peter! Does death itself stare you in the face? Remember Him who, "being found in fashion as a man, humbled Himself, and became obedient unto death, even the death of the cross." We should never be alone if we could see Jesus; or at least, if we were, it would be a blessed solitude. We should never feel deserted if we could see Jesus; we should have the best of helpers. I know not if we should feel weak if we always saw Him, for He would be our strength and our song, He would become our salvation. The bitter waters of Marah, the afflictions and troubles of the day, would all be sweet if this tree were cast into the flood for us, and if Jesus were brought, in solemn meditation, into contact with our spirits. Oh! to see Jesus. You have seen Him as your Saviour: you desire to see Him as your Master. Oh! to see Him as your friend, upon whose bosom you can still lean your aching head, into whose ear you can ever pour your tale of sorrow.

20

Through the wilderness you may continually come up leaning on your Beloved, and with Him you may have perpetually such sweet enjoyments, that earth, desert as it is, shall seem to blossom like a garden of roses, and your spirit shall enjoy heaven below.

Again, would it not be much better for us, dear friends, if we were to see Jesus as our Forerunner? I do not know whether it is so with the most of you, but while some of us rejoice in the prospect of heaven, yet the thought of death is sometimes surrounded with much gloom. It cannot be an easy thing to go down amidst the chill darkness of the river, and there to be separated, the soul from the body, and to leave this earthly tabernacle behind, an inheritance to worms: it is a hideous appearance to us sometimes. Even the apostle himself shuddered a little at it when he said, "Not that we would be unclothed, but clothed upon." Death seemeth a bitter pill to us all; and unless it is swallowed up in victory, and the victory takes away the sting of death, the hour of dissolution will be too bitter. But do you not think that our thoughts of gloom about death sometimes arise from a forgetfulness that Jesus will be with us? If our faith could see Jesus as making our bed in our sickness, and then standing by our side in the last solemn article, to conduct us safely through the iron gates, should we not then look upon death in a very different light? You know how Watts's hymn puts it—

"Oh! if my Lord would come and meet,
  My soul should stretch her wings in haste,
Fly fearless through death's iron gate,
  Nor feel the terrors as she pass'd,

Jesus can make a dying bed
  Feel soft as downy pillows are,
While on His breast I lean my head,
  And breathe my life out sweetly there."

My dear brethren and sisters, gathering up all I should like to have said, but cannot say, into one, it is this: if we see Jesus, being always with us, from morn till eve, in life and in death, what noble Christians it will make us! Now we shall not get angry with each other so quickly. We shall see Jesus; and we cannot be angry when that dear loving face is in view. And when we have been affronted, we shall be very ready to forgive when we see Jesus. Who can hate his brother when he sees that face, that tender face, more marred than that of any man? When we see Jesus, do you think we shall get worldly? Would you have spoken as you did across the counter to-day, brother, had you seen Jesus? My dear friend, would you have been as you have been to your work-fellow? would you have spoken as you did to your servants? would you have acted as you did to your master, had you seen Jesus? They say "a master's eye doeth much"; certainly the presence of Jesus would do much. "The master's eye doeth more than both his hands," they say, O! for that consciousness of the eye of Jesus, which shall be like the hand of Jesus, moulding us according to His will. "We see Jesus."

Now, I hope you do see Jesus as you sit in the pews there. Sometimes on Sabbath days, when the Lord helps the preacher, and Christ is evidently set forth amongst you, you have seen Jesus; but will you see Him after you have gone down those steps? Will you see Him when you get home to your houses? Will you see Him next morning in the workroom, or at the business, or in the market? This is not quite so easy, and yet I hold that, if we had more grace, we should see Christ just as well in the market, among the baskets of fruit, as we can at the Tabernacle sitting in our pews. We should see Him quite as well if we were driving a horse, or walking along Cheapside, as when we are in our closets, bowing the knee; for that is true grace which is with us always, and that is the presence of Jesus which abides with us for ever, and that is true piety which shines the fairest in the midst of worldly cares. May we each one of us have this, and may it be the expression of our life—"We see Jesus"; and then we shall be able to go farther and say,

"For me to live is Christ, and to die is gain."

III. I shall detain you just a minute or two longer, for a third point about our sight of Jesus, namely: we have said that faith is like sight, and that our faith should be a present grace, in active operation; but there may be this reflection about our present sight of Christ, that SOMETIMES OUR FAITH, LIKE OUR SIGHT, IS NOT QUITE CLEAR.

You do not always see, I suppose, equally well. There are many things that affect the optic nerve, and we know that in fair weather we can see a longer distance than we can in cloudy weather. I was at Newcastle some time ago, in a friend's house, and when I went up to the top window and looked out, he said, "There is a fine view, sir, if you could but see it; we can see Durham Cathedral from here on a Sunday." "On a Sunday!" I said, "how is that?" "Well, you see all that smoke down there, all those furnaces, and so on; they are all stopped on a Sunday, and then, when the air is clear, we can see Durham Cathedral." In a moment, I thought—ah! we can see a great deal on a Sunday, when the smoke of the world is gone for a little time; we can see all the way to heaven then; but sometimes, what with the smoke we make in business, and the smoke the devil makes, and the smoke that sin makes, we can scarcely see anything at all. Well, since the natural sight has to undergo variations, both from itself within and from the smoke without, and from the state of the weather, we must not wonder if our faith undergoes variations too. It ought not to do so, but sometimes it does. There are seasons when we realise that Christ is ours. Glory be to His name, if all the devils in hell should speak to the contrary, yet we know that our Beloved is ours, and that we are His. We are sure of it. Though all the angels in heaven should come and deny it, we would face them out, and say, "I know whom I have believed, and am persuaded that He is able to keep that which I have committed unto Him against that day." But there are other times when the same believer sings Newton's hymn, but whenever he does, he ought to sing it alone, for fear anybody should catch the contagion of it—

"'Tis a point I long to know,
    Oft it causes anxious thought:
Do I love the Lord or no,
    Am I His, or am I not?"

There are hours when some of us would be glad to creep into a mouse-hole or hide ourselves in a nutshell. We feel so little, so insignificant. Our faith is at so miserable an ebb, that we know not what to do. Well, let us not be astonished, as though we were not the children of God, because of this. Everything that has life has variations. A block of wood is not affected by the weather, but a living man is. You may drive a stake into the ground, and it will feel no influence of spring, summer, autumn, or winter; but if the stake be alive, and you drive it into the soil where there is moisture, it will soon begin to sprout, and you will be able to tell when spring and winter are coming by the changes that take place in the living tree. Life is full of these changes; do not wonder, then, if you experience them.

Again, faith, like sight, is not only subject to variations, but it has great growth. Our children, in a certain sense, see as truly when they are a day old as when they are grown up to be twenty years old; but we must not suppose that they see as accurately, for they do not. I think observations would teach us that little children see all things as on a level surface, and that distant objects seem to them to be near, for they have not yet received experience enough to judge of the relative position of things. That is an acquired knowledge, and no doubt very easily acquired, but still it is learned as a matter of mental experience. And let me say, though you may not have noticed it, all our measures of distance by the eye are matters which have to be gained by habit and observation. When I first went to Switzerland with a friend from Lucerne, we saw a mountain in the distance which we were going to climb. I pointed out a place where we should stop half-way up, and I said, "We shall be there in about four hours and a half." "Four hours and a half!"

my friend said, "I'd undertake to walk it in ten minutes." "No, not you." "Well, but half an hour!" He looked again, and said, "Anybody could get there in half an hour!" It seemed no distance at all. And yet when we came to toil up, the four hours and a half turned into five or six, before we reached the place. Our eyes were not accustomed to mountains, and we were not able to measure them; and it is only by considerable experience that you get to understand what a mountain is, and how a long distance appears. You are altogether deceived, and do not know the position of things till you become wiser. And it is just so with faith. Faith in the Christian when he first gets it, is true and saving; but it is not in proportion. The man believes one doctrine, perhaps, and it is so delightful that it swallows up every other. Then he gets hold of another, and he swings that way like a pendulum; no doctrine can be true but that one. Perhaps in a little time he swings back like a pendulum the other way. He is unsteady because, while his faith perceives the truth, it does not perceive the harmonies of truth: his faith, for instance, may perceive the Lord Jesus Christ, but as yet it has not learned the position which Christ occupies in the great economy of grace. He is half-blind, and cannot see far. He has sight, but it is not the sight which he will yet receive. Like the blind man who, when our Lord healed him, saw men at first as trees walking. He came in due time to see clearly, for grace always goes on in its work—it will never halt half-way; but at first all was obscure and confused. Just as when you pass from darkness into light, you are unable to bear it, you are dazzled, and need a short time to accustom the eye to the brilliance; but in due time the eye is strengthened, and you can bear more and more light, till we again see with comfort. Let us ask, then, of the Lord, that He will increase our faith till the mental eye shall become clear and bright, and we shall be made meet to be partakers of the inheritance of the saints in light, to be with Christ, and to see Him as He is. If you have but little faith, remember that that will save you. The little diamond is as much a diamond as the Koh-i-noor. So little faith is as truly the faith of God's elect as the greatest faith. If you do but see Jesus, though it be but by the corner of your eye, yet if you see Him, you shall be saved; and though you may not see as much of Him to trust Him, to rely on Him entirely, your sins which are many are forgiven, and you shall yet receive grace for grace, until you shall see Him in His glory. However, always be praying, "Lord, increase our faith."

The last thing I have to notice about this true faith in Christ as sight, is, that it is at all times a very simple thing to look. Look! No one need to go to a grammar school or to a university to look. Look! The smallest child, as we have said, can look; the most illiterate and untaught can look. If there be life in a look, glory be to God for such a provision, because it is available for each one of us! Sinner, if thou wouldst be saved, there is nothing for thee to think upon but Christ. Do thy sins trouble thee? Go to Him, and trust in Him, and the moment thou lookest to Him thou art saved. "Oh," says one, "but I cannot do that; my faith is so weak." Well, when I walk about and see a beautiful sight, very seldom do I think about my own sight; my mind is occupied with the sight, and so let it be with you. Never mind that eye; think more about the vision to be seen. Think of Christ. It would be a pitiful thing if, when there were some great procession in the streets, all you thought about was your own eye; you would see but very little. Think less about your faith, and more about Jesus.

"Weary sinner! keep thine eyes
On the atoning sacrifice;
View Him bleeding on the tree,
Pouring out His life for thee.

Cast thy guilty soul on Him,
Find Him mighty to redeem;
At His feet thy burden lay;
Look thy doubts and fear away."

Turn over and over in your mind the great transaction on the cross. I have sometimes said to young seekers, Go home and spend an hour deliberately in reading about the death of Christ, and then in picturing it to your mind's eye, for it is in that way that faith comes. Through the Holy Spirit's power, we come to believe that story by thinking upon it, seeing Jesus in it, and then following on, and giving it the full credence of our spirit. Go to the cross for faith if you cannot go with faith, and the Lord grant that you may find in Jesus

"True belief and true repentance,
Every grace that brings us nigh."

so that you, too, may say with us, "We see Jesus." What is there in this world which is worth looking at in comparison with Him? All else is like the mirage of the desert, which appears but to fade away, deluding the weary traveller with hopes of rest and refreshing, and leaving him sick at heart, because all has passed as the baseless fabric of a dream, leaving not a wreck behind. Can you gain aught by watching the bubbles on the stream of time? Will they slake your death-thirst and cool your brow in the article of death? Is there aught of healing in the uplifted images of earthly gold, and honour, wisdom, and power? You have tried them—well, how do they answer? I know of one who, travelling over a pass in Italy, one evening, secured a light to help him over a dangerous and difficult part of the way further on. It was not needed till the narrow steep descent was reached, in fact, it was in the way till then, but just as the traveller came to the very spot where it was required, it went out and left him in utter darkness. So it is full often in the sinner's experience, who travels in the dark, his lights go out when most needed. Oh! far better than to walk in daylight, using the eye of faith, in the clear sunshine of gospel light from the Sun of Righteousness. Walk in the light. Come to the light, and live seeing Jesus.

" 'We would see Jesus,' for the shadows lengthen
Across this little landscape of our life;
'We would see Jesus,' our weak faith to strengthen,
For the last weariness, the final strife.

'We would see Jesus,' the great rock foundation,
Whereon our feet were set by sovereign grace:
Nor life nor death, with all their agitation,
Can thence remove us if we see His face.

'We would see Jesus'—sense is all too binding,
And heaven appears too dim, too far away;
We would see Thee, to gain a sweet reminding
That Thou hast promised our great debt to pay.

'We would see Jesus:' this is all we're needing—
Strength, joy, and willingness, come with the sight;
'We would see Jesus,' dying, risen, pleading;
Then welcome day, and farewell mortal night!"

The Lord send you away with His blessing, for Jesus' sake.

LITTLE FAITH AND GREAT FAITH

"O thou of little faith, wherefore didst thou doubt?"–Matthew xiv. 31.
"O woman, great is thy faith: be it unto thee even as thou wilt."–Matthew xv. 28.

Between the very lowest degree of faith and a state of unbelief there is a great gulf. An abyss immeasurable yawns between the man who has even the smallest faith in Christ and the man who has none. One is a living man, though feeble, the other is "dead in trespasses and sins"; the one is a justified man, the other is "condemned already, because he hath not believed in the name of the only begotten Son of God." The weakest believer is on the road to heaven; the other, having no faith, is going the downward road, and he will find his portion at last among the unbelievers–a terrible portion indeed.

Although we thus speak of believers as all of one company, yet there is a great distance between weak faith and strong faith. Thank God, it is a distance upon the one safe road–the King's highway. No gulf divides little faith from great faith; on the contrary, little faith has only to travel along the royal road, and he shall overtake his stronger brother, and himself become "strong in the Lord, and in the power of His might." I want to quicken some of the more tardy travellers along the sacred way. I would have doubts slain and faith revived. I want Mr. Feeble-Mind, and Mistress Much-Afraid, and Miss Despondency, and the whole tribe of the little ones, to take heart of hope this morning, and observe that they have not yet enjoyed all that the Lord has prepared for them. Although a little faith saves, there is more faith to be had: faith which strengthens, gladdens, honours, and makes useful in a most desirable grace. It is written, "He giveth more grace," and therefore God has more in readiness for us. Little faith may increase exceedingly until it ripens into full assurance with all its mellowness and sweetness.

There are three things I am going to attend to. The first is little faith gently censured: "O thou of little faith, wherefore didst thou doubt?" In the second place, little faith tenderly commended; for it is no small boon to have any faith at all, even though it has to be called little. Thirdly, I shall conclude by speaking of great faith as much more to be commended. In this last matter I shall dwell upon our Master's gracious words: "O woman, great is thy faith: be it unto thee even as thou wilt."

I have read in your hearing two stories in the fourteenth and fifteenth chapters of this Gospel according to Matthew. It is memorable that the incidents illustrating little and great faith, come so closely together. I shall take it for granted that you have the stories of Peter and the Canaanitish woman clearly before your minds. Keep your Bibles open while I preach; and may the Spirit of God open your hearts to understand them!

I. First, we have LITTLE FAITH GENTLY CENSURED.

What shall I say about it, to begin with, but this?–that it is frequently found where we expected greater things. This man who is chided for little faith is Peter. Peter, to whom the Lord had communicated a very clear knowledge of Himself; Peter, the foreman of the twelve; Peter, in after-days the great preacher of Pentecost; Peter, who has been exalted by some into the primate or pope of the apostolic church, though he claimed no such position; this is Peter, who was a true piece of stone from the foundation rock, Peter, to whom the Master gave the keys, and to whom He delivered the commission, "Feed My sheep," and "Feed My lambs." It is Peter, to whom Jesus says, "O thou of little faith." And, my dear brother or sister, may it not be true that you have obtained great mercy, enjoyed high privileges, received gracious protection, and been eminently favoured with fellowship with Christ, most near and dear? By this time you ought to be strong in faith. But yet you are not so. You will soon be home; your grey hairs are silvered with the light of Immanuel's land; you can almost hear the singing of the saints across the narrow stream. At your time of life, so long taught of God, so deeply experienced in the things of Christ, you ought to be fathers in faith, whereas you are still children; you ought to be mothers in Israel, and yet you are mere babes. Is it not so? Why is this sad fact so undeniable? Solomon spake of the cedar in Lebanon, and of the hyssop on the wall; but I have too often seen a hyssop on Lebanon, and I have sometimes seen a cedar upon a wall: I mean, that I have seen great grace where there seemed to be nothing to assist it, and I have seen little grace where everything was advantageous to its growth. These things ought not so to be. You and I, who are no children now; you and I, who are no longer coasters, but have launched out into the deep, and have had experience in many a storm; you and I who are no strangers to our Lord now, for the King hath often brought us into His banqueting-house, and His banner over us has been love; we ought to be ashamed if we are still lamenting our little faith. It is an infirmity in which we cannot glory, for unbelief is exceeding sinful. Well might the Master lift His finger to some who are sitting in these pews this morning, and say to us one by one, "O thou of little faith, wherefore didst thou doubt?"

Continuing our very gentle censure, we note that little faith is far too eager for signs. I do not think that Peter's faith became suddenly little; it was always little, and the sight of the boisterous wind made its littleness apparent. When he said, "Lord, if it be Thou, bid me come unto Thee on the water," his faith was weak. Why did he want to walk on the water? Why did he seek such a wonder? It was because his faith was little. Strong faith is content without signs, without tokens, without marvels. It believes God's bare word, and asks for no confirming miracle; its trust in Christ is such that it asks for no sign in the heavens above, or in the seas beneath. Little faith, with her "If it be Thou," must have signs and wonders, or she yields to doubt. Joyful meditations, remarkable dreams, singular providences, choice answers to prayer, special fellowships—little faith must be having something out of the common, or she collapses. The perpetual cry of little faith is, "Show me a token for good." Little faith is not satisfied with the bow which God doth set in the cloud, but she would have the whole heavens painted with celestial colours. It is not satisfied with the usual portion of the saints, but must have more, do more, and feel more than the rest of the disciples. Why could not Peter have kept in the ship like the rest of his brethren? But, no; because his faith was weak he must quit the deck for the deep; he cannot think it really is his Master walking on the sea unless he walks with Him. How dare he ask to do what His divine Lord was doing? Let him be content to share his Lord's humiliation: he ventures far when he asks to partake in a miracle of Omnipotence. Am I to doubt unless I can do miracles like those of my Lord? But this is one of the failings of weak faith: it is not content to drink of His cup and be baptized with His baptism; it would share His power, and partake in His throne.

Weak faith is apt to have too high an opinion of its own power. "Oh," says one, "Surely you are wrong. Is it not the error of weak faith to have too low an opinion of its own ability?" Brethren, no man can have too low an opinion of his own power; because he has no power whatever. The Lord Jesus Christ said, "Without Me ye can do nothing"; and His witness is true. If we have strong faith we shall glory in our powerlessness, because the power of Christ doth rest upon us. If we have weak faith, we shall diminish our trust in Jesus and put into our hearts instead of it so many measures of confidence in self. Just in proportion as faith in our Lord is weakened, our idea of ourselves will be strengthened. "But I thought," says one, "that a man who had strong self-reliance was a man of great faith." He is the man who has no faith at all; for self-reliance and Christ-reliance will not abide in the same heart. Peter has an idea that he can go upon the water to his Master; he is not so sure of the others, but he is clear about himself. James, and John, and Andrew, and the rest of them, are in the ship: it does not occur to Peter that any one of these can tread the waves; but he cries, "Lord, if it be Thou, bid me come unto Thee on the water." Self-consciousness is no attribute of faith; but it is a nest for doubt. Had he known himself, he might have said, "Lord, bid John come to Thee on the water; I am unworthy of so high a dignity." But, no: being weak in faith, he was strong in his own opinion of himself, and he hurried to the front, as usual; hastened into a pathway that was quite unfit for his trembling feet to tread, and before long found out his error. It is weak faith that allows of high ideas of self. Great faith hides self under its mighty wings.

Note another point about weak faith: it is too much affected by its surroundings. Peter went on pretty well till he noticed that the wind tossed the waves about tremendously, and then he was afraid. Are not many Christians too apt to live by what they feel and see? Do we not often hear a young beginner say, "I know that I am converted, for I feel so happy?" Well, but a new frock will make many a girl happy, or a few shillings in the pocket will make a youth rejoice. Is this the best evidence that you can bring? Why, if you are very troubled, it may be a better sign of conversion than feeling happy. It is well to mourn over sin, and struggle against it, and try to overcome it: this is a sure mark of grace; a far surer one than overflowing joy. Ah, believer! you will be happy in the highest and best sense if you trust in Jesus; but you will soon lose your happiness if your happiness becomes the ground of your confidence. Happiness is a thing that depends upon how things happen. It is too often hap-ness, and nothing more. It is too much a hap-hazard thing. But faith rests in Christ whatever hap may happen; and so it is happy in the happening of sorrow and grief, because it relies wholly upon God. Faith rests upon the Lord's faithful word and promise, come what may. "Ah!" says another, "I feel very low and dull. I am heavy even when I try to pray; I cannot pray as I would like." And so you doubt your salvation because of that, do you? Does your salvation depend upon the liveliness of your prayers? It is the mark of weak faith, that it is all up, and then all down. If we live by feelings, brethren, we shall live a very wretched life; we shall not dwell in the Father's house, but we shall be a kind of gipsies, whose tents are too frail to shut out the weather. God save us from being like the barometer, which at one time is "set fair"; but "set fair" with the barometer does not last long, it is back again to "rain," and it drops down to "much rain," before we know where we are. Strong faith knows where its true standing is, and, perceiving this to be unchanging, it concludes that its foundation is as good one day as another day; for its standing is in Christ. As the promise upon which strong faith leans is not a variable quantity, but is always the same, so its rest is the same. Our faithful God will save all those who put their trust in Him; and there is the top and the bottom of it: we need not go any further. But poor weak faith is always looking out to see whether the wind is in the east; and if it be so, down she goes. Is the wind quiet? Peter walks on the wave. Does the wind howl? Peter begins to sink. This is weak faith all over. It pins us down to its environment. God help us to rise out of it!

Weak faith, in the next place, is forgetful of its constant danger, and has not learned to believe in the teeth of it. When Peter was walking on the waves, he was in as much danger as when he began to sink. Practically, he never was in any danger at all; for Jesus, who enabled him to tread the sea, was equally near all the way. When he was standing, he could not have walked another step if the Master had not upheld him; and when he began to sink, his Master was still able to prevent his drowning. Would his Master withdraw the divine strength, and suffer His poor servant to perish? Peter's strength is gone; but will his Master take away the divine strength, and leave him to perish? Weak faith frequently makes this mistake; she does not know that she is at all times in extreme danger, wherever she may be, when she looks to herself; and that she is never in any danger, wherever she may be, if she looks to her Lord. If you get a cloudy view of your confidence, and begin to trust, not in Christ pure and simple, but in Christ Jesus as you enjoy Him, in Christ as you are like Him, or in Christ and yourself as taught by Him; if you allow any amalgamations in your trust, they will turn out to be adulterations; and when a sense of danger falls upon your mind, you will not know where to turn for the re-establishment of your confidence. Strong faith takes Jesus only as her basis; but feeble faith tries to add thereto. Beloved, weak faith tries to make up for want of confidence in the Lord Jesus Christ with an indistinct confidence in herself, or her works, or prayers, or something else. If Peter had been trusting wholly in Jesus, whether he walked on the billows, or sank in the waves, he had done what his Master told him to do, and the reason of this safety was not in the least affected by the wind. If his reliance be on Jesus only, the ground of his confidence is never questionable. I pray that we may climb above that weak faith

27

which rises and falls with the passing incidents of this life's story.

Weak faith, when conscious of her danger, swings as a pendulum to the opposite extreme, and in an instant exaggerates her peril. One moment Peter walks upon the sea; the next moment he is going to be drowned. It is a curious thing that he never thought of swimming. When the soul trusts Christ it is spoiled for reliance upon self. When once a man has found out the way to walk upon the top of the water, he forgets his skill in swimming in it. Self-confidence goes when confidence in Christ comes in. It was the Lord's will that Peter should know his weakness, and should most clearly see that his standing depended upon his faith, and that faith found all its strength in the Lord Jesus. Down goes Peter; and now it is, "Lord save me." He is at his wits' end. Peter is going to be drowned—drowned with the Master standing by! He will die while Jesus lives. Will he? He will perish when he is doing what Jesus bade him do? Do you think he will? It is evident he has that fear upon him. I have been foolish enough to feel that I should sink under trouble and need. It is folly. Having mixed up our confidence in brighter days, when dark days·come, a larger part of our confidence is gone, and we fear that we shall perish. Have not some of you that believed in the doctrine of the final perseverance of the saints, yet said, "I shall one day fall by the hand of the enemy"? You know that Christ has promised to keep you; and yet, because you are not quite keeping yourself as you ought to do, you dream that He will not keep you. You know that He will never give you up, and yet you are almost ready to give it all up yourself, and say, "I shall prove an apostate after all." In this way little faith forgets her Lord. She is too bold one day, and too timid another, and all because she mixes up her confidences.

Little faith speaks unreasonably. Notice how our Lord puts it: "O thou of little faith, wherefore didst thou doubt?" Faith is spiritual common sense; unbelief is unreasonable. For look; if Christ was worth trusting at all, and Peter had proved that he thought He was, by throwing himself into the sea, to come to Him; then, if He was worth trusting at all, He was worthy to be trusted to the full. You cannot say of a man, "He is a faithful man, for you may at times rely upon his word." That qualifying word, "at times," is fatal to his character. Unless he is always to be relied upon, he is not an honest, truth-speaking man. And if you say of God's promises, "I can believe some of them, and therefore I expect Him to help me under certain difficulties," you are accusing the Lord of unfaithfulness. O sir, you are cutting away the foundation of what little faith you have. Your Lord might ask you, "Why do you believe as much as you do believe? Having gone so far, why do you not go on to the end? The reason which makes you believe as much as you do believe, should make you believe to a still greater degree. O thou of little faith, wherefore didst thou doubt? If thou hast any faith, why dost thou doubt? If any doubt, why any faith?" The two things are inconsistent with each other. You are not occupying a logical position in being a weak believer in a strong Christ. Why wavering faith in an unwavering promise? Why feeble faith in a mighty Saviour? Let your faith take its colour from Him on whom it rests, and from the Word which you believe, and then you will be standing upon good, solid, reasonable ground, which can be justified to conscience and understanding.

One word more about our trembling apprehensions. Weak faith often gets a wetting. Although Peter was not drowned, yet you may be sure he was soaked to the skin with the water. If you have strong faith you will often escape a sea of troubles, which weak faith will be immersed in. Weak faith is a great fabricator of terrors. I know friends who have a trouble-factory in their back-garden, where they are always making rods for their own backs. They disbelieve God about this and about that, and hence they are always fretting and worrying, and getting wet through with trouble. I have heard say that home-made clothes very seldom fit; and, certainly, home-made troubles are very hard to bear. I have also heard that a home-made suit will last longer than other garments, and I believe that home-made troubles stick to us far longer than those which God appoints for us. Shut up that fear-factory, and make songs instead! If God send thee a trouble, it comes not amiss to thee. But who wetted Peter through and through, and soaked him in the deep? Who but Peter himself? Peter, afflicted Peter! If he had possessed strong faith, he might have had a dry coat. His Master prevented the waters destroying him; but He suffered them to make him very uncomfortable. If thou hast weak faith, thou wilt have broken joys and many discomforts.

Thus have I very gently censured weak faith. I did not mean to hurt a hair of its head. It is a blessed thing, this little faith—not its littleness, but its faith. If I could kill the weakness, and quicken the faith; if the littleness could be removed, and the faith could be increased, how glad should I be!

II. Now, LITTLE FAITH SHALL BE TENDERLY COMMENDED. I shall praise it, not because it is little, but because it is faith. Little faith requires to be tenderly handled, and then it will be seen to be a precious thing.

First of all, it is true faith. Faith which begins and ends with Jesus is true faith. The least faith in Jesus is the gift of God; and it is "like precious faith," though it is not like strong faith. If thou hast faith as a grain of mustard seed, thou canst do wonders. Though thy faith be so little that thou hast to look for it with all thine eyes, yet if it be there, it is of the same nature as the strongest faith. A three-penny piece is silver, as surely as the crown piece, and it bears the mint-mark quite as certainly. A drop of water is of the same nature as the sea; a spark is fire as assuredly as the flames of Vesuvius. Nobody knows what may come of a spark of faith: behold, it sets a thousand souls on fire! Little faith is true faith, for did not our Lord say to this Peter: "Blessed art thou, Simon Bar-jona: for flesh and blood hath not revealed it unto thee, but My Father which is in heaven?" Peter had true faith; and yet it was little faith. O my hearer, "If thou believest that Jesus is the Christ, thou art born of God." If thou dost feebly cast thyself on Christ's finished work, thy weakness in the act of reliance does not alter the fact that thou hast fallen into strong hands, which will surely save thee. Jesus saith, "Look unto Me, and be ye saved"; and though thy look be a very unsteady one, and though tears of sorrow dim thine eyes so that thou canst not see Him as He is, yet thy looking to Him hath saved thee. Little faith is born from above, and belongs to the family of the saved. The weakest faith is real faith.

Next, notice that little faith obeys the precept, and will not go a step without it. Little faith cries, "If it be Thou, bid me come unto Thee on the water. And He said, Come. And when Peter was come down out of the ship, he walked on the water to go to Jesus." If Jesus saith, "Come," little faith answers, "Behold, I come!" Though her gait be staggering, and her knees be feeble, yet she will go where Jesus calls her, whether it be through flood or flame. I know some of the Lord's children who very seldom have much enjoyment; and yet I almost envy them for their tenderness of conscience. Their shrinking from the least contact with sin, their carefulness to keep the way of the Lord's commandments, are admirable traits in their character. Gracious walking is, after all, more precious than comfortable feeling. How can I blame thee, poor little faith, when I see these afraid to put one foot before the other for fear thou shouldest step aside? I had rather see thee in all thy timidity thus carefully obedient than hear thee talking loudly about thy great faith, and then see thee tampering with sin and folly, and feeling as if when thou hast greatly erred it is a matter of no great consequence. When tenderness of conscience flourishes side by side with little faith, they are as two lilies for delicate beauty.

Peter's little faith did not try to walk upon water until Jesus gave the word of permission. Peter asked, "Bid me come." Oftentimes have I noticed men and women much despondent, greatly fearful, and yet they would not do anything for the life of them, until they heard the voice behind them saying, "This is the way, walk ye in it." They hesitate till they have consulted the map of the Word; they dare not go at a venture, but they kneel and cry for guidance, for they are afraid of taking even a single step, apart from their Master's will. They have a holy dread of running without warrant from the Lord. Little faith, if this be thy mind and temper, we commend thee much!

And, next, little faith struggles to come to Jesus. Peter did not leave the ship for the mere sake of walking the waters; but he ventured on the wave that he might come to

29

Jesus. He sought not a promenade upon the waves, but the presence and company of his Lord. "When Peter was come down out of the ship, he walked on the water to go to Jesus." That was the one point he aimed at—to get to Jesus. Some of you, I know, have but little faith; but you long to get nearer to Jesus. Your daily panting is, "Lord, reveal Thyself to me, reveal Thyself in me, and make me more like to Thee." He who seeks Jesus has his face turned in the right direction. Though your knees knock together, and your hands hang down, yet what little headway you do make is towards Jesus: you strive to serve Him, and to honour Him; is it not so? Though the winds be contrary, you still pull for the shore. Well, though thou be little in faith, yet am I glad thou art struggling, despite thy feebleness, to reach thy Lord. Struggle on, for Jesus comes to meet thee; and when thou dost begin to sink, through mistrust, He will catch thee up and set thee on thy feet again. Wherefore, be of good cheer!

Little faith deserves commendation again, in that it does behave grandly for a time. Though Peter had little faith, yet he walked from one billow to another, in rare style. I think I see him after he had leapt out of the ship, astonished to find himself standing upon the waters, which lay beneath him like solid glass. Then he takes one step, like a child that begins to walk; and, with growing confidence, he takes another. Though the waves roll under his feet, yet he stands firmly upon them, for a time. Little faith can play the man for a while. When Jael took the nail and slew Sisera, the timorous woman became a warrior, as she slew the enemy of Israel. Many a time the lame and the feeble, who could not usually lift a hand in the holy war, have felt stimulated, and have developed heroism for the time being. Little faith, like David's sling, has slain the giant; like Ehud's lefthanded dagger, little faith has wrought deliverance. So I commend thee, little faith; for thou hast thy high days and holidays, and thou too canst count thy victories, wrought in the name of Jesus. If it were always with thee as it is at times, thou wouldest be glorious indeed! Even now thou canst move mountains, and pluck up trees by the roots.

Little faith I must commend yet further; because when it finds itself in trouble it betakes itself to prayer. Peter begins to sink. What does Peter do? Peter prays: "Lord, save me." Little faith knows where her strength lies. When she is in trouble, she does not then turn her face to human confidences, or natural forces; but she turns immediately to prayer. Little faith pours out her heart before the Lord. I love to see a man, in the hour of his distress, begin to pray at once, as naturally as frightened birds take to their wings. Some of you run to your neighbours, or hold a council with your own wits: but the profit of this course has never made you rich. Let us try a surer method. Instead of stopping to turn over all the old stock we have, let us go at once to Jesus for new help. Alas! we do not go to Jesus until we have knocked at every other door; and then the mercy is that He does not turn us away from His gate. Peter did not try the natural resort of swimming; he took to praying, "Lord, save me." O little faith, thou art great at pleading in prayer. Perhaps thy very weakness drives thee oftener to thy knees. Thou art not so prevalent in prayer as strong faith; but thou art quite as abundant in it. I see thee trembling and faint; then dost thou cry unto the Lord for strength, and He helps thee. This cry of thine proves thee to be of the spiritual stock; even as it was with one of old, of whom it was said, "Behold, he prayeth."

Weak faith has this commendation again, that it is always safe, because Jesus is near. Peter was safe on the water, because Christ was on the water. Though his faith was weak, he was not saved by the strength of his faith; he was saved by the strength of that gracious hand which was stretched out to catch him when he was sinking in the flood. If thou believest in Christ with all thy heart, if He is the first and last of thy confidence, then, though thou be full of trembling and alarm, Jesus will never let thee perish. If thou art depending upon Him, and upon Him alone, it is not possible that He should slight thy faith, and let thee die. God forbid we should so insult our Lord as to suppose He would let a believer drown, however weak his faith! Since Christ lives, how can we die? Since Christ standeth on the waters, how can we sink beneath them? Are we not one with Him?

One thing I may say in commendation of weak faith, and that is, that Jesus Himself acknowledges that it is faith. He said to Peter, "O thou of little faith." He rebuked him because it was little, but He smiled on him because it was faith. I love to feel that the Holy Ghost is the Creator, not of the littleness of our faith, but of our faith, be it ever so little. Our Lord acknowledges that to be faith which we suspect to be a little better than unbelief. "Lord, I believe; help thou mine unbelief," is an admirable prayer for many of us. Christ forgives the unbelief, but He very graciously accepts the faith, despite its weakness. He can spy out faith when, like a lone spark, it is all but smothered under a heap of rubbish.

Once more, I commend little faith because, though it may sometimes sink, it recovers itself, and does its old wonders over again. Peter is ready to sink; but when his Master has caught him, what do you see? There is not one person now walking on the water; there are two. Christ is there, and Peter too. Peter, my man, you walk on the sea as one to the manner born! Oh, yes; his little faith has learned, by a touch from the Lord, to do what it did at first: He walked the waves at first, and now he does it again. See! he comes up with his Lord into the ship. You that used to have good times, and at this hour look back upon them with deep regret, may have the like again. You that have grown despondent and sad, be of good courage; you shall have your festival days back again, and much brighter than they. "Oh, but I have wasted so much time," says one, "through this feeble faith of mine." Well, it is a great pity; but there is a promise which I commend to your faith: "I will restore to you the years that the locust hath eaten." The locust has eaten up our harvests—this locust of weakness has devoured our pleasant fruits; yet our Lord Jesus Christ can restore to us those wasted years; He can pack ten years of usefulness into one; He can put seven days of joy into one day, and so make up to us the lost past. Our Lord can make you to forget the shame of your youth, and not to remember the reproach of your widowhood any more. Be of good courage, little faith! Thou comest of a good family, though thou be but a babe as yet. Be of good courage, little faith! Thou mayest be sick on board the vessel; but the vessel in which thou hast embarked is safe for all that, and thou wilt get to shore as surely as strong faith will do. Put thy trust in the Lord, and quietly wait for Him, so shall thy morning surely come in due time. Thus I have gently censured and kindly commended little faith.

III. But now I want to say a few words to finish with; and this is the motto of them—GREAT FAITH IS MUCH MORE COMMENDED.

It is sometimes found where we least expected it. Our Lord beheld it, not in the manly Peter, but in the tender woman who pleaded for her child. She was a woman; but she had faith which put the men to shame. She was a Canaanitish woman, of a race concerning which it was said, "Cursed be Canaan," and yet she had stronger faith than Israelitish Peter, who had known the Scriptures from his youth up. She was a woman who had great discomfort at home; for the devil was there, tormenting her daughter. It is a dreadful thing to have the devil in your husband, or a devil in your daughter, when you go home; yet many a Christian woman has this to bear. Notwithstanding this grave trial, though there was nothing to comfort her at home she was a woman of great faith. And why should not we be like her? My brother, although your condition and circumstances are greatly against your growth in grace, yet why should not you grow to manhood in Christ? The Lord Jesus can cause you to do so. Though it seems to you that you must be stunted by the chill blast and the cruel soil which environ you, yet the great husbandman can so foster you that you shall become a plant of renown. God can turn disadvantageous circumstances into means of growth. By the holy chemistry of His grace He can bring good out of evil. I commend great faith with special emphasis when I see it where all its surroundings are hostile to it.

Next, great faith is to be commended because it perseveres in seeking the Lord. This woman came to Jesus to have her daughter healed; and at first He answered her never a word. Oh, the misery of silent suspense! Next, He speaks coolly of her to His disciples; but she seeks on. She has come for a boon, and she so believes in the Lord, the Son of David, that she will not take "no" for an answer; she means to be heard, and so she presses her suit with importunity even to the end. Oh for a strong faith, a persevering faith! Brethren, have you got it? You men are you using it? Here is a woman that had it, and kept it at work till she won her object. May we have it abundantly!

Great faith also sees light in the thickest darkness. I do not think Peter was half so tried as the Canaanite was. What was it that frightened Peter? The wind. What might have frightened her? Why, the harsh words of Jesus Himself. Who is afraid of the wind? Who would not be afraid of a rejecting Christ, speaking hard words? "It is not meet to take the children's bread, and to cast it to dogs." Why if, our Lord had spoken thus to any one of us, we should never have dared to pray again. We should have said, "No, that hard sentence shuts me out altogether." But not so strong faith. "No," says she, "He called me a dog. Dogs have a position in society; little dogs are carried by their little masters indoors at dinner time, that they may get a crust or a crumb; and Lord, I will be a dog, and get my crumb: it is only a crumb for Thee to give it, though it would be everything to me to get it." So she pleads with Him as readily as if He had given her a promise instead of a rebuff. Great faith can see the sun at midnight: great faith can reap harvests at mid-winter, and find rivers in high places. Great faith is not dependent upon sunlight: she sees that which is invisible by other light. Great faith rests upon the certainty that such a thing is so because God has said it, and she is satisfied with His bare word. If she neither sees, nor hears, nor feels anything to corroborate the divine testimony, she believes God for His own sake, and all is well with her. O brethren, I hope you will be brought to this condition—that you will believe in God, though your feelings give God's promise the lie, and though your circumstances give it the lie. Though all your friends and companions give the Lord the lie, may you come to this, Let God be true with every man, and every man a liar; but doubt God we dare not, and we will not. His sure promise must stand. Such a faith as this deserves to be commended, and our Lord Himself praises it. "O woman, great is thy faith!"

Great faith prays and prevails. How did she prevail! Her daughter was made whole, and she received a broad grant of whatever she willed. "Be it unto thee even as thou wilt." I wish we had this mighty faith in connection with prayer. One man praying with faith will get more from God than ten men, or, for the matter of that, ten thousand men, who are unstable and unbelieving. Believe me, there is a way of praying in which you may have what you will of God. You may go up to your closet, and ask and have; ay, and come out of your solitude saying, "I have it." Even though you have it not as a matter of actual enjoyment, yet your faith has grasped it, realized it, and believed in it, and so has taken immediate possession. Did not Luther often, in his worst times, come down from his chamber crying, "Vici," "I have conquered?" He wrestled with God in prayer, and then he felt that all else that he had to wrestle with was just nothing: if he had overcome heaven by prayer, he could overcome earth, and death, and hell. Strong faith doth all this, and goes on to do more.

She has extraordinary reverence for God; but she has a wonderful familiarity with Him. If you were to hear what strong faith sometimes dared to say to God, you would think it profane; and profane it would be from any lips but hers. But when God indulges her to know the secret of the Lord, which is with them that fear Him, and when He says, "Ask what thou wilt, and it shall be done unto thee," she has a blessed liberty with God, which is to be commended, and not forbidden. If the Son make you free in prayer, you shall be free indeed. Strong faith is ever on the winning side. It wears the keys of heaven at its girdle. The Lord can deny nothing to the pleadings of an unstaggering faith.

I commend strong faith, because Jesus, our Lord, was delighted with it. What music there was in His words, "O woman, great is thy faith!" There was no smile on His face when He said to Peter, "O thou of little faith": it grieved Him that His follower should have such little faith in Him. But now it gladdened Him that this poor woman had much splendid faith. He looks at her faith as jewellers do at some famous stone worth more than they can tell. "O woman," said He, "great is thy faith. I am charmed with thy faith. I am amazed at thy faith. I am delighted with thy faith." Well, brethren, you and I long to do something to please our Redeemer. I know we have often cried, "Oh, what shall I do my Saviour to praise?" Believe Him then. Believe His promise without doubt. Believe Him greatly. Believe Him unstaggeringly. Believe Him to the full, and go on in faith till there seems to be nothing further to believe. Believe evermore in Christ Jesus.

How enriched that woman became! She had pleased her Lord, and then her Lord pleased her: "Be it unto thee even as thou wilt." She went away the happiest woman under the skies. God had given her her desire, and she was over-glad and ever glad.

What benefits we could confer upon others if we had strong faith! Her daughter was made whole. Mother, if thou hadst more faith, thy child would soon be brought to Jesus. Father, if thou hadst more faith, thy boy would not be such a plague to thee as he now is. Have more faith in thy God; and when thou dost treat thy Father better, thy children shall treat thee better. If thou wilt dishonour thy God by doubting Him, do you wonder your children dishonour you by disobeying you! O preacher, if thou hadst more faith, thou wouldest have more converts! Sunday-school teacher, if thou hadst more faith, more children would be brought to the Saviour out of thy class. "Lord increase our faith"! I hope we are all saying that in our hearts at this moment.

I will conclude by asking: Is there not great reason why our faith in Christ should be strong? Is there not every reason why we should have the strongest faith in Him? I told you, the other day, of John Hyatt, when he was dying. Someone said to him: "Mr. Hyatt, can you trust your soul with Christ now?" He said, "I would trust Him with ten thousand souls, if I had them." We can go even further than that. If all the sins that men had committed since the world was made, and time began, were laid upon one poor sinner's head, that sinner would be justified in believing that Christ could take that sin away. Whosoever thou art, and whatever thou art, bring your burdens, and lay them at His feet, casting all your care upon Him, for He careth for you; and henceforth may He never have to say to you, "O thou of little faith, wherefore didst thou doubt?" Oh, may He often exclaim, with joy, of you, "O woman, great is thy faith: be it unto thee even as thou wilt"! May the Holy Spirit bless these simple words of mine to your edification! Amen.

FAITH ESSENTIAL TO PLEASING GOD

"But without faith it is impossible to please Him: for he that cometh to God must believe that He is, and that He is a rewarder of them that diligently seek Him."–Hebrews xi. 6.

Men have lived who have pleased God: Enoch was one of them, but he was not the only one. In all ages certain persons have been well-pleasing to God, and their walk in life has been such as was His delight. It should be the aim of every one of us to please God. The thing is possible, notwithstanding all our imperfections and infirmities: let us aim at it in the power of the Holy Ghost. What has been wrought in one man may be wrought in another. We, too, may be well-pleasing unto God; therefore let us seek after it with hopefulness. If we so live as to please the Lord, we shall only be acting as we ought to act; for we ought to please Him who made us and sustains us in being. He is our God and Lord, and obedience to Him is the highest law of our being. Moreover, the glorious Jehovah is so perfectly good, so supremely holy, that the conduct which pleases Him must be of the best and noblest sort, and therefore we should seek after it. Should we not aspire to that character upon which God Himself can smile? The approbation of our fellow-men is pleasant in its way; but they are always imperfect, and often mistaken; and so we may be well-pleasing to them, and yet may be far removed from righteousness. It may be a calamity to be commended in error, for it may prevent our becoming really commendable. But God makes no mistake; the Infinitely Holy knows no imperfection; and if it be possible for us to be pleasing to Him, it should be our one object to reach that condition. As Enoch, in a darker age, was pleasing to Him, why should not we, upon whom the gospel day has dawned? God grant us to find grace in His sight!

If we please God, we shall have realized the object of our being. It is written concerning all things, "For His pleasure they are and were created"; and we miss the end of creation if we are not pleasing to the Lord. To fulfil God's end in our creation is to obtain the highest joy. If we are pleasing to God, although we shall not escape trial, for even the highest qualities must be tested, yet we shall find great peace and special happiness. He is not an unhappy man who is pleasing to God: God hath blessed him, yea, and he shall be blessed. By pleasing God we shall become the means of good to others: our example will rebuke and stimulate; our peace will convince and invite. Being himself well-pleasing to God, the godly man will teach transgressors God's way, and sinners shall be converted unto Him. I therefore, without the slightest hesitancy, set it before you as a thing to be desired by us all, that we should win this testimony—that we are pleasing unto God.

Here the apostle comes in with a needful instruction. He asserts that faith is absolutely needful, if we would please God. Then, to help us still further, he mentions two essential points of faith, "He that cometh to God must believe that He is, and that He is a rewarder of them that diligently seek Him." When I have spoken on these two points, I shall close, as God shall help me, by showing that He then teaches us many valuable lessons.

I. First, then, THE APOSTLE ASSERTS THAT FAITH IS ABSOLUTELY ESSENTIAL TO THE PLEASING OF GOD. Take, as a key-word, the strong word "impossible." "Without faith it is impossible to please God." He does not say it is difficult, or so needful that without it success is barely possible; but, point-blank, He declares it to be "impossible." When the Holy Spirit says that a thing is impossible, it is so in a very absolute sense. Let us not attempt the impossible. To attempt a difficulty may be laudable, but to rush upon an impossibility is madness. We must not, therefore, hope to please God by an invention of our own, however clever, nor by any labour of our own, however ardent; since infallible inspiration declares that, "without faith it is impossible to please God."

We are bound to believe this statement, because we have it in the sacred volume, stated upon divine authority; but, for your help, I would invite you to think of some few matters which may show you how impossible it is to please God without faith in Him.

For, first, without faith there is no capacity for communion with God at all. The things of God are spiritual and invisible: without faith we cannot recognize such things, but must be dead to them. Faith is the eye which sees; but without that eye we are blind, and can have no fellowship with God in those sacred truths which only faith can perceive. Faith is the hand of the soul, and without it we have no grasp of eternal things. If I were to mention all the images by which faith is set forth, each one would help you to see that you must have faith in order to know God and enter into converse with Him. It is only by faith that we can recognize God, approach Him, speak to Him, hear Him, feel His presence, and be delighted with His perfections. He that has not faith is toward God as one dead; and Jehovah is not the God of the dead, but of the living. The communion of the living goes not forth toward death and corruption; His fellowship is with those who have spiritual life, a life akin to His own. Where there is no faith, there has been no quickening of the Holy Spirit, for faith is of the very essence of spiritual life; and so the man who has no faith can no more commune with the living God, and give Him pleasure, than can a stock or a stone, a horse or an ox, hold converse with the human mind.

Again, without faith the man himself is not pleasing to God. We read, "Without faith it is impossible to please God"; but the Revision has it better: "Without faith it is impossible to be well-pleasing unto God." The way of acceptance described in Scripture is, first, the man is accepted, and then what that man does is accepted. It is written: "And He shall purify the sons of Levi, that they may offer unto the Lord an offering in righteousness." First, God is pleased with the person, and then with the gift, or the work. The unaccepted person offers of necessity an unacceptable sacrifice. If a man be your enemy you will not value a present which he sends you. If you know that he has no

34

confidence in you, but counts you a liar, his praises are lost upon you; they are empty, deceptive things which cannot possibly please you. O my hearers, in your natural state you are so sinful that God cannot look upon you with complacency! Concerning our race it is written: "It repented the Lord that He had made man on the earth, and it grieved Him at His heart." Concerning many God has said, "My soul loathed them, and their soul also abhorred Me." Is this true of us? "Ye must be born again," or ye cannot be pleasing to the Lord. Ye must believe in Jesus; for only to as many as receive Him does He give power to become the sons of God. When we believe in the Lord Jesus, the Lord God accepts us for His beloved's sake, and in Him we are made kings and priests, and permitted to bring an offering which pleases God. As the man is, such is his work. The stream is of the nature of the spring from which it flows. He who is a rebel, outlawed and proclaimed, cannot gratify his prince by any fashion of service; he must first submit himself to the law. All the actions of rebels are acts done in rebellion. We must first be reconciled to God, or it is a mockery to bring an offering to His altar. Reconciliation can only be effected through the death of the Lord Jesus, and if we have no faith in that way of reconciliation we cannot please God. Faith in Christ makes a total change in our position towards God—we who were enemies are reconciled; and from this comes towards God a distinct change in the nature of all our actions: imperfect though they be, they spring from a loyal heart, and they are pleasing to God.

Remember, that, in human associations, want of confidence would prevent a man's being well-pleasing to another. If a man has no confidence in you, you can have no pleasure in him. If you had a child, and he had no trust in his father, no belief in his father's kindness, no reliance on his father's word—it would be most painful, and it would be quite impossible that you should take any pleasure in such a child. If you had a servant in your house who always suspected your every action, and believed in nothing that you said or did, but put a wrong construction upon everything, it would make the house very miserable, and you would be well rid of such an inmate. How can I take pleasure in a man who associates with me, and pretends to serve me, but all the while thinks me a sheer impostor, and gives me no credit for truthfulness? Such a person would be an eye-sore to me. It is clear that want of confidence would destroy any pleasure which one man might have in another. When the creature dares to doubt his Creator, how can the Creator be pleased? When the word which wrought creation is not enough for a man to rest upon, he may pretend what he will of righteousness and obedience, but the whole affair is rotten at the core, and God can take no pleasure in it.

Note again: unbelief takes away the common ground upon which God and man can meet. Two persons who are pleasant to one another, must have certain common views and objects. God's great object is the glorification of His son; and how can we be pleasing to Him if we dishonour that Son? The Father delights in Jesus: the very thought of Him is a pleasure to God. He said, as if to Himself only, "This is My beloved Son, in whom I am well pleased." This He said, afterwards, to others, that they might regard it—"This is My beloved Son; hear ye Him." He delights in what His Son has done: He smells a sweet savour of rest in His glorious sacrifice. If you and I believe in God's plan of salvation through Jesus Christ, we have a common ground of sympathy with God; but if not, we are not in harmony. How can two walk together except they be agreed? If we have thoughts of Jesus such as the Father has, we can live together and work together; but if we are opposed to Him on a point which is as the apple of His eye, we cannot be well-pleasing to Him. If Jesus be despised, rejected, distrusted, or even neglected, it is not possible for us to be pleasing to God. According to the well-worn fable, two persons who are totally different in their pursuits cannot well live together: the fuller and the charcoal-burner were obliged to part; for whatever the fuller had made white, the collier blackened with his finger. If differing pursuits divide, much more will differing feelings upon a vital point. It is Jesus whom Jehovah delights to honour; and if you will not even trust Jesus with your soul's salvation, you grieve the heart of God, and He can have no pleasure in you. Unbelief deprives the soul of the divinely-appointed meeting-place at the mercy-seat, which is the person of the lord Jesus, where God and man unite in one Mediator, and the Lord shines forth on the suppliant.

Assuredly, again, want of faith destroys all prospect of love. Although we may not perhaps see it, there lies at the bottom of all love a belief in the object loved, as to its loveliness, its merit, or its capacity to make us happy. If I do not believe in a person, I cannot love him. If I cannot trust God, I cannot love Him. If I do not believe that He loves me, I shall feel but slight emotions of love to Him. If I refuse to see anything in the greatest display of His love, if I do not value the gift of His dear Son, then I cannot love Him. We love Him because He first loved us; but if we will not believe in His love, the motive power is gone. If we reject the word which saith, "God so loved the world, that He gave His only begotten Son, that whosoever believeth in Him should not perish, but have everlasting life," then we have put from out of the heart the grand incentive to love. But love on our part is essential to our pleasing God: how can He be pleased with an unloving heart? Is not the Lord's chief demand of men that we love Him with all our heart, with all our soul, with all our mind, and with all our strength? Without faith love is impossible, and God's pleasure in us must be impossible.

Again, dear friends, want of faith will create positive variance on many points. Note a few. If I trust God, and believe in Him, I shall submit myself to His will; even when it becomes very painful to me I shall say, "It is the Lord: let Him do what seemeth Him good." But if I do not believe that He is God, and that He is aiming at my good, then I shall resent his chastisements, and shall kick against His will. What He wills me to suffer, I shall not be willing to suffer; but I shall rebel, and murmur, and proudly accuse my Maker of injustice, or want of love. I shall be in a rebellious state towards Him, and then He cannot have pleasure in me. "The Lord taketh pleasure in them that fear Him, in those that hope in His mercy"; but He will walk contrary to us, if we walk contrary to Him by refusing to bow ourselves before His hand.

Without faith, moreover, I get to be at variance with God in another way; for inasmuch as I desire to be saved, I shall seek salvation in my own way, and go about to establish a righteousness of my own. Whatever it may be, whether it be by ceremonies, or by good works, or by feelings, or what not, I shall, in some way or other, set up a way of salvation other than that which God has appointed through Christ Jesus. God's love to Christ is supreme, and He will not endure that a rival should be set up in opposition to Him. Another way of salvation is Antichrist, and this provokes the Lord to jealousy. If you are labouring to be saved in one way, while God declares that through His Son is the only way of salvation, you are acting in distinct opposition to the Lord in a matter which does not admit of any compromise. Rejectors of Christ are enemies to God. If you pretend that you are God's servants, you are convicted of falsehood if you refuse to honour His Son by trusting in Him. If you believe in Christ, whom He has sent, you work the work of God; and not else. Self-righteousness is an insult to Christ, and a distinct revolt from God. He who has no faith seeks salvation by a way that is derogatory to the Lord Jesus, and it is impossible for him to please God.

We must be at variance with God if we are without faith; for it is a solemn truth that "He that believeth not God hath made Him a liar; because he believeth not the record that God gave of His Son." This is the crime of the unbeliever: so is it stated by the Holy Spirit speaking by the beloved John. Could you take any pleasure in a man who made you out to be a liar? Perhaps with great patience you could bear with him, but you could not be pleased with him: that would be out of the question. Does a man daily, by the mode of his life, and by the evident drift of his actions, give you the lie?—how can he talk of giving you pleasure? Nothing he could do would please you while he calls you a liar. He that makes God to be a liar, makes Him to be no God; to the best of his ability he undeifies the Deity; he uncrowns the Lord of all, and even stabs at the heart of the Eternal. To talk of being well-pleasing to God in such a case is absurd.

Let us conclude this point by asking, by what means can we hope to please God, apart from faith in Him? By keeping all the commandments? Alas! you have not done so. You have already broken those commands; and what is more, you still break them, and are in a chronic state of disobedience. If you do not believe in Him you are not obedient to Him; for true obedience commands the understanding as well as every other power and faculty. We are bound to obey with the mind by believing, as well as with the hand by acting. The spiritual part of our being is in revolt against God until we believe; and, while the very life and glory of our being is in revolt, how can we please God?

But what will you bring to the Lord wherewith to please Him? Do you propose to bribe Him with your money? Surely you are not so foolish! Is the Lord to be bought with a row of almshouses, or a chapel, or a cathedral? To most of you it would be impossible to try the plan for lack of means; but if you were wealthy enough to lavish gold out of the bag, would this please Him? The silver and the gold are His, and the cattle on a thousand hills. If He were hungry, He would not tell you. What can you give to Him to whom all things belong? Truly, you can assist in an ornate worship, or build a gorgeous church, or embroider the furniture of an altar, or emblazon the windows of a church. But are you so weak as to believe that such trifles as these can cause any delight to the mind of the Infinite? Solomon built Him a house, but "the Most High dwelleth not in temples made with hands." To what shall I liken the most glorious erections of human genius but to the ant-hills of the tropics, which are wonderful as the fabrication of ants, even as our cathedrals are marvellous as the handicraft of men. But what are ant-hills or cathedrals when measured with the Infinite? What are all our works to the Lord? He who with a single arch has spanned the world, cares little for our carved capitals and groined arches. The prettinesses of architecture are as much beneath the glory of Jehovah as the dolls and boxes of bricks of our children would be beneath the dignity of a Solomon. God is not a man that He should take delight in these things. "Will the Lord be pleased with thousands of rams, or with ten thousands of rivers of oil? shall I give my first-born for my transgression, the fruit of my body for the sin of my soul?" It is not this that He asks of you, but to walk humbly with Him, never daring arrogantly to doubt His truth and mistrust His faithfulness. Go not about by a thousand inventions to aim at what you will never compass, but believe your God, and be established. So much upon that painful point. Remember the impossibility of pleasing the Lord without faith, and do not dash your ship upon this ironbound coast.

II. Now, secondly, THE APOSTLE MENTIONS TWO ESSENTIAL POINTS OF FAITH.

He begins by saying, "He that cometh to God must believe that He is." Note the key-word "must": it is an immovable, insatiable necessity. Before we can walk with God, it is clear that we must come to God. Naturally, we are at a distance from Him, and we must end that distance by coming to Him, or else we cannot walk with Him, nor be pleasing to Him. That we may come to Him, we must first believe that there is a God to come to. More; we must not only believe that there is a God—for only a fool doubts that: "The fool hath said in his heart, There is no God"—but we must believe that Jehovah is God, and God alone. This was Enoch's faith: he believed that Jehovah was the living and true God. You are to believe, and must believe in order to be pleasing with God, that He is God, that He is the only God, and that there can be none other than He. You must also accept Jehovah as He reveals Himself. You are not to have a God of your own making, nor a God reasoned out, but a God such as He has been pleased to reveal Himself to you. Believe that Jehovah is, whoever else may be or may not be.

But the devils believe and tremble, and yet they are not pleasing to God, for more is wanted. Believe that God is in reference to yourself; that He has to do with your life, and your ways. Many believe that there is a hazy, imaginary power which they call God; but they never think of Him as a person, nor do they suspect that He thinks of them, or that His existence is of any consequence to them one way or another. Believe that God is as truly as you are; and let Him be real to you. Let the consideration of Him enter into everything that concerns you. Believe that He is approachable by yourself, and is to be pleased or displeased by you. Believe in Him as you believe in your wife or your child whom you try to please. Believe in God beyond everything, that "He is" in a sense more sure that that in which anyone else exists. Believe that He is to be approached, to be realized, to be, in fact, the great practical factor of your life.

Hold this as the primary truth, that God is most influential upon you; and then believe that it is your business to come to Him. But there is only one way of coming to Him, and you must have faith to use that way. He that died and lives for ever saith, "I am the way. No man cometh unto the Father, but by Me." He that cometh to God must believe in God as He is revealed, and must come to God as God reveals the way of approach; and this is an exertion of faith. Faith as to this point is essential. You cannot come to Him in whom you do not believe. Are not many hearers of the Word really as far from God as infidels? Let me ask you, how many atheists are now in this house? Perhaps not a single one of you would accept the title, and yet, if you live from Monday morning to Saturday night in the same way as you would live if there were no God, you are practical atheists; and as actions speak more loudly than words, you are more atheists than those doctrinal unbelievers who disavow God with their mouths, and, after all, are secretly afraid of Him. A life without God is as bad as a creed without God. You cannot come to God unless you believe in him as the All-in-all, the Lord God beside whom there is none else.

Yet all this would be nothing without the second point of belief. We must believe that "He is the rewarder of them that diligently seek Him." How do we seek Him, then? Well, we seek Him, first, when we begin by prayer, by trusting to Jesus, and by calling upon the sacred name, to seek salvation. "Whosoever shall call upon the name of the Lord shall be saved." That is a grand promise, and it teaches how we come to God; namely, by calling upon His name. Afterwards we seek God by aiming at His glory, by making Him the great object for which we live. One man seeks money, and another seeks reputation, another seeks pleasure; but he that is pleasing to God seeks God as his object and end. "Seek ye first the kingdom of God, and His righteousness; and all these things shall be added unto you." The man with whom God is pleased, is pleased with God; he sets the Lord always before him, and seeks to live for Him. This he would not do, unless he believed that God would reward him in so doing. Take this as a certainty, that we must believe that "God is the rewarder of them that diligently seek Him," or we shall not seek Him. We are sure that, somehow or other, it will be to our highest benefit to honour the Lord and trust on Him. Albeit we deserve nothing at His hands but wrath, yet we perceive from the gospel that if we seek Him through His Son, we shall be so well-pleasing to Him as to get a reward from His hands. This must be of grace—free, sovereign grace! And what a reward it is! Free pardon, graciously bestowed; a change of heart, graciously wrought; perseverance graciously maintained, comfort graciously poured in, and privilege graciously awarded. The reward of godliness, even in this world, is immeasurable, and in the world to come it is infinite. We may have respect unto the recompence of the reward; indeed, we should have respect to it, and therefore boldly seek God, and seek nothing else.

The Lord is "a rewarder of them that diligently seek Him." That is not quite an exact translation: the Greek word means not only to seek Him, but "seek Him out"; that is, seek Him till they find Him, and seek Him above all others. It is a very strong word; we hardly know how to transfer its meaning into English, for though it does not say "diligently," it implies it. We must seek, and seek out; that is, seek till we really find. Those who with their hearts follow after God, shall not be losers if they believe that He will reward them. You have to believe God so as to seek His glory. Even when you do not obtain any present reward for it, you are to say, "I shall have a reward ultimately, even if I am for a while a loser through His service. If I lose money, respect, friendship, or even life from following God, yet still He will be a rewarder, and I shall be repaid ten thousandfold, not of debt, but according to His grace." He, then, that would please God, must first believe that He is; and then, dedicating himself to God, must be firmly assured that this is the right, the wise, the prudent thing to do. Be certain that to serve God is in itself gain: it is wealth to be holy; it is happiness to be pleasing to God. To us it is life to live to God—to know Him, to adore Him, to commune with Him, to become like Him. It is glory to us to make Him glorious among the sons of men. For us to live is Christ. This, we are persuaded, is the best pursuit for us; in fact, it is the only one which can satisfy our hearts. God is our shield, and our exceeding great reward; and in the teeth of everything that happens we hold to this, that to serve God is gain. If God helps us to trust Him, and therefore to live unto Him and to seek to be well-pleasing in His sight, we shall succeed in pleasing Him. We cannot conceive that the heavenly Father sees, without pleasure, a man struggling against sin, battling against evil, enduring sorrow contentedly through a simple faith, and labouring daily to draw nearer and nearer to Him. God is not displeased with those who, by faith, live to please Him, and are content to take their reward from His hand. He must be pleased with the work of His own grace. The desire to come to God, the way to come to God, the power to come to God, the actual coming to God—these are all gifts of sovereign grace. Coming to God, however feebly we come, and seeking Him, however much else we miss, must be well-pleasing in His sight; for it is the result of His own purpose and grace which He gave us in Christ Jesus before the world began. But all this hangs upon faith. Without faith there is no coming to God who is, and no seeking of God who is a rewarder; and therefore without faith it is impossible to please God.

III. WE WILL NOW GATHER A FEW LESSONS FROM WHAT THE APOSTLE HAS TAUGHT US. Help us, O gracious Spirit!

First, then, the apostle teaches us here by implication that God is pleased with those that have faith. The negative is often the plainest way of suggesting the positive. If we are so carefully warned that without faith it is impossible to please God, we infer that with faith it is possible to please God. If you believe that He is, and that He is a rewarder of them that diligently seek Him; if you are willing to believe all that He teaches you because he teaches it, and are really a believer in Himself and in all that He is pleased to reveal, then are you pleasing to Him. He that believes in God believes in all the words that God speaks, and he surrenders himself to all that God does; and such a man must be pleasing to God. We believe in one God, and in one Mediator between God and man, the Man Christ Jesus; and we trust in the Lord as He thus draws near to us: thus are we in the way of pleasing God. By faith we ourselves have become pleasing to God, and our actions performed with a view to His honour are pleasing to Him. What a joy is this! It is bliss to think that I, who, in my unregenerate state, grieved the Holy Spirit, and vexed Him day by day, am now the object of pleasure to Him. I, whose actions were contrary to the law of God, and the bent of whose mind was against the gospel of Christ, I, even I, who was once obnoxious to Divine anger, an heir of wrath, even as others, have now, through faith, become to God an object of His complacency. This is very wonderful. If the Holy Spirit leads you to feel the full sweetness of this truth, you will rejoice with joy unspeakable. I feel like singing rather than preaching. Oh, guilty one, wilt thou not now believe thy God? This is the way to come back to Him. When the prodigal said, "In my father's house there is bread enough and to spare," he believed in his father's power to supply all his needs. When he thought in his heart that his father would receive him, then he said, "I will arise and go to my father, and will say unto him, Father, I have sinned." You must have so much belief in God as to believe Him to have the heart of a father towards you, or you will never come back to Him; but when you begin to trust your God your face is already towards the heavenly home, and before long your head will be in your Father's bosom. If faith can make the vilest and guiltiest pleasing to God, will they not believe in Him? What a transformation this would work in them! Oh, that this morning all of us may stand out in the clear sunlight of Jehovah's good pleasure, and know ourselves to be well-pleasing to Him through Jesus Christ!

Learn, next, that those who have faith make it the great object of their life to please God. Am I speaking the truth? Will each one ask whether it is true about himself? Do I, as a believer, live to please God? We need personal heart-searching on this point. The believer in the invisible God delights to act as in His sight, and in secret to serve Him. I take a choice pleasure in rendering to my God a service unknown to others, not done for the sake of my fellows, but distinctly that I may do something for my Lord's own self. It is sweet to give or do simply to please Him, without respect to the public eye. Even such actions as must come under the gaze of others are not to be done with the view of winning their approbation, but only to please God. The doing of such actions is a singular fountain of strength to a man's mind. It is ennobling to feel you have only one Master, and that you live to please Him, even God. To please men is poor work. To live to follow everybody's whim is slavery. If you let one man pull you by the ear in his direction, another will tug at you from another direction, and you will have very long ears before long. Happy is he who, pleasing God, feels that he has risen above seeking to please men. It is grand to say, "This is what God would have me do, and I will do it in happy fellowship with others, or alone by myself, as the case may be; but do it I must." This gives a man backbone, and at the same time removes the selfishness which is greedy of popular applause. It is a grand thing to be no longer looking down for cheer, but to be distinctly looking up for it. The man who truly believes in God makes small account of men. Put them together, they are vanity; heap them up in their thousands, they are altogether lighter than vanity. Nations upon nations, what are they but as grasshoppers! The lands in which they live, what are they before God! "He taketh up the isles as a very little thing." To please God even a little is infinitely greater than to have the acclamations of all our race throughout the centuries. The true believer feels that God is, and that there is none beside Him; none that needs to be thought of in comparison with Him. The theology of the present aims at the deification of man, but the truth of all time magnifies God. We shall stand by the old paths, wherein we hear a voice which bids us worship Jehovah, our God, and serve Him alone. He shall be all in all. Only as we see men loved of Him can we live for men; we seek their good in God, and for His glory, and regard them as capable of being made mirrors to reflect the glory of the Lord.

Note, next, the apostle teaches us here that they that have faith in God are always coming to God; for He speaks of the believer as "He that cometh to God." If you once learn to believe God, and to please Him, you are coming to Him day by day. You not only come to Him, and go away with Him, as in acts of prayer and praise; but you are always coming; your life is a march towards Him. The way of the believer is toward God; by his faith he comes ever nearer and yet nearer to the eternal throne. What is his reward? Why, He that sitteth on the throne will say, "Come, ye blessed of My Father, inherit the kingdom prepared for you from the foundation of the world." Come! Come on! You have been coming, keep on coming for ever. There is a gentle, constant, perpetual progress of the believer's heart and mind nearer and closer to God. I could not wonder at Enoch being translated after walking with God hundreds of years; for it is such a small step from close communion with God on earth to perfect communion with God in heaven. A thin partition divides us which a sigh will remove. The breaking of a blood-vessel, the snapping of a cord, the staying of a breath, and he that had God with him shall be with God. Sometimes he could not tell whether he was in the body or out of the body, but had to leave that question with God; he will soon be able to answer the question for himself, and know that he is absent from the body, and present with the Lord. O beloved, please God, please God; and as you please Him by your simple confidence and childlike trust, you are coming nearer to Him.

The next lesson is one I have already spoken of: God will see that those who practise faith in Him shall have a reward. I say, God will see to it, for the text says, "He is a rewarder of them that diligently seek Him." The Lord will not leave the reward of faith to the choicest angel: He Himself will adjudge the recompense. Here we may get but scant reward from, those whom we benefit: indeed, they usually return us base ingratitude. Joseph was a faithful servant to Potiphar; but Potiphar put him in prison on a groundless charge. Joseph helped the butler, and interpreted his dream, yet he remembered not Joseph, but forgat him. You may not reckon upon due returns from your fellow-men, or you will be disappointed. Like David, you may guard Nabal's sheep, and when the sheep-shearing comes you may hope to be remembered, and he will insult you with a churlish answer. Expect little from men and much from God, for by nature and by office He is a rewarder. No work done for Him will go unrewarded. In His service the wages are sure. Rise into the Abrahamic life which stays itself upon the Lord's word, "Fear not, Abraham: I am thy shield and thy exceeding great reward." It is enough reward to have such a God to be our God. What if He gives us neither vineyards nor olive gardens, neither sheep nor oxen; He Himself is ours, and this is a greater reward than if He gave us all the world. God Himself is enough for the believer. If his faith be true and deep, and intelligent, he cries. "Whom have I in heaven but Thee? and there is none upon earth that I desire beside Thee."

The last lesson we gather from it is this: those who have no faith are in a fearful case. I speak not of the heathen, but of unbelievers who reject the gospel. "Without faith it is impossible to please God." Some of you are always fashioning fresh nets of doubt for your own entanglement. You invent snares for your own feet, and are greedy to lay more and more of them. You are mariners who seek the rocks, soldiers who court the point of the bayonet. It is an unprofitable business. Practically, morally, mentally, spiritually, doubting is an evil trade. You are like a smith, wearing out his arm in making chains with which to bind himself. Doubt is sterile, a desert without water. Doubt discovers difficulties which it never solves: it creates hesitancy, despondency, despair. Its progress is the decay of comfort, the death of peace. "Believe!" is the word which speaks life into a man; but doubt nails down his coffin. If thou canst believe, O guilty one, that Jesus Christ bore the guilt of sin upon the cross, and by His death has made atonement to the insulted government of God; if thou canst so believe in Him as to cast thyself just as thou art at His dear feet, thou shalt be pleasing to God. I entreat thee to look up and see the pierced hands, and feet, and side of the dear Redeemer, and read eternal mercy there; read full forgiveness there, and then go thou away in peace, for thou art well-pleasing to God. The sinner who believes God's testimony concerning His Son has begun to please Him, and is himself well-pleasing to the Lord. Oh that you would now trust Him who justifieth the ungodly and passeth by the iniquities of sinful men! He will receive you graciously and love you freely. Oh, come to Him, for He is a rewarder of them that diligently seek Him. God help you to do so at once. But without faith you cannot please Him. Do what you may, feel what you like, you will labour as in the very fire, and nothing will come of it but eternal despair. The Lord help you to believe and live. Amen.

FAITH AND LIFE

"Simon Peter, a servant and an apostle of Jesus Christ, to them that have obtained like precious faith with us through the righteousness of God and our Saviour Jesus Christ; grace and peace be multiplied unto you through the knowledge of God, and of Jesus our Lord, according as His divine power hath given unto us all things that pertain unto life and godliness, through the knowledge of Him that hath called us to glory and virtue: whereby are given unto us exceeding great and precious promises: that by these ye might be partakers of the divine nature, having escaped the corruption that is in the world through lust."—2 Peter i. 1-4.

The two most important things in our holy religion are faith and life. He who shall rightly understand these two words is not far from being a master in experimental theology. Faith and life! these are vital points to a Christian. They possess so intimate a connection with each other that they are by no means to be severed; God hath so joined them together, let no man seek to put them asunder. You shall never find true faith unattended by true godliness; on the other hand, you shall never discover a truly holy life which has not for its root and foundation a living faith upon the righteousness of our Lord Jesus Christ. Woe unto those who seek after the one without the other! There be

41

some who cultivate faith and forget holiness; these may be very high in orthodoxy, but they shall be very deep in damnation, in that day when God shall condemn those who hold the truth in unrighteousness, and make the doctrine of Christ to pander to their lusts. There are others who have strained after holiness of life, but have denied the faith; these are comparable unto the Pharisees of old, of whom the Master said, they were "whitewashed sepulchres"; they were fair to look upon externally, but inwardly, because the living faith was not there, they were full of dead men's bones and all manner of uncleanness. Ye must have faith, for this is the foundation; ye must have holiness of life, for this is the superstructure. Of what avail is the mere foundation of a building to a man in the day of tempest? Can he hide himself among sunken stones and concrete? He wants a house to cover him, as well as a foundation upon which that house might have been built; even so we need the superstructure of spiritual life if we would have comfort in the day of doubt. But seek not a holy life without faith, for that would be to erect a house which can afford no permanent shelter, because it has no foundation on a rock—a house which must come down with a tremendous crash in the day when the rain descends, and the floods come, and the winds blow, and beat upon it. Let faith and life be put together and, like the two abutments of an arch, they shall make your piety strong. Like the horses of Pharaoh's chariot, they pull together gloriously. Like light and heat streaming from the same sun, they are alike full of blessing. Like the two pillars of the temple, they are for glory and for beauty. They are two streams from the fountain of grace; two lamps lit with holy fire; two olive-trees watered by heavenly care; two stars carried in Jesus' hand. The Lord grant that we may have both of these to perfection, that His name may be praised.

Now, it will be clear to all, that in the four verses before us, our apostle has most excellently set forth the necessity of these two things—twice over he insists upon the faith, and twice over upon holiness of life. We will take the first occasion first.

I. Observe, in the first place, what he says concerning the character and the origin of faith, and then concerning the character and origin of spiritual life.

"Simon Peter, a servant and an apostle of Jesus Christ, to them that have obtained like precious faith with us through the righteousness of God and our Saviour Jesus Christ." So far the faith. "Grace and peace be multiplied unto you through the knowledge of God, and of Jesus our Lord, according as His divine power hath given unto us all things that pertain unto life and godliness, through the knowledge of Him that hath called us to glory and virtue." These two verses, you see, concern the spiritual life which comes with the faith.

Let us begin where Peter begins, with the FAITH. You have here a description of true saving faith.

First, you have a description of its source. He says, "to them that have obtained like precious faith." See, then, my brethren, faith does not grow in man's heart by nature; it is a thing which is obtained. It is not a matter which springs up by a process of education, or by the example and excellent instruction of our parents; it is a thing which has to be obtained. Not imitation, but regeneration; not development, but conversion. All our good things come from without us, only evil can be educed from within us. Now, that which is obtained by us must be given to us; and well are we taught in Scripture that "faith is not of ourselves, it is the gift of God." Although faith is the act of man, yet it is the work of God. "With the heart man believeth unto righteousness"; but that heart must, first of all, have been renewed by divine grace before it ever can be capable of the act of saving faith. Faith, we say, is man's act, for we are commanded to "believe on the Lord Jesus Christ," and we shall be saved. At the same time, faith is God's gift, and wherever we find it, we may know that it did not come there from the force of nature, but from a work of divine grace. How this magnifies the grace of God, my brethren, and how low this casts human nature! Faith. Is it not one of the simplest things? Merely to depend upon the blood and righteousness of the Lord Jesus Christ, does it not seem one of the easiest of virtues? To be nothing, and to let Him be everything—to be still, and to let Him work for me, does not this seem to be the most elementary of all the Christian graces? Indeed, so it is; and yet, even to this first principle and rudiment, poor human nature is so fallen and so utterly undone, that it cannot attain unto! Brethren, the Lord must not only open the gates of heaven to us at the last, but He must open the gates of our heart to faith at the first. It is not enough for us to know that He must make us perfect in every good work to do His will, but we must be taught that He must even give us a desire after Christ; and when this is given, He must enable us to give the grip of the hand of faith whereby Jesus Christ becomes our Saviour and Lord. Now, the question comes (and we will try and make the text of to-day a text of examination all the way through) have we obtained this faith? Are we conscious that we have been operated upon by the Holy Spirit? Is there a vital principle in us which was not there originally? Do we know to-day the folly of carnal confidence? Have we a hope that we have been enabled through divine grace to cast away all our own righteousness and every dependence, and are we now, whether we sink or swim, resting entirely upon the Person, the righteousness, the blood, the intercession, the precious merit of our Lord Jesus Christ? If not, we have cause enough to tremble; but if we have, the while the apostle writes, "Unto them that have obtained like precious faith," he writes to us, and across the interval of centuries his benediction comes as full and fresh as ever, "Grace and peace be multiplied unto you."

Peter having described the origin of this faith, proceeds to describe its object. The word "through" in our translation, might, quite as correctly, have been rendered "in"—"faith in the righteousness of our God and our Saviour Jesus Christ." True faith, then, is a faith in Jesus Christ, but it is a faith in Jesus Christ as divine. That man who believes in Jesus Christ as simply a prophet, as only a great teacher, has not the faith which will save him. Charity would make us hope for many Unitarians, but honesty compels us to condemn them without exception, so far as vital godliness is concerned. It matters not how intelligent may be their conversation, nor how charitable may be their manners, nor how patriotic may be their spirit, if they reject Jesus Christ as very God of very God, we believe they shall without doubt perish everlastingly. Our Lord uttereth no dubious words when He said "He that believeth shall not be damned," and we must not attempt to be more liberal than the Lord Himself. Little allowance can I make for one who receives Jesus the prophet, and rejects him as God. It is an atrocious outrage upon common sense for a man to profess to be a believer in Christ at all, if he does not receive His divinity. I would undertake, at any time, to prove to a demonstration, that if Christ were not God, He was the grossest impostor who ever lived. One of two things, He was either divine or a villain. There is no stopping between the two. I cannot imagine a character more vile than that which would be borne by a man who should lead his followers to adore him as God, without ever putting in a word by way of caveat, to stop their idolatry; nay, who should have spoken in terms so ambiguous, that two thousand years after His death, there should be found millions of persons resting upon Him as God. I say, if He were not God, the atrocity of His having palmed Himself upon us, His disciples, as God, puts aside altogether from consideration any of the apparent virtues of His life. He was the grossest of all deceivers, if He was not "very God of very God." O beloved, you and I have found no difficulties here; when we have beheld the record of His miracles, when we have listened to the testimony of His divine Father, when we have heard the word of the inspired apostles, when we have felt the majesty of His own divine influence in our own hearts, we have graciously accepted Him as "the Wonderful, the Counsellor, the mighty God, the everlasting Father;" and, as John bare witness of Him and said, "The Word was in the beginning with God, and the Word was God," even so have we received Him; so that at this day, He that was born of the virgin Mary, Jesus of Nazareth, the king of the Jews, is to us "God over all, blessed for ever."

"Jesus is worthy to receive
Honour and power divine:

And blessings more than we can give,
　Be Lord for ever Thine."

Now, beloved friends, have we heartily and joyfully received Jesus Christ as God? My hearer, if thou hast not, I pray thee seek of God the faith which saves, for thou hast it not as yet, nor art thou in the way to it. Who but a God could bear the weight of sin? Who but a God shall be the "same yesterday, to-day, and for ever?" Concerning whom but a God could it be said, "I am the Lord, I change not: therefore ye sons of Jacob are not consumed." We have to do with Christ, and we should be consumed if He changed; inasmuch, then, as He does not change, and we are not consumed, He must be divine, and our soul rolls the entire burden of its care and guilt upon the mighty shoulders of the everlasting God, who—

"Bears the earth's huge pillars up,
And spread the heavens abroad."

Remark in further dwelling upon the text, that the apostle has put in another word beside "God," and that is, "of God and our Saviour." As if the glory of the Godhead might be too bright for us, he has attempered it by gentler words "our Saviour." Now, to trust Jesus Christ as divine, will save no man, unless there be added to this a resting in Him as the great propitiatory sacrifice. Jesus Christ is our Saviour because He became a substitute for guilty man. He having taken upon Himself the form of manhood by union with our nature, stood in the room, place and stead of sinners. When the whole tempest of divine wrath was about to spend itself on man, He endured it all for His elect; when the great whip of the law must fall, He bared His own shoulders to the lash; when the cry was heard, "Awake, O sword!" it was against Christ the Shepherd, against the man who was the fellow to the eternal God. And because He thus suffered in the place and stead of man, He received power from on high to become the Saviour of man, and to bring many sons into glory, because He had been made perfect through suffering. Now, have we received Jesus Christ as our Saviour? Happy art thou, if thou hast laid thy hand upon the head of Him who was slain for sinners. Be glad, and rejoice in the Lord without ceasing, if to-day that blessed Redeemer who has ascended upon high has become thy Saviour, delivered thee from sin, passing by thy transgressions, and making thee to be accepted in the beloved. A Saviour is He to us when He delivers us from the curse, punishment, guilt, and power of sin, "He shall save His people from their sins." O Thou great God, be Thou my Saviour, mighty to save.

But be pleased to notice the word "righteousness." It is a faith in the righteousness of our God and our Saviour. In these days, certain divines have tried to get rid of all idea of atonement; they have taught that faith in Jesus Christ would save men, apart from any faith in Him as a sacrifice. Ah, brethren, it does not say, "faith in the teaching of God our Saviour;" I do not find here that it is written, "faith in the character of God our Saviour, as our exemplar." No, but "faith in the righteousness of God our Saviour." That righteousness, like a white robe, must be cast around us: I have not received Jesus Christ at all, but I am an adversary and an enemy to Him, unless I have received Him as Jehovah Tsidkenu, the Lord our righteousness. There is His perfect life; that life was a life for me; it contains all the virtues, in it there is no spot; it keeps the law of God, and makes it honourable, my faith takes that righteousness of Jesus Christ, and it is cast about me, and I am then so beauteously, nay, so perfectly arrayed, that even the eye of God can see neither spot nor blemish in me. Have we, then, to-day a faith in the righteousness of God our Saviour? For no faith but this can ever bring the soul into a condition of acceptance before the Most High. "Why," saith one, "these are the very simplicities of the gospel." Beloved, I know they are, and, therefore, do we deal them out this morning, for, thanks be to God, it is the simplicities which lie at the foundation; and it is rather by simplicities than by mysteries that a Christian is to try himself and to see whether he be in the faith or no. Put the question, brethren, have we, then, this like precious faith in God and our Saviour Jesus Christ?

Our apostle has not finished the description, without saying that it is "like precious faith." All faith is the same sort of faith. Our faith may not be like that of Peter, in degree, but if it be genuine, it is like it as to its nature, its origin, its objects, and its results. Here is a blessed equality. Speak of "liberty, equality, and fraternity," you shall only find these things carried out within the Church of Christ. There is indeed a blessed equality here, for the poorest little-faith who ever crept into heaven on its hands and knees, has a like precious faith with the mighty apostle Peter. I say, brethren, if the one be gold, so is the other; if the one can move mountains, so can the other; for remember, that the privileges of mountain-moving, and of plucking up the trees, and casting them into the sea, are not given to great faith, but "if ye have faith as a grain of mustard seed," it shall be done. Little faith has a royal descent and is as truly of divine birth as is the greatest and fullest assurance which ever made glad the heart of man, hence it ensures the same inheritance at the last, and the same safety by the way. It is "like precious faith."

He tells us too, that faith is "precious;" and is it not precious? for it deals with precious things, with precious promises, with precious blood, with a precious redemption, with all the preciousness of the person of our Lord and Saviour Jesus Christ. Well may that be a precious faith which supplies our greatest want, delivers us from our greatest danger, and admits us to the greatest glory. Well may that be called "precious faith," which is the symbol of our election, the evidence of our calling, the root of all our graces, the channel of communion, the weapon of prevalence, the shield of safety, the substance of hope, the evidence of eternity, the guerdon of immortality, and the passport of glory. O for more of this inestimably precious faith. Precious faith, indeed it is.

When the apostle, Simon Peter, writes "to them that have obtained like precious faith with us, through the righteousness of God, and our Saviour Jesus Christ," does he write to you? does he write to me? If not, if we are not here addressed, remember that we can never expect to hear the voice which says, "Come ye blessed of My Father;" but we are to-day in such a condition, that dying as we now are, "Depart ye cursed" must be the thunder which shall roll in our ears, and drive us down to hell. So much, then, concerning faith.

Now we shall turn to notice with great brevity, the LIFE. "Grace and peace be multiplied unto you through the knowledge of God and of Jesus our Lord, according as His divine power hath given unto us all things that pertain unto life and godliness, through the knowledge of Him that hath called us to glory and virtue." Here we have, then, brethren, the fountain and source of our spiritual life. Just as faith is a boon which is to be obtained, so you will perceive that our spiritual life is a principle which is given. A thing which is given to us, too, by divine power—"according as his divine power hath given unto us all things that pertain unto life and godliness." To give life at all is the essential attribute of God. This is an attribute which He will not alienate; to save and to destroy belong unto the Sovereign of heaven. "He can create, and He destroy," is one of the profoundest notes in the ascription of our praise. Suppose a corpse before us. How great a pretender would he be who should boast that it was in his power to restore it to life. Certainly, it would be even a greater pretence if anyone should say that he could give to himself or to another the divine life, the spiritual life by which a man is made a Christian. My brethren, you who are partakers of the divine nature, know that by nature you were dead in trespasses and sins, and would have continued so until this day if there had not been an interposition of divine energy on your behalf. There you lay in the grave of your sin, rotten, corrupt. The voice of the minister called to you, but you did not hear. You were often bidden to come forth, but you did not and could not come. But when the Lord said, "Lazarus, come forth," then Lazarus came forth; and when He said to you, "Live," then you lived also, and the spiritual life beat within you, with joy and peace through believing. This we ought never to forget, because, let us never fail to remember, that if our religion is a thing which sprang from ourselves, it is of the flesh, and must die.

45

That which is born of the flesh in its best and most favourable moments, is flesh, and only that which is born of the Spirit is spirit. "Ye must be born again." If a man's religious life be only a refinement of his ordinary life, if it be only a high attainment of the natural existence, then it is not the spiritual life, and does not prepare him for the eternal life before the throne of God. No, we must have a supernatural spark of heavenly flame kindled within us. Just as nothing but the soul can quicken the body and make it live, so the Spirit alone can quicken the soul and make the soul live. We must have the third master-principle infused, or else we shall be but natural men, made after the image of the first Adam. We must have, I say, the new spirit, or else we shall not be like the second Adam, who was made by a quickening spirit. Only of the Christian can we say that he is spirit, soul, and body; the ungodly man has only soul and body, and as to spiritual existence, he is as dead as the body would be if there were no soul. Now the implantation of this new principle, called the spirit, is a work of divine power. Divine power! what stupendous issues are grasped in that term, divine power! It was this which digged the deep foundations of the earth and sea! Divine power, it is this which guides the marches of the stars of heaven! Divine power! it is this which holds up the pillars of the universe, and which one day shall shake them, and hurry all things back to their native nothingness. Yet the selfsame power which is required to create a world and to sustain it, is required to make a man a Christian, and unless that power be put forth, the spiritual life is not in any one of us.

You will perceive, dear friends, that the apostle Peter wished to see this divine life in a healthy and vigorous state, and therefore he prays that grace and peace may be multiplied. Divine power is the foundation of this life; grace is the food it feeds upon, and peace is the element in which it lives most healthily. Give a Christian much grace, and his spiritual life will be like the life of a man who is well clothed and nurtured; keep the spiritual life without abundant grace, and it becomes lean, faint, and ready to die; and though die it cannot, yet will it seem as though it gave up the ghost, unless fresh grace be bestowed. Peace, I say, is the element in which it flourishes most. Let a Christian be much disturbed in mind, let earthly cares get into his soul, let him have doubts and fears as to his eternal safety, let him lose a sense of reconciliation to God, let his adoption be but dimly before his eyes, and you will not see much of the divine life within him. But oh! if God shall smile upon the life within you, and you get much grace from God, and your soul dwells much in the balmy air of heavenly peace, then shall you be strong to exercise yourself unto godliness, and your whole life shall adorn the doctrine of God your Saviour.

Observe, again, that in describing this life, he speaks of it as one which was conferred upon us by our being called. He says, "We were called unto glory and virtue." I find translators differ here. Many of them think the word should be "By"—"We are called by the glory and virtue of God"—that is, there is a manifestation of all the glorious attributes of God, and of all the efficacious virtue and energy of His power in the calling of every Christian. Simon Peter himself was at his fishing and in his boat, but Jesus said to him, "Follow me;" and at once he followed Christ. He says there was in that calling, the divine glory and virtue; and, doubtless, when you and I shall get to heaven, and see things as they are, we shall discover in our effectual calling of God to grace, a glory as great as in the creation of worlds, and a virtue as great as in the healing of the sick, when virtue went from the garments of a Saviour. Now, can we say to-day, that we have a life within us which is the result of divine power, and have we, upon searching ourselves, reason to believe, dear friends, that there is that within us which distinguishes us from other men, because we have been called out of mankind by the glory and energy of the divine power? I am afraid some of us must say "Nay." Then the Lord in His mercy yet bring us into the number of His people. But if we can, however, tremblingly say "Yes, I trust there is something of the life in me;" then as Peter did, so do I wish for you that benediction, "Grace and peace be multiplied unto you through the knowledge of our Lord and Saviour Jesus Christ." O brethren, whatever men may say against the faith of God, there is nothing in the world which creates virtue like true faith. Wherever true faith enters, though it be into the heart of a harlot or of a thief, what a change it makes! See her there; she has polluted herself many times; she has gone far into sin. Mary has been a sinner; she heard the preaching of the Saviour; standing the crowd she listens to Him one day as He preaches concerning the prodigal, and how the loving Father pressed Him to his bosom; she comes to Jesus and she finds forgiveness. Is she a harlot any longer? Nay, there she is, washing His feet with her tears, and wiping them with the hairs of her head. The woman who was a sinner, hates her evil ways and loves her gracious Lord. We must say of her, "But she is washed, but she is sanctified, but she is saved." Take Saul of Tarsus. Foaming with blood, breathing out threatenings, he is going to Damascus to drag the saints of God to prison. On the road he is struck down; by divine mercy he is led to put his trust in Jesus. Is he a persecutor any longer? See that earnest apostle beaten with rods—shipwrecked—in labours more abundant than all the rest of them—counting not his life dear unto him, that he may win Christ and be found in Him. Saul of Tarsus becomes a majestic proof of what the grace of God can do. See Zaccheus, the grasping publican, distributing his wealth, the Ephesians burning their magical books, the gaoler washing the apostle's stripes. Take the case of many now present. Let memory refresh itself this morning, with the recollection of the change which has been wrought in you. We have nothing to boast of; God forbid that we should glory, save in the cross of Christ, but yet some of us are wonderful instances of renewing grace. We were unclean, our mouths could utter blasphemy; our temper was hot and terrible; our hands were unrighteous; we were altogether as an unclean thing, but how changed now! Again, I say, we boast of nothing which we now are, for by the grace of God we are what we are, yet the change is something to be wondered at. Has divine grace wrought this change in you? Be not weary with my reiteration of this question. Let me put it again to you till I get an answer; nay, till I force you to an answer: Have you this precious faith? Can you not answer the question? Then, have you not that divine life, that life which is given by divine calling? If you have the one, you have the other; and if you have not both, you have neither, for where there is the one, the other must come, and there the one has come, the other has been there.

II. I have thus fully but feebly brought the subject before you, allow me to remind you that another verse remains which handles the same topics. In the fourth verse, he deals with the privileges of faith, and also with the privileges of the spiritual life.

Notice the PRIVILEGE OF FAITH first. "Whereby are given unto us exceeding great and precious promises"—here is the faith, "That by these ye might be partakers of the divine nature, having escaped the corruption that is in the world through lust." Here is the life resulting from the faith. Now, the privileges of faith first. The privileges of faith are, that we have given to us "Exceeding great and precious promises." "Great and precious"—two words which do not often come together. Many little things are great which are not precious, such as great rocks, which are of little value; on the other hand, many things are precious which are not great—such as diamonds and other jewels, which cannot be very great if they be very precious. But here we have promises which are so great, that they are not less than infinite, and so precious, that they are not less divine. I shall not attempt to speak about their greatness or their preciousness, but just give a catalogue of them, and leave you to guess at both. We have some of them which are like birds in the hand—we have them already; other promises are like birds in the bush, only that they are just as valuable and as sure as those which are in the hand.

Note here, then, we have received by precious faith the promise and pardon. Hark thee, my soul, all thy sins are forgiven thee. He who hath faith in Christ hath no sin to curse him, his sins are washed away, they have ceased to be; they have been carried on the scape-goat's head into the wilderness; they are drowned in the Red Sea; they are blotted out; they are thrown behind God's back, they are cast into the depths of the sea. Here is a promise of perfect pardon. Is not this great and precious?—as great as your sins are; and if your sins demanded a costly ransom, this precious promise is as great as the demand.

Then comes the righteousness of Christ: you are not only pardoned, that is, washed and made clean, but you are dressed, robed in garments such as no man could ever weave. The vesture is divine. Jehovah Himself has wrought out your righteousness for you; the holy life of Jesus the Son of God, has become your beauteous dress, and you are covered with it. Christian, is not this an exceeding great and precious promise? The law was great—this righteousness is as great as the law. The law asked a precious revenue from man, more than humanity could pay—the righteousness of Christ has paid it all. Is it not great and precious?

Then next comes reconciliation. You were strangers, but you are brougut nigh by the blood of Christ. Once aliens, but not fellow-citizens with the saints and of the household of God. Is not this great and precious?

Then comes your adoption. "Beloved, now are we the sons of God, and it doth not yet appear what we shall be: but we know that, when He shall appear, we shall be like Him: for we shall see Him as He is." "And if children, then heirs, heirs of God, joint heirs with Jesus Christ, if so be we suffer with Him that we may be glorified together." Oh, how glorious is this great and precious promise of adoption!

Then we have the promise of providence: "all things work together for good to them that love God, to them that are called according to His purpose." "Thy place of defence shall be the munitions of rocks." "Thy bread shall be given thee and thy waters shall be sure." "As thy day thy strength shall be." "Fear not, I am with thee; be not dismayed, I am thy God." "When thou passest through the rivers I will be with thee, the floods shall not overflow thee. When thou goest through the fire, thou shalt not be burned, neither shall the flame kindle upon thee." When I think of providence, the greatness of its daily gifts, and the preciousness of its hourly boons, I may well say, here is an exceeding great and precious promise.

Then you have the promise too, that you shall never taste of death but shall only sleep in Jesus. "Write, blessed are the dead which die in the Lord from henceforth. Yea, saith the Spirit, that they cease from their labours: and their works do follow them." Nor does the promise cease here, you have the promise of resurrerection. "For the trumpet shall sound, and the dead shall be raised incorruptible, and we shall be changed. For this corruptible must put on incorruption, and this mortal must put on immortality." Beloved, we know that if Christ rose from the dead, so also them who sleep in Jesus, will the Lord bring with Him. Nor is this all, for we shall reign with Jesus; at His coming, we shall be glorified with Him, we shall sit upon His throne, even as He has overcome and sits with His Father upon His throne. The harps of heaven, the streets of glory, the trees of paradise, the river of the water of life, the eternity of immaculate bliss—all these, God hath promised to them who love Him. "Eye hath not seen, nor ear heard, the things which God hath prepared for them that love Him, but He hath revealed them unto us by His Spirit;" and by our faith we have grasped them, and we have to-day "the substance of things hoped for, and the evidence of things not seen." Now, beloved, see how rich faith makes you!—what treasure!—what a costly regalia!—what gold mines!—what oceans of wealth—what mountains of sparkling treasures has God conferred upon you by faith!

But we must not forget the life, and with that we close. The text says, He has given us this promise, "that"—"in order, that." What then? What are all these treasures lavished for? For what these pearls? For what these jewels? For what, I say, these oceans of treasure? For what? Is the end worthy of the means? Surely God never giveth greater store than the thing which He would purchase will be worth. We may suppose then, the end to be very great when such costly means have been given; and what is the end? Why, "that by these ye might be partakers of the divine nature, having escaped the corruption that is in the world through lust." O, my brethren, if you have these mercies to-day by faith, do see to it that the result is obtained. Be not content to be made rich in these great and precious promises, without answering God's design in your being thus enriched. That design, you perceive, is twofold: it is first that you may be partakers of the divine nature; and, secondly, that you may escape the corruption which is in the world.

To be a partaker of the divine nature is not, of course, to become God. That cannot be. The essence of Deity is not to be participated in by the creature. Between the creature and the Creator there must ever be a gulf fixed in respect of essence; but as the first man Adam was made in the image of God, we, by the renewal of the Holy Spirit, are in a yet diviner sense made in the image of the Most High, and are partakers of the divine nature. We are, by grace, made like God. "God is love;" we become love—"He that loveth is born of God." God is truth; we become true, and we love that which is true, and we hate the darkness and the lie. God is good, it is His very name; He makes us good by His grace, so that we become the pure in heart who shall see God. Nay, I will say this, that we become partakers of the divine nature in even a higher sense than this—in fact, in any sense, anything short of our being absolutely divine. Do we not become members of the body of the divine person of Christ? And what sort of union is this—"members of His body, of His flesh, and of His bones?" The same blood which flows in the head flows in the hand, and the same life which quickens Christ, quickens His people; for, "Ye are dead, and your life is hid with Christ in God." Nay, as if this were not enough, we are married into Christ. He hath betrothed us unto Himself in righteousness and in faithfulness; and as the spouse must, in the nature of things, be a partaker of the same nature as the husband, so Jesus Christ first became partaker of flesh and blood that they twain might be one flesh; and then He makes His Church partaker of the same spirit, that they twain may be one spirit; for He who is joined unto the Lord is one spirit. Oh, marvellous mystery! we look into it, but who shall understand it? One with Jesus, by eternal union one, married to Him; so one with Him that the branch is not more one with the vine than we are a part of the Lord, our Saviour, and our Redeemer. Rejoice in this, brethren, ye are made partakers of the divine nature, and all these promises are given to you in order that you may show this forth among the sons of men, that ye are like God, and not like ordinary men; that ye are different now from what flesh and blood would make you, having been made participators of the nature of God.

Then the other result which follows from it, was this, "Having escaped the corruption that is in the world through lust." Ah, beloved, it were ill that a man who is alive should dwell in corruption. "Why seek ye the living among the dead?" said the angel to Magdalene. Should the living dwell among the dead? Should divine life be found amongst the corruptions of worldly lusts? The bride of Christ drunken. Frequenting the ale-house! A member of Christ's body found intoxicated in the streets, or lying, or blaspheming, or dishonest! God forbid. Shall I take the members of Christ, and make them members of a harlot? How can I drink the cup of the Lord, and drink the cup of Belial? How can it be possible that I can have life, and yet dwell in the black, dark, foul, filthy, pestiferous tomb of the world's lusts? Surely, brethren, from these open lusts and sins ye have escaped: have ye also escaped from the more secret and more delusive lime-twigs of the Satanic fowler? O, have ye come forth from the lust of pride? Have ye escaped from slothfulness? Have ye clean escaped from carnal security? Are we seeking day by day to live above worldliness, the love of the things of the world, and the ensnaring avarice which they nourish? Remember, it is for this that you have been enriched with the treasures of God. Do not, oh, I conjure you, do not, chosen of God and beloved by Him, and so graciously enriched, do not suffer all this lavish treasure to be wasted upon you.

There is nothing which my heart desires more than to see you, the members of this Church distinguished for holiness: it is the Christian's crown and glory. An unholy Church! it is of no use to the world, and of no esteem among men. Oh! it is an abomination, hell's laughter, heaven's abhorrence. And the larger the Church, the more influential, the worse nuisance does it become, when it becomes dead and unholy. The worst evils which have ever come upon the world, have been brought upon her by an unholy Church. Whence came the darkness of the dark ages? From the Church of Rome. And if we want to see the world again sitting in Egyptian darkness, bound with fetters of iron, we have only to give up the faith, and to renounce holiness of life, and we may drag the world down again to the limbo of superstitition, and bind her fast in chains of ignorance and vice. O Christian, the vows of God are upon you. You are God's priest: act as such. You are God's king: reign over your lusts. You are God's chosen: do not associate with Belial. Heaven is your portion, live like a heavenly spirit, so shall you prove that you have the true faith; but except ye do this, your end shall be to lift up your eyes in hell, and find yourself mistaken when it will be too late to seek or find a remedy. The Lord give us the faith and the life, for Jesus' sake. Amen.

THE NECESSITY OF GROWING FAITH

"We are bound to thank God always for you, brethren, as it is meet, because that your faith groweth exceedingly, and the charity of every one of you all toward each other aboundeth."—2 Thessalonians i. 3.

Last Lord's day I tried to say cheering and encouraging words to "Little-faith." I trust that the Holy Spirit, the Comforter, did thereby strengthen some to whom the Saviour said, "O thou of little faith, wherefore didst thou doubt?" But none of us would desire to remain among the Little-faiths; we long to press forward in our march to the better land. If we have just started in the heavenly race, it is well; there are grounds of comfort about the first steps in the right way; but we are not going to stop at the starting-point; our desire is towards the winning-post and the crown. My prayer at the commencement of this discourse is, that we may each of us rise out of our little faith into the loftier region of assurance, so that those who love us best may be able to say, "We are bound to thank God always for you, brethren, as it is meet, because that your faith groweth exceedingly."

The church of Jesus Christ at Thessalonica did not commence under very propitious circumstances. Remember that oft-quoted text about the Bereans: "These were more noble than those in Thessalonica, in that they searched the Scriptures daily whether those things were so." That record does not relate to the converts in Thessalonica, but to those Jews who heard Paul preach in the synagogue, and refused to test his teaching by a reference to the Old Testament. They were not a noble sort of people, and yet from among them there were taken by almighty grace a certain company who were led to believe in the true Messiah. Thus they became more noble than even the Bereans; for we do not hear a church in Berea, neither was an epistle written to the Bereans. Thessalonica received two epistles, bright with hearty commendations. Paul praised the Philippians, but the Thessalonians he praised yet more, thanking God at every remembrance of them, and glorying in them among the churches of God for their patience and faith.

I shall ask you, with your Bibles open, to see whether we cannot account in some measure for this remarkable condition of things. The verse before us is full of thanksgiving to God for the growth of the Thessalonians in faith and in love; and to my mind it sounds like an echo of the First Epistle to the Thessalonians. The First Epistle is the key and the cause of the Second. Very often a man's success in this place, or in that, will tally with his own condition of heart in relation to that place. As we sow we reap. The grace of God enabled Paul to sow toward the Thessalonians with great hopefulness, and trust, and prayerfulness, and consequently he reaped plentifully.

Observe how (1 Thess. i. 2. 3) Paul began by distinctly recognizing the existence of faith and love in that Church. "We give thanks to God always for you all, making mention of you in our prayers; remembering without ceasing your work of faith, and labour of love, and patience of hope in our Lord Jesus Christ, in the sight of God and our Father." Recognize the root, and then look for the flower. See that faith is in the soul, smile upon it and foster it, and then you may expect that the faith will steadily increase. In our text Paul mentions faith as growing and love as abounding, while in the next verse he mentions patience, which is the outgrowth of hope—"the patience of hope." He noticed in the Thessalonians the birth of those three divine sisters—faith, hope, and

50

charity. That which he recognised with pleasure he afterwards saw growing exceedingly: those who cherish the seed shall rejoice in the plant. Observe in the children under your care the first blossoms of any good thing, and you shall observe its increase. Despise not the day of small things. When you have learned to recognize faith in its buds, you shall soon see faith in its flowers, and faith in its fruits. Do not overlook feeble grace, or criticize it because it is as yet imperfect; but mark its beginnings with thankfulness, and you shall behold its advance with delight.

In addition to recognizing the beginnings of faith, Paul laboured hard to promote it. Look in the second chapter, and read verses 7, 8, 11, 12:—"But we were gentle among you, even as a nurse cherisheth her children: so being affectionately desirous of you, we were willing to have imparted to you, not the gospel of God only, but also our own souls, because you were dear unto us. As ye know how we exhorted and comforted and charged every one of you, as a father doth his children, that ye would walk worthy of God, who hath called you unto His kingdom and glory." He threw his whole strength into the work of upholding that church, toiling night and day for it; and consequently he obtained his desire; for still it is true in the husbandry of God, that those who sow, and steep their seed in the tears of earnestness, shall doubtless come again rejoicing, bringing their sheaves with them.

Paul had accompanied his public labours with his private prayers. See how I Thessalonians iii. 12 tallies with our text:—"And the Lord make you to increase and abound in love one toward another, and toward all men, even as we do toward you." This was his prayer; and he received exactly what he prayed for. He saw abounding love in each one towards every other. The Lord seemed to have noted the wording of Paul's prayer, and to have answered him according to the letter of his request. If we open our mouth wide, the Lord will fill it. Brethren, what we comfortably recognize in its gracious beginnings, what we labour to increase and what we earnestly guard with prayer, shall in due time be granted to us!

More than this: Paul had gone on to exhort them to abound in love and faith. Look at Chapter iv. verse 9: "As touching brotherly love ye need not that I write unto you: for ye yourselves are taught of God to love one another. And indeed ye do it toward all the brethren which are in all Macedonia: but we beseech you, brethren, that ye increase more and more." Paul did not only quietly pray for the church, but he added his earnest admonitions. He bids them increase more and more; and in response they do increase, so that he says, "Your faith groweth exceedingly." When a man says, "more and more," it is only another way of saying, "exceedingly": is it not so? There was a big heart in Paul towards the Thessalonians. He wanted them to grow in faith and love "more," and then to take another step, and add another "more" to it. The exhortation being given out of a full heart, behold, God has fulfilled it to His servant, and the people have willingly followed up the apostolic precept.

But Paul had added faith to his prayers and his exhortations. Look at chapter v. verses 23, 24, and see if it is not so. "And the very God of peace sanctify you wholly; and I pray God your whole spirit and soul and body be preserved blameless unto the coming of our Lord Jesus Christ. Faithful is He that calleth you, who also will do it." When we are sure that God will do it, it will surely be done. We miss many a blessing because we ask without faith. The apostle believed that he had the petition which he had sought of the Lord; and he received according to his faith. He who can firmly believe shall ere long fervently pour out thanksgiving. The church of Thessalonica, the child of Paul's prayers, the child of his labours, and at last the child of his faith, obtained a remarkable degree of faith, and a singular warmth of love. The Lord give to us who are workers the mind and spirit of Paul, and lead us to follow him in our conduct to others, and then I do not doubt that our good wishes shall be realized. If we are right ourselves, we shall see prosperity in the churches, or classes, or families whose good we seek; and as we feel bound to pray about them, we shall also feel bound to thank God concerning them.

Before I plunge into the sermon, I should like to pause, and ask whether we as

Christian men and women are such that Paul could say of us, "We are bound to thank God always for you, brethren, as it is meet, because that your faith groweth exceedingly, and the charity of every one of you all toward each other aboundeth." What think you? Could your pastor bless God for you? Could your nearest and dearest Christian friend feel that he was bound to thank God always for you? If not, why not? Oh that we may rise into such a happy state that we shall be the cause of gratitude in others! It ought to be so; we ought to glorify God, causing men to see our good works, and praise our Father in heaven.

One more question: Do you think we are in such a condition that it would be safe for anybody to praise us? Would it be safe to ourselves for us to be thus commended, and made subjects of thankfulness? It takes a great deal of grace to be able to bear praise. Censure seldom does us much hurt. A man struggles up against slander, and the discouragement which comes of it may not be an unmixed evil; but praise soon suggests pride, and is therefore not an unmixed good. "As the fining-pot for silver, and the furnace for gold; so is a man to his praise." Would it be safe if Paul were here to say good things about you as he did about the Thessalonians? Did it not prove that the brethren there were sober, well-established believers?

Once more, do you ever feel it in your heart to talk like this about your fellow-Christians? Paul himself was in a fine condition when he could thus extol his brethren. Few men are ready with hearty commendations of others. We are greedy in receiving praise, and niggardly in dispensing it. We seldom speak too kindly of one another. Now and then you hear a person say, "There is no such thing as love in the church at all." I know that gentleman very well, and I never saw any excess of love in him. I heard one say, "Brotherly love is all a mockery; there is no reality in Christian charity"; and truly he measured his own corn very accurately. Most men would see others better if their own eyes were clearer. When a man honestly feels that his fellow-Christians are for the most part much better than himself, and that he would willingly sit at the feet of many of them, then he is himself in a healthy state. I admire the grace of God in many around me. I see their imperfections as though I did not see them. I am not looking for the thorns, but for the roses; and I see so many of them that my heart is glad, and in spirit I bless the name of the Lord.

The man who can commend the work of the Lord in others without saying a word upon their liberality. To use a very rough word, cadgers were multiplied among them, as they always are where generosity abounds. Shame that it should be so. Read chapter iii, envy, and self, or he would not have so seen or so spoken. I love the text because it is an instance of a man of great grace, of a man under the inspiration of the Spirit of God, who yet delighted to speak enthusiastically of a church which certainly was far from perfect. I delight in that eye which can be a little blind to faults while it exercises a clear vision in seeing all that is good and praiseworthy towards God.

So, then, we come to our text, and the subject runs thus: for us to grow in faith is a subject for devout thanksgiving; and in the second place, it is an object for diligent endeavour. Thirdly, if we greatly grow in faith it will be the source of other growths; for as faith increases, love, patience, and every other virtue, will flourish.

I. For us to grow, and increase in faith is A SUBJECT FOR DEVOUT THANKSGIVING. Paul gives a commendation of the Thessalonian church which is exceedingly warm and hearty. One critic says the word may be regarded as somewhat extravagant, after the mode of the Apostle when he wishes to be emphatic. He writes fervidly: "Your faith groweth exceedingly, and the charity of every one of you all toward each other aboundeth." It is an intense and unreserved commendation. As I have already said, this church was not absolutely perfect; for, because of the love of every one towards another, and their great kindness towards the poor, certain unworthy persons encroached upon their liberality. To use a bery rough word, cadgers were multiplied among them, as they always are where generosity abounds. Shame that it should be so. Read chapter iii., verse 11: "For we hear that there are some which walk among you disorderly, working not at all, but are busybodies." There had been also among them here and there a person of loose life and of sharp business dealings, and to such he spoke in the First Epistle; but these flies in the pot of ointment did not destroy its sweetness. They were so few comparatively that Paul speaks of the whole body with approbation. When our faith shall grow and our love abound, it may be proper for a pastor to speak with unrestricted admiration of what the Lord has done.

The blessing of increased faith is of unspeakable value, and therefore should be largely rendered for it. Little faith will save, but strong faith is that which builds up the church, which overcomes the world, which wins sinners, and which glorifies God. Little-faith is slow and feeble, and to suit his pace the whole flock travel softly. Little-faith is a wounded soldier, and has to be carried in an ambulance by the armies of the Lord; but faith which grows exceedingly, lifts the banner aloft, leads the van, meets hand to hand the foes of our Prince, and puts them to the rout. If we were invoking blessings upon a church we could scarcely ask for a larger boon than that all the brethren might be strong in faith, giving glory to God. Strong-faith ventures into large endeavours for Christ, and hence missions are projected: Strong-faith carries out the projects of holy zeal, and hence daring ideals are turned into facts: Strong-faith is a shield against the darts of error, and hence she is the object of the contempt and hatred of heresy. Strong-faith builds the walls of Zion, and casts down the walls of Jericho. Strong-faith smites the Philistines hip and thigh, and makes Israel to dwell in peace. Oh that the night of Little-faith were over, and that the day of glorious faith would come! Soon would our young men see visions, and our old men dream dreams, if faith were more among us. When the Son of man cometh shall He find faith in the earth? At the revival of faith we shall see another Pentecost, with its rushing mighty wind, and its tongues of flame; but during our lack of faith we still abide in weakness, and the enemy will exact upon us. O God, we beseech thee, make Thy face to shine upon us, cause our faith to grow exceedingly, and out love to abound yet more and more; then shall there be times of refreshing from the presence of the Lord.

Paul thus fervently gave thanks to God because the blessing came to the church at a remarkably seasonable time. The people of Thessalonica had risen against the church and persecuted it; thus, without were fightings, but within there were no fears; for the brethren were firm in faith and fervent in love. The church was subject to constant tribulation; but its faith grew exceedingly. Has it not often been so with the Lord's people? Times of cloud and rain have been growing times. Pharaoh dealt hardly with Israel; but the more he oppressed them, the more they multiplied. The more the Church of God is down-trodden, the more it rises into power and influence. The bush burns and is not consumed; nay, rather, it flourishes in the flame. I say not that this increase of faith is the immediate effect of persecution, but it is singularly the attendant upon it. God knew that when His poor servants were haled to prison, when they were brought before rulers and kings for His name's sake, and when they were spoiled of their goods, they wanted increased strength, and therefore He gave it to them by growth in faith. As the persecution rose upon them like the deluge, their confidence in God rose above it, like Noah's ark, which rose the higher the deeper the waters became. They stood fast in the day of trial, and became an example to all other churches, whether persecuted or not; and this because their faith grew exceedingly. Beloved, I pray for each member of this church that your confidence in God may rise from ebb to flood. We need it much just now. This is a time of depression in trade, when many are suffering want, and almost all find their means decreased. We need to be rich in faith, for we are growing poor in pocket. Many children of God cannot find employment wherewith to earn their bread. This is, moreover, a time of abounding vice. Perhaps never in our memories were any of us so shocked as we have been of late by the discoveries of unspeakable abominations. We need that our faith should grow exceedingly, for sin runs down our streets in torrents. It is also a period of grievous departure from the faith once delivered to the saints. Looking back to our younger days, we are amazed at the progress of error. We mourned in those days that men trifled with the doctrines of the gospel; but what shall we now say, when men deride those doctrines, and mock at them as antiquated fables? The foundations of the earth are removed, and only here and there will you find a man who beareth up the pillars thereof; therefore do we need that our faith should be exceedingly steadfast. I charge you, brethren, to be rooted and grounded in faith, seeing the times are evil! I cannot speak emphatically enough upon the abounding dangers of the times; they demand of us that we be not of doubtful mind, but that we take firm hold of infallible truth, and endure as seeing Him who is invisible. He that cannot say, "I believe, and am sure," is one born out of due time.

The apostle's commendation was meet and fit, since, if there be any growth in faith, it is the work of God's Spirit. Faith is the gift of God in its beginnings, and it is equally the gift of God in its increase. If thou hast faith as a grain of mustard seed, God gave it thee; and if thou hast faith as a spreading tree, God has given the increase. The infancy of faith is of God, and so is its perfect manhood. In the natural world we ought as much to admire God's hand in growth as in creation; for, indeed, the outbursting of spring, the advance of summer, and the maturity of autumn, are all a sort of creation, seen in detail. Even thus the progress of faith reveals the same power as the commencement of faith. If thou dost not look to God for more faith, thou wilt never have more faith: great faith in its strong broad current flows as much from the fountainhead of grace as in its first trickling streamlet of hope in Christ. Let God have all the glory of faith from its Alpha to its Omega. If thou be a strong man in Christ Jesus take heed that thou do not sacrifice to thine own net, nor burn incense to thine own drag, and glorify thine own experience as if thou madest thyself strong and rich in the things of God. We are bound to render all the thanksgiving unto God; it is meet that it should be so. Look how the apostle puts it: "We are bound to thank God always for you." I like the modesty of that. He does not so much say that he did thank God, though he did do so; but in deep humility he admits the debt which he could not fully pay. He did not judge his thanksgivings to be sufficient, but owned that he was still under bonds to render more praise. I rejoice to be bound with these bonds, to be bound to thank God every day, and all the day. I wear these golden fetters and count them my best ornaments. "Bind the sacrifice with cords, even with cords to the horns of the altar." I would be bound over, not to keep the peace, but to keep praise for ever. Let the altar of incense be always burning, yea, flaming higher and higher with the sweet spices of love and gratitude. Blessed be God for what He is doing for His people, when He causes their faith to grow; for it is a blessing so immense, so incalculable, that our praises ought to rise to the height and glory of loud-sounding hallelujahs. Brethren, let us bless God for every good man who know whose faith has grown, for every holy woman whose love in the church is manifest unto all; and when we have done so, let us turn our eye to God, and say, "Lord, make me such a one that others may glorify in me also; I am as yet sadly weak and undeveloped; make me to grow till all Thy image shall be seen in me, and my fellow-Christians shall bless God concerning me." Thus have I set growth in faith before you as a subject for thanksgiving. It is indeed a jewel worth more than both the Indies.

II. In the second place, it is worthy to be AN OBJECT FOR DILIGENT ENDEAVOUR. If you have it not, labour speedily to attain it. As the merchantman seeketh goodly pearls, so seek a growing faith. Covet earnestly the best gifts and the noblest graces. Never be self-satisfied, but cry with Jabez, "Oh that the Lord would bless me indeed, and enlarge my coast."

Why? Because the proof of faith lies in the growth of faith. If thou hast a dead faith, it will always be the same; but if thou hast the faith of God's elect, it must grow. If I heard of a child that was born some years ago, and had never grown, I should begin to guess that my friend was entrapping me, and that the child was dead from the birth. Life in its earliest stages is ever attended with growth. Brother, thou must have more faith, or we shall fear that thou hast no faith; thou must have more love, or else for sure thou hast no love at all. That which does not grow unto God does not live unto God.

We ought to have more faith because God's truth deserves it. It ought to be the easiest thing in the world for us to trust God; to believe every word of the Lord should be an act to which we need not to be exhorted; it should be as natural as for the lungs to heave, or the heart to beat. We ought, as children of God, to believe our Father by instinct, even as young eaglets hide under the mother's wing. We ought to exercise faith even as the eye sees, and the ear hears, because thereunto we were created by the Holy Spirit. It should be a necessity of our spiritual existence, that we must and will trust the Lord Jesus Christ yet more and more. I pray that it may be so; for unbelief is a horrible crime. Have you doubted God? Have you in any sense mistrusted Him? Have you limited the Holy One of Israel? Then continue not the slave of such a sin, but give unto God your heart's confidence from this time henceforth, and for ever.

Moreover, we ought to grow in faith, because it will be so much for our own spiritual health, and strength, and joy. Does Little-faith know what it might be, and do, and enjoy if it could only quit its littleness? There are many ways of being a Christian, as there are many ways of being an Englishman: but all are not equally desirable. I may be an Englishman in banishment, or in the workhouse, or in prison; but I prefer to be an Englishman at home, in health, and at liberty. So you may be a Christian, and be weak, timorous, and said; but this is not desirable; it is better to be a happy, holy, vigorous, useful Christian. As your being an Englishman does not depend on your health or wealth, so neither does your salvation turn upon the strength or joy of your faith; yet much does depend on it. Why not glorify God on the road to heaven? Why not have foretastes of it now? It is not my desire to go through the world in miserable style, singing always—

"Do I love the Lord or no?
Am I His, or am I not?"

Infinitely do I prefer so to trust God that my peace may be like a river, and my righteousness like the waves of the sea. Look at the difference between Abraham, the Father of the faithful, and his nephew Lot. Lot was righteous, but he was by no means so strong in faith as Abraham, neither was he so great or so happy. Abraham is calm, bold, royal; Lot is greedy, timid, trembling. Lot, in Sodom, is with difficulty made to run for his life, while Abraham alone with God is interceding for others. Lot escapes from a burning city with the loss of all things, while Abraham dwells peacefully with the Lord who is the possessor of heaven and earth. Abraham's faith makes him rise like some lone Alp till he touches the very heaven of God. It is well to be Lot, but it is infinitely better to be Abraham. Do seek the utmost degree of faith; for if this be in you and abound, you shall not be barren or unfruitful. Heaven lies that way. More faith, more rest of heart. To grow heavenly we must grow more believing.

The question is, How is this to be done? How is my faith to be made to grow exceedingly? I have already told you that it is the work of the Holy Spirit; but still He uses us for the increase of our own faith. If we are to grow in faith, certain evils are to be avoided with scrupulous care. Avoid continual change of doctrine. If you have a tree in your garden and you transplant it often, it will yield you scanty fruit. Those who are everything by turns, and nothing long, are "ever learning, but never able to come to the knowledge of the truth." Unstable as water, they shall not excel. Those brethren who believe this to-day, and that to-morrow, and the other thing the next day, do not believe anything in downright earnest. They cannot grow; they are not rooted and grounded. Like the moon, they are always changing, and what light they have is cold and sickly. He who can change his religion has none to change. Those who prefer philosophy to Christ never knew Him.

Then, again, if you had a tree, and did not transplant it, but began to dig away the earth from it, removing the ground in which it stood, you would impoverish it, and prevent its fruitfulness. I know certain professors who are giving up the ground which their souls should grow in. One doctrine after another is forsaken, till nothing is held to be important. They do not believe much now, and they are on the line to believe nothing at all. The experiment of the Frenchman who had just brought his horse to live on a straw a day when it died, is being repeated among us, faith literally starved to death. What low diet do some men prescribe for their souls! Marrow and fatness they do not even smell at! How can your faith grow when vital truths are abandoned, or held with feeble grasp? Oh for a band of Puritan believers! Oh for a troop of spiritual Ironsides!

Next, a tree cannot grow if it is shut out from sun, and rain, and dew. Without heavenly influences we must be barren. Plant a little tree right under a great oak so that it is always in the shade, and it cannot grow; clear the big tree away, or the sapling will dwindle to death. Some men's faith cannot grow because it is overshadowed by worldliness, by tolerated sin, by love of riches, by the pride of life, by cares of lower things. The pursuit of Christ crucified must be all-absorbing, or it will be ineffectual. To know what you believe, and to abide steadfast in it, is the way to be robust in faith. Men whose hearts are not in their trades, men who chop and change—these are the men whose names appear in the *Gazette*; are not many spiritual bankruptcies due to the same cause?

There are methods which the spiritual husbandman uses to cause faith to grow. First, faith grows by an increase of knowledge. Many persons doubt because they are not instructed. Some doubt whether they shall hold on to the end; they are ignorant of the doctrine of the final perseverance of the saints. Some are in despair because they find evil desires arising in their hearts; they do not know the teaching of Scripture as to the two natures and the warfare between flesh and spirit. Many think themselves condemned because they cannot wholly keep the law; they forget that they are justified by faith. A great deal of unbelief vanishes when knowledge, like the morning sun, drives away the mists. Unbelief is an owl of the night, and when the sun rises it hides away in a dark corner. Study the word of God: give your heart to searching it; seek to get at the inner teaching, and learn the analogy of faith; practise deep sea-fishery, and you will reach those mysterious truths which are the secret riches of the soul. These truths are much despised now; but those who rejoice in them will find their faith growing exceedingly.

Better still than mere knowledge, which alone would puff you up, faith grows by experience. When a man has tried and proved a thing, then his confidence in it is largely increased. Take a promise and test it, and then you will say, "I know that is so." When you have tested it again, and again, and again, nobody will be able to shake you, for you will say, "I have tasted and handled of this good word; I have made it my own, and I am not to be driven from it." The experienced Christian is the established Christian. The man who has proved all things is the man who holds fast that which is good. God gives grace to increase our faith by knowledge and by experience!

Faith also grows by much meditation and walking with God. If you want to believe in a man, you must know him. Half the disputes between Christian people arise from their not knowing one another. There is a hymn of Mr. Sankey's which I venture to alter thus:

"When we know each other better,
The mists will roll away."

When we know each other, our suspicions, prejudices, and dislikes will speedily disappear. I am sure it is so with our God. When you walk with Him, when your communion with Him is close and constant, your faith in Him will grow exceedingly. Some of you, I am afraid, do not give five minutes in the day to meditation. You are in too great a hurry for that. In London life men get up in a hurry even as they went to bed in a hurry and slept in a hurry. They swallow their breakfast in a hurry; they have no time to digest it; the bell is ringing at the station, and they must hurry to catch the train; they reach business in a hurry; they hurry through it, and they hurry to get back from it. Men cannot think, for they have barely time to wink their eyes. As to an hour's meditation and reading the Scriptures, and communing with God, many professors nowadays would think they committed robbery against the god of this world if they took half-an-hour out of his service to give it to fellowship with the world to come. If our faith is to grow exceedingly, we must maintain constant intercourse with God.

Another way of increasing faith is by much prayer. Pray for faith and pray with faith; thus shall thy soul become firm in its reliance on the promises. It is while we wrestle with the angel that we find out our weakness, as the sinew of our thigh shrinks; but at the same time we prove our God-given strength, since as princes we wrestle with God and prevail. Power from prayer as well as power in prayer is what we want. On our knees we gather strength, till doubting and fearing disappear.

We must be careful to render obedience to God. A man cannot trust God while he lives in sin; every act of disobedience weakens confidence in God. Faith and obedience are bound up in the same bundle. He that obeys God, trusts God; and he that trusts God, obeys God. He that is without faith is without works; and he that is without works is without faith. Do not oppose faith and good works to one another, for there is a blessed relationship between them; and if you abound in obedience your faith shall grow exceedingly.

Again, faith grows by exercise. The man who uses the little faith he has will get more faith; but he that says, "I have not enough faith for such and such work," and therefore shrinks back, shall become more and more timid, till at last, like a coward, he runs away. Go forward with thy little faith, and to thy surprise it shall have grown as thou hast advanced. Accomplish much, and then endeavour something more, and something more. I have often used an illustration taken from a person who teaches the art of growing taller. I do not believe in that art: we shall not add a cubit to our stature just yet. But part of this professor's exercise is, that in the morning, when you get up, you are to reach as high as ever you can, and aim a little higher every morning though it be only the hundredth part of an inch. By that means you are to grow. This is so with faith. Do all you can, and then do a little more; and when you can do that, then do a little more than you can. Always have something in hand that is greater than your present capacity. Grow up to it, and when you have grown up to it, grow more. By many little additions a great house is built. Brick by brick up rose the pyramid. Believe and yet believe. Trust and have further trust. Hope shall become faith, and faith shall ripen to full assurance and perfect confidence in God Most High.

This, then, brethren, is what I commend to you. May God the Holy Ghost help you all to go from faith to faith.

III. Finally, this growing faith becomes THE CENTRE OF OTHER CHRISTIAN GRACES. "Your faith groweth exceedingly, and the charity of every one of you all toward each other aboundeth." A firm faith in gospel verities will make us love one another, for each doctrine of truth is an argument for love. If you believe in God as having chosen His people, you will love His elect; if you believe in Christ as having made atonement for His people, you will love His redeemed, and seek their peace. If you believe in the doctrine of regeneration, and know that we must be born again, you will love the regenerate. Whatever doctrine it is that is true, it ministereth toward the love of the heart. I am sure you will find a deep, firm, fervent unity with one another in those that hold the truth in the love of it. If you are not filled with brotherly love, it must be because you are not firmly believing that truth which worketh toward love.

Firmness in the faith ministers toward the unity of the church. The church of Thessalonica did not have a secession, or a split, as some call it: the church at Thessalonica did not divide under the pressure of persecution: they adhered closely to one another, and the more they were hammered, the more they were consolidated. They were welded into one solid mass by the hammer of persecution and the fire of love, and the reason was because they each one held the truth with all firmness. I am always afraid of a church that is made up of mixed elements, when some are Calvinistic, some Arminian, some Baptist and some Paedobaptist. When the minister who holds them together dies, they will disintegrate. When certain reasons that now make them cohere cease to exist, the church will divide like quicksilver, each little bit breaking into smaller bits, and so they will go rolling about in innumerable factions. But given a church that holds the truth firmly, with deep and strong faith, then if the pastor dies, or twenty pastors die, they believe in a Pastor who lives for ever, and whoever comes or does not come, the truth they hold, holds them in living unity. I cannot imagine a greater blessing for you as a church in years to come than for each man and woman to be intelligently established in the truth you have received. Who shall separate the men who are one in Christ by the grip of mighty faith? I commend firm faith to you with all my heart, as the source of love and the means of unity in years to come.

This faith breeds patience in men, and patience assists love. Truth to tell, God's people are, some of them, a singular tribe. A countryman was accustomed to say that if God had not chosen His people before they were born, He would never have done so afterwards. There is truth in that saying. Therefore if a man loves His fellow-Christian as an act of mere nature, he will often feel himself baffled; he will say, "They acted very unkindly to me. Who can love people that are so ill-mannered, so ungrateful?" But when faith is strong, you will say, "What is that to me? I love them for Christ's sake. If I am to have a reward, it shall come from my Lord Christ. As for God's people, I love them despite their faults; over the head of the mistaken judgments they form of me, I love all my brethren." The way to make men better is not to be always censuring them, but to love them better. The quickest way to win a sinner, is to love him to Christ; the quickest way to sanctify a believer is to love him into purity and holiness. Only faith can do this. May faith, therefore, grow exceedingly; for faith by working patience helps us to bear with others. If there be anything grand, and good, and desirable, anything Christ-like, anything God-like, the way to it is to let your faith grow exceedingly. If this church is to become a missionary church more and more, as I pray God it may, your faith must grow exceedingly. If you are to stand fast as a break-water in these times of departure from the faith once delivered to the saints, your faith must grow exceedingly. If you are to be made a blessing to this wicked city, and shine like a lighthouse over this sea of London, your faith must grow exceedingly. If God has brought you as a church, together with other churches, to the kingdom for such a time as this; if you are to achieve your destiny, and work for God and glorify His name, your faith must grow exceedingly. The man who is timorous and faint-hearted, let him go home; he is not fit for the day of battle. The age requires heroes. The chicken-hearted are out of their place in this perilous century. You that know what you know, and believe what you believe, whose tramp is that of fearless warriors, you have a high calling; fulfil it. You shall see what God will do for you and with you; and it shall be written in the pages of eternity that at such a time the church grew in its faith, and therefore God used it for His glory. May it be so. May those among us who have no faith be led to Jesus. O believers, try your own faith by speaking to unbelievers as they go away this morning: this afternoon in the Sunday-school, prove your faith by winning your dear children for Christ: try your faith every day in the week by giving sinners no rest until they come to Christ. God bless you each one for His name's sake. Amen.

THE SHIELD OF FAITH

"Above all, taking the shield of faith, wherewith ye shall be able to quench all the fiery darts of the wicked."–Ephesians vi. 16.

Like the Spartans, every Christian is born a warrior. It is his destiny to be assaulted; it is his duty to attack. Part of his life will be occupied with defensive warfare. He will have to defend earnestly the faith once delivered to the saints; he will have to resist the devil; he will have to stand against all his wiles; and having done all, still to stand. He will however, be but a sorry Christian if he acteth only on the defensive. He must be one who goes against his foes, as well as stands still to receive their advance. He must be able to say with David, "I come against thee in the name of the Lord of hosts, the God of the armies of Israel whom thou hast defied." He must wrestle not with flesh and blood, but against principalities and powers. He must have weapons for his warfare—not carnal—but "mighty through God to the pulling down of strongholds." He must not, I say, be content to live in the stronghold, though he be then well guarded, and munitions of stupendous strength his dwelling place may be; but he must go forth to attack the castles of the enemy, and to pull them down, to drive the Canaanite out of the land. Now, there are many ways in which the Christian may to a great degree forget his martial character. And alas! there are not a few who, if they be Christians at all, certainly know but very little of that daily warfare to which the Captain of our salvation calleth His disciples. They will know most of fighting who cleave closest to king David; who are willing not merely to be with him when he is in Saul's court with his fingers amid the strings of the harp, going in and out before the people, and behaving discreetly, so that "all Israel and Judah loved David because he went out and came in before them;" but men who are willing to go with David into the cave of Adullam when he is outlawed, when his character has become a stench in the nostrils of every proud hypocrite, and when Saul the king—in his day the representative of that worldly religion which is not of God but standeth in the strength of man—when he hunteth David to seek his life. Thus the men who are willing to follow Christ in the midst of an ungodly and perverse generation, to come right out from it and be separate; their life will have to be like the life of the men of Napthali, who hazarded their lives unto the death in the high places of the field. You will remember that Jonathan, one of the sweetest characters in the word of God, is one of whom after all there is little to be said. His life was inglorious from the very time that he forsook David, and his death was amongst the slain of the Philistines upon the dewless mountains of Gilboa. Alas, poor Jonathan, he could give David his bow, but he could not draw the bow for David; he could give David his garments, even to his armour, but he could not put on the armour for David. The attraction of his father's court was too much for him, and there he stayed. In that Book of the Chronicles, where the Holy Ghost has recorded the names of the mighty men that were with David in Adullam, we find not the name of Jonathan. We find the names of those who broke through the Philistines to give David a drink of water of the well of Bethlehem; we find the name of the man who went down into the pit in the time of winter and smote the lion; but Jonathan has not the honour to stand recorded in the list of the great host which was like the host of God. And there are Christians of that kind nowaday. They have a soft religion—a religion which shuns opposition, a reed-like religion which bows before every blast, unlike that cedar of godliness which standeth aloft in the midst of the storm, and claps its boughs in the hurricane for very joy of triumph, though the earth be all in arms abroad. Such men, like those who shunned David in Adullam, lack the faith that shares the glory. Though saved, yet their names shall not be found written among the mighty men who for our Great Commander's sake are willing to suffer the loss of all things and to go forth without the camp bearing His reproach. Those Christians too, who, having come clean out from the world, are diligently engaged in building up the Church, will have to fight more than others who are rather built up than builders. You remember, in Nehemiah's day, how the Jews wrought in their work when they built the walls of Jerusalem. With one hand they held the trowel, and in the other they held a weapon. "The builders, every one had his sword girded by his side and so builded." Moreover there were master masons along the wall, and the labourers all actually engaged, yet here and there you might see a sentinel ready to sound the trumpet so that the workmen might prove warriors, rush to the fray, and drive away their foes. Be you but very diligent in doing good to the Church of Christ, and you shall soon have reason to defend your cause. Do you but serve your Master zealously and diligently, and let but the Lord's blessing rest upon your labours, the Lord's blessing will entail Satan's curse, the smile of God will necessarily incur the frown of man. According to your nonconformity to the world, your daring to be singular—when to be singular is to be right,—according to your diligence in building up the walls of Jerusalem, you shall be compelled to recognize your soldierly character. To you the text shall come with greater emphasis than to more cowardly souls. "Above all, take the shield of faith wherewith ye shall be able to quench all the fiery darts of the wicked."

Having treated the character of the persons who will most require the shield provided in the text, let us proceed at once to discuss the words before us. We will do so thus. First, let us expound the comparison; secondly, enforce the exhortation; and thirdly propound it as a word of comfort to any trembling sinners who are now specially attacked with the fiery darts of the wicked.

I. First, then, let us EXPOUND THE METAPHOR. Faith is here compared to a shield. There are four or five particulars in which we may liken faith to a shield.

The natural idea which lies upon the very surface of the simile is, that faith, like a shield, protects us against attack. Different kinds of shields were used by the ancients, but there is a special reference in our text to the large shield which was sometimes employed. I believe the word which is translated "shield," sometimes signifies a door, because their shields were as large as a door. They covered the man entirely. You remember that verse in the Psalms which exactly hits the idea, "Thou Lord wilt bless the righteous, with favour wilt thou compass him as with a shield." As the shield enveloped the entire man, so we think faith envelops the entire man, and protects him from all missiles wherever they may be aimed against him. You will remember the cry of the Spartan mother to her son when he went out to battle. She said, "Take care that you return with your shield, or upon it." Now, as she meant that he could return upon his shield dead, it shows that they often employed shields which were large enough to be a bier for a dead man, and consequently quite large enough to cover the body of a live man. Such a shield as that is meant in the text. That is the illustration before us. Faith protects the whole man. Let the assault of Satan be against the head, let him try to deceive us with unsettled notions in theology, let him tempt us to doubt those things which are verily received among us; a full faith in Christ preserves us against dangerous heresies, and enables us to hold fast those things which we have received, which we have been taught, and have learned, and have made our own by experience. Unsettledness in notion generally springs from a weakness of faith. A man that has strong faith in Christ, has got a hand that gets such a grip of the doctrines of grace, that you could not unclasp it, do what you would. He knows what he has believed. He understands what he has received. He could not and would not give up what he knows to be the truth of God, though all the schemes that men devise should assail him with their most treacherous art. While faith will guard the head, it will also guard the heart. When temptation to love the world comes in, then faith holds up thoughts of the future and confidence of the reward that awaits the people of God, and enables the Christian to esteem the reproach of Christ greater riches than all the treasures of Egypt, and so the heart is protected. Then when the enemy makes his cut at the sword-arm of a Christian, to disable him, if possible, from future service, faith protects the arm like a shield, and he is able to do exploits for his Master, and go forth, still conquering, and to conquer, in the name of Him that hath loved us. Suppose the arrow is aimed at his feet, and the enemy attempts to make him trip in his daily life—endeavours to mislead him in the uprightness of his walk and conversation. Faith protects his feet, and he stands fast in slippery places. Neither does his foot slip, nor can the enemy triumph over him. Or suppose the arrow is aimed at the knee, and Satan seeks to make him weak in prayer, and tells him that God will shut out his cry, and never listen to the voice of his supplication; the faith protects him, and in the power of faith, with confidence, he has access to God, and draws near unto His mercy-seat. Or let the arrow be aimed at his conscience, and let it be winged with the remembrance of some recent sin; yet faith protects the conscience, for its full assurance of atonement quenches the fiery darts with that delightful text, "The blood of Jesus Christ His Son cleanseth us from all sin." So there is no part of a man which is not secure. Although Satan will certainly attack him in every direction, yet, let him come where he will.

"He that hath made his refuge God,
Shall find a most secure abode."

Nor does faith only protect the whole man, but if you will think for a moment you will see that the apostle suggests the idea that it protects his armour too. After recounting various pieces, he says, "Above all." The man of God is to put on the girdle and the breast-plate, and he is to be shod, and he is to wear his helmet. But though these are all armour, yet faith is an armour for his armour; it is not only a defence for him, but a defence for his defences. Thus faith not only shields the man, but shields his graces too. You may easily perceive how this is. Satan sometimes attacks our sincerity; he tries to cut the girdle of truth which is about our loins. But faith enables us to be all sincere; like Moses who forsook Egypt, not fearing the wrath of the king, and refused to be called the son of Pharaoh's daughter. Then the enemy will often make an attack against our righteousness, and try to batter our breastplate. Yet doth faith come in and enable us like Joseph to exclaim, "How can I do this great wickedness and sin against God." Or like Job we cry, "Till I die I will not remove mine integrity from me." Or like David we can cry, even in the worst of slanders, "Thou Lord that delivered me out of the jaw of the lion, and out of the paw of the bear, wilt deliver me out of the hand of this Philistine." You see how faith guards the breastplate and protects the girdle. All our virtues are unable to live of themselves, they need grace to preserve them, and that grace is given us through faith. Are you meek? cover your meekness with faith, or else you will give way to a hasty speech. Are you full of decision? let your decision be shielded with confidence in God, or else your decision may waver, and your firmness may give way. Have you the spirit of love and gentleness? take care that you have the shield of faith, or your gentleness may yet turn to anger and your love be changed to bitterness. We must protect our graces with faith as well as the nature they adorn. It is not simply the head, but the helmet; not the feet merely, but the shoes; not the loins, but the girdle;—all must be shielded and secure by this all-covering, all-triumphant shield of faith.

In the second place, let me suggest, that faith like a shield receives the blows which are meant for the man himself. Some Christians think that faith would enable them to escape blows,—that if they had faith everything would be quiet, everything would be peaceful and calm. I know how young Christians imagine this. They think as soon as ever they have come out of their first convictions of their own sinfulness and found the Saviour, oh! now they are going to ride softly to heaven, singing all the way. What did they put their armour on at all for if there were to be no battles? What have they put their hand to the plough for if they are not to plough to the end of the furrow and often to wipe the sweat from their face through their hard toil? Why enlist, young men, if you are not wanted to fight? What is the good of a fair-weather soldier,—one who stays at home to feed at the public expense? No! let the soldier be ready when war comes; let him expect the conflict as a part and necessary consequence of his profession. But be armed with faith, it receives the blows. The poor shield is knocked and hammered and battered like a pent-house exposed in the time of storm; blow after blow comes rattling upon it, and though it turns death aside yet the shield is compelled itself to bear the cut and the thrust. So must our faith do—it must be cut at, it must bear the blows. Some people, instead of using the shield of faith to bear the blow, use the skulking place of cowards. Ashamed of Christ they make no profession of him, or having professed Christ, ashamed of the profession, they hide themselves by deserting their colours, by conformity to the world. Perhaps they are even called to preach the gospel, but they do it in so quiet and gentle a way, like men that wear soft raiment, and ought to be in kings' houses. Unlike John the Baptist, they are "reeds shaken with the wind." Of them no one saith anything ill, because they have done no ill to Satan's kingdom. Against them Satan never roars—why should he! He is not afraid of them, therefore he need not come out against them. "Let them alone," saith he, "thousands such as these will never shake my kingdom." But this is not to use the shield of faith; this, I repeat it, is to use the skulking-places of an ignoble cowardice. Others use the shield of presumption, they think it is right with them when it is not, but so they are proof, not against the attacks of Satan, but against the weapons of our spiritual warfare. Seared in their conscience as with a hot iron they fear not the rebukes of God's law. Deadened even to the voice of love they bow not before the invitations of Christ; they go on their way caring for none of those things; presumption has made them secure. Some people have no blows to suffer. Their shield lets them go through the world quietly, saying, "Peace, peace, where there is no peace." But only uplift the shield of faith, bearing the blood-red escutcheon of the cross, and there are plenty of the knights of hell who are ready to unhorse you. On, champion, on! in the name of Him that is with you. No lance can pierce that shield; no sword shall ever be able to cut through it; it shall preserve you in all battle and in all strife; you shall bring it home yourself, through it you shall be more than conqueror. Faith, then, is like a shield, because it has to bear the blows.

Thirdly, faith is like a shield, because it hath good need to be strong. A man who has some pasteboard shield may lift it up against his foe, the sword will go through it and reach his heart. Or perhaps in the moment when the lance is in rest, and his foe is dashing upon him, he thinks that his shield may preserve him, and lo it is dashed to shivers and the blood gushes from the fountain and he is slain. He that would use a shield must take care that it be a shield of proof. He that hath truth faith, the faith of God's elect, hath such a shield that he will see the scimitars of his enemies go to a thousand shivers over it every time they smite the bosses thereof. And as for their spears, if they but once come in contact with this shield, they will break into a thousand splinters, or bend like reeds when pressed against the wall,—they cannot pierce it, but they shall themselves be quenched or broken in pieces. You will say, how then are we to know whether our faith is a right faith, and our shield a strong one? One test of it is, it must be all of a piece. A shield that is made of three or four pieces in this case will be of heaven's forging or your shield will certainly fail you; you must have the faith of God's elect which is of the operation of the Holy Spirit who worketh it in the soul of man. Then you must see to it that your faith is that which rests only upon truth, for if there be any error or false notion in the fashioning of it, that shall be a joint in it which the spear can pierce. You must take care that your faith is agreeable to God's word, that you depend upon true and real promises, upon the sure word of testimony and not upon the fictions and fancies and dreams of men. And above all, you must mind that your faith is fixed in the person of Christ, for nothing but a faith in Christ's divine person as "God over all, blessed for ever," and in His proper manhood when as the Lamb of God's passover He was sacrificed for us—no other faith will be able to stand against the tremendous shocks and the innumerable attacks which you must receive in the great battle of spiritual life. Look to your shield, man. Not so fast there with that painted God! Not so fast there with that proud heraldic symbol which has no strength in it. See to thy shield. See if it be like the shields of Solomon which were borne before the king, each one made of gold. Or at least let them be like the shields of Rehoboam, every one of the best brass, so that there be found no wooden shield in thy hand which may be dashed in pieces when most thou needest its help.

made of gold. Or at least let them be like the shields of Rehoboam, every one of the best brass, so that there be found no wooden shield in thy hand which may be dashed in pieces when most thou needest its help.

But to pass on—for we must not pause long on any one particular—faith is like a shield because it is of no use except it be well handled. A shield needs handling, and so does faith. He was a silly soldier who, when he went into the battle, said he had a shield but it was at home. So there be some silly professors who have a faith, but they have not got it with them when they need it. They have it with them when there are no enemies. When all goeth well with them, then they can believe; but just when the pinch comes their faith fails. Now there is a sacred art in being able to handle the shield of faith. Let me explain to you how that can be. You will handle it well if you are able to quote the promises of God against the attacks of your enemy. The devil said "One day you shall be poor and starve." "No," said the believer, handling his shield well, "He hath said 'I will never leave thee, nor forsake thee;' " "bread shall be given thee and thy water shall be sure." "Aye," said Satan, "but thou wilt one day fall by the hand of the enemy." "No," said faith, "for I am persuaded that He that hath begun a good work in me will perform it until the day of Jesus Christ." "Aye," said Satan, "but the slander of the enemy will overturn you." "No," said faith, "He maketh the wrath of man to praise Him; the remainder of wrath doth He restrain." "Aye," said Satan, as he shot another arrow, "you are weak." "Yes," said faith, handling his shield, "but 'My strength is made perfect in weakness.' Most gladly therefore will I rather glory in my infirmities, that the power of Christ may rest upon me." "Aye," said Satan, "but thy sin is great." "Yes," said faith, handling the promise, "but He is able to save to the uttermost them that come unto God by Him." "But," said the enemy again, drawing his sword and making a tremendous thrust, "God hath cast thee off." "No," said faith, "He hateth putting away; He does not cast off His people, neither doth He forsake His heritage." "But I will have thee, after all," said Satan. "No," said faith, dashing the bosses in the enemy's jaws, "He hath said, 'I give unto My sheep eternal life, and they shall never perish, neither shall any pluck them out of My hand.' " This is what I call handling the shield.

But there is another way of handling it, not merely with the promises, but with the doctrines. "Ah," says Satan, "what is there in thee that thou shouldst be saved? Thou art poor, and weak, and mean, and foolish!" Up came faith, handling the shield doctrinally, this time, and said, "God hath chosen the base things of this world, and things which are despised hath God chosen, yea, and things which are not, to bring to nought the things that are"; for "not many wise men after the flesh, not many mighty, not many noble are called." "Hath not God chosen the poor of this world, rich in faith, and heirs of the kingdom which He hath promised to them that love Him?" "Aye," said he, "if God should have chosen you, yet after all you may certainly perish!" And then, Christian handling his shield of faith doctrinally again, said, "No, I believe in the final perseverance of the saints, for is it not written 'the righteous shall hold on His way, and he that hath clean hands shall wax stronger?' " Those that thou gavest Me I have kept, and none of them is lost," and so forth. So by well understanding the doctrines of grace, there is not a single doctrine which may not in its way minister to our defence against the fiery darts of the wicked. Then, the Christian soldier ought to know how to handle the shield of faith according to the rules of observation. "Aye," saith the enemy, "thy confidence is vain, and thy hope shall soon be cut off." "No," saith faith, "I have been young and now am old, yet have I not seen the righteous forsaken." "Yes, but thou hast fallen into sin, and God will leave thee." "No," saith faith, "for I saw David, and he stumbled, but yet the Lord surely brought him out of the horrible pit, and out of the miry clay." To use this shield in the way of observation, is very profitable when you mark the way whereby God has dealt with the rest of His people; for as He deals with one, so He will deal with the rest, and you can throw this in the teeth of your enemy. "I remember the ways of God. I call to remembrance His deeds of old. I say hath God cast off His people, hath He forsaken one of His chosen? And since He has never done so, I hold up my shield with great courage, and say He never will; He changes not; as He has not forsaken any, He will not forsake me."

Then there is another way of handling this shield, and that is experimentally. When you can look back, like the Psalmist, to the land of Jordan and of the Hermonites, from the hill Mizar, when you can return to those days of old, and call to remembrance your song in the night, when your spirit can say, "Why art thou cast down, O my soul, why art thou disquieted within me. Hope thou in God, for I shall yet praise Him." Why, brethren, some of us can talk of deliverances so many, that we know not where to end, scarcely do we know where to begin. Oh! what wonders has God done for us as a Church and people! He has brought us through fire and through water. Men did ride over our heads, but hitherto all things have worked together for our good. His glory has appeared amidst all the villanies and slanders of men to which we have been exposed. Let us handle our shield then, according to the rules of experience, and when Satan tells us that God will fail us at the last, let us reply, "Now thou liest, and I tell it to thee to thy face, for what our God was in the past, He will be in the present, and in the future, and so on even to the end." Young soldiers of Christ, learn well the art of handling your shield.

Lastly for the matter of the figure. The shield in olden times was an emblem of the warrior's honour, and more especially in later days than those of Paul. In the age of chivalry, the warrior carried his escutcheon upon his shield. Now, faith is like a shield, because it carries the Christian's glory, the Christian's coat of arms, the Christian's escutcheon. And what is the Christian's coat of arms? Well, good Joseph Irons used to say it was a cross and a crown, with the words "No cross, no crown"—a most blessed coat of arms too. But methinks the Christian's best coat of arms is the cross of his Saviour—that blood-red cross; always stained, yet never stained; always dyed in blood, yet always resplendent with ruby brightness; always trodden on, yet always triumphant; always despised, yet always glorified; always attacked, yet always without resistance, coming off more than conqueror. Some of the old Reformers used to have an anvil for their coat of arms, and a significant one too, with this motto, "The anvil hath broken many hammers." By which they meant that they stood still, and just let men hammer at them till their hammers broke of themselves. Another old coat of arms with some of the Reformers, was wont to be a candle with a great many enemies all puffing to blow it out, and though they all blew as hard as they could, yet the candle did but burn the brighter. Out of darkness came light, and from all their attacks, the light grew stronger. This morning put thy coat of arms upon thy shield, and lift it up. Let that blood-red cross be your choice; then when thy battle is over, they will hang thy escutcheon up in heaven; and when the old heraldries have gone, and the lions, and tigers, and griffins, and all manner of strange things have vanished from remembrance, that cross and thy old shield indented with many a blow, shall be honourable with many a triumph before the throne of God. Above all things, then, take the shield of faith.

II. I now leave the expounding of the figure in haste, and pass on to ENFORCE THE EXHORTATION. "Above all taking the shield of faith."

If you sent a servant upon an errand, and you said to him, "Get so-and-so, and so-and-so, and so-and-so, but above all now see to such-and-such a thing"; he would not understand that he ought to neglect any, but he would perceive that there was some extra importance attached to one part of his mission. So let it be with us. We are not to neglect our sincerity, our righteousness, or our peace, but above all, as the most important we are to see to it that our faith is right, that it be true faith, and that it covers all our virtues from attack. The necessity of true faith is clearly explained by the text. Faith is here said to have a quenching power. The ancients were wont to use small arrows, perhaps light cane arrows, which were tinged with poison. They would be called fiery darts, because they no sooner touched the flesh or even grazed the skin than they left a fiery poison in the veins. Sometimes too they employed darts which were tipped with tow that had been dipped in some inflammable spirit, and were blazing as they flew through the air in order to set the tents of their antagonists on fire, or burn down houses in besieged cities. Now faith has a quenching power; it sees the temptation or the blasphemy, or the insinuation coming against it with poison and with fire in it to take away its life or to burn up its comforts. Faith catches the dart, not only receives it, but takes away its sting, and quenches its fire. Oh it is wonderful how God sometimes enables His people to live in the midst of temptations and tribulations as though they had none of them. I believe so that some of the martyrs when they were burning in the fire suffered hardly any pain, because the joy and peace which God gave them delivered them from the vehement heat. This I know. There are times when everybody is speaking well of some of us, and we are wretched by reason of the world's fawnings. We do not want to be called "Son of Pharaoh's daughter." And yet there are other times when, though every one speaks ill, our peace is like a river, and our righteousness like the waves of the sea. Truly at such times we can say, "Now I am in my proper place; this is where I should be—outside the camp, bearing the reproach of Christ." The praise of man is deadly and damnable; his censure is goodly and godlike. Let it come; it cannot dishonour, it does but ennoble. Thus does it often happen that faith quenches the fire of attack, nay, more, turns the attack into comfort, extracts honey from the nettle, and sweets of joy from the wormwood and the gall. "Above all, take the shield of faith."

Another commendation which the text gives is this—that faith alone, out of all the pieces of armour, is able to quench all the darts. The helmet can only keep off those that are aimed against the head. The foot is only and alone protected by the sandals, the breast alone is guarded by the breastplate, but faith protects against all attacks. Have all other virtues, but most of all have faith is the *Catholica*, it is the cure-all, it is the universal remedy, it is good not only for the heat of fever, but for the shaking of ague. It is good for everything,—good for the timid to make them strong, good for the rash to make them wise; it is good for those who are desponding to make them brave, and good for those who are too daring, to make them discreet. There is no respect in which faith is not useful to us, therefore, whatever you leave out, see to your faith; if you forget all besides, be careful above all that ye take the shield of faith.

And then, again, we are told above all to take the shield of faith, because faith preserves from all sorts of enemies. The fiery darts of the wicked? Does that refer to Satan? Faith answers him. Does it refer to wicked men? Faith resists them. Does it refer to one's own wicked self? Faith can overcome that. Does it refer to the whole world? "This is the victory that overcometh the world, even our faith." It matters not who the enemy may be; let the earth be all in arms abroad, this faith can quench all the fiery darts of the wicked. Above all then, take the shield of faith. I know there are some ministers who seem to teach doubting as a duty. I cannot; I dare not. Above all, take the shield of faith. You know in the old Grecian contests the aim of the enemy was to get near enough to push aside the shield, and then to stab under the armour. And that is what Satan wants to do. If he can knock aside the shield and get under it, then he can stab us mortally. Take care of your shield. Do not live in perpetual unbelief. Be not always cast down. Pray unto thy God till thou canst say—"I know whom I have believed, and am persuaded that He is able to keep that which I have committed unto Him." Oh! the old saints were not always doubting. "My beloved is mine, and I am His," said Solomon. David said—"Say unto my soul, I am thy salvation." "The Lord is my salvation." "The Lord is my shepherd." Job too could say, "I know that my Redeemer liveth." Paul could speak very confidently in full many places. And why should we be content to say—"I hope, I trust,"—when they said they knew, and were persuaded—all was well between God and their souls? Let it be so with us. Unbelief dishonours us, weakens us, destroys our comforts, prevents our usefulness. Faith will make us happy, and make us useful, and what is best of all, it will enable us to honour God on earth, and to enjoy His presence while yet we are in the low-lands of this present world.

III. Lastly, I have a word or two to say by way of conclusion to some POOR SINNER WHO IS COMING TO CHRIST, BUT WHO IS GREATLY VEXED WITH THE FIERY DARTS OF THE WICKED ONE.

You remember how John Bunyan in his *Pilgrim's Progress* represents Christiana and Mercy and the children coming to knock at the gate. When they knocked, the enemy who lived in a castle hard by sent out a big dog, which barked at them at such a rate that Mercy fainted, and Christiana only dared to knock again, and when she obtained entrance, she was all in a tremble. At the same time hard by in the castle there were men who shot fiery darts at all who would enter; and poor Mercy was exceedingly afraid because of the darts and the dog. Now, it generally happens that when a soul is coming to Christ the devil will dog him. As sure as ever he feels his need of a Saviour and is ready to put his trust in Christ, it will be true of him as of the poor demoniac child;—as he was a coming, the devil threw him down and tore him. Now, poor tempted sinner, there is nothing that can bring joy and peace into your heart but faith. Oh, that you may have grace this morning to begin to use this shield. "Ay, sir," say you, "I have been looking within and I cannot see anything that is good; I have been looking to my experiences and I am afraid I have never felt as So-and-so did." That is the way to ruin yourself. Did you ever hear of a man who in cold winter's weather got warm by rolling on the ice, and saying, "I don't feel any heat as some people do." No, because he is looking in the wrong place to get the heat. If you expect to get anything in yourself you expect more than Paul ever got, for he said after he had long known his Master, "I know that in me—(that is, in my flesh)—there dwelleth no good thing." "Oh, sir," you reply again, "I find I am willing to do a great many things, but I cannot; and when I would be what I should be, I find a resistance somewhere within my own breast." Well, and what of that? Even so did the apostle: "When I would do good, evil is present with me." The fact is you have no business to look there. These things are not shields against Satan. What cares he for your experiences? Were they never so good he would still roar at you. What he is afraid of is your faith. Throw down these things, then, which only encumber you and expose you, and lay your breast bare to his attacks, and take up the shield of faith. What has Satan said to you? "You are too great a sinner to be saved." Well, quote this text, "Him that cometh unto Me, I will in nowise cast out." I had a lesson this week in the case of a good

Christian man, who through feebleness of mind has fallen at last into the deepest despair. I never met a person in such awful despair as he was, and you cannot tell how it puzzled me to give him any sort of comfort; indeed, I failed after all. He said, "I'm too big a sinner to be saved." So I said, "But the blood of Jesus Christ His Son cleanseth us from all sin." "Aye," said he, "but you must remember the context, which says, 'if we walk in the light, as He is in the light, we have fellowship one with another, and the blood of Jesus Christ His Son cleanseth us from all sin.' Now, I do not walk in the light," said he; "I walk in the dark, and I have no fellowship with the people of God now, and therefore it does not apply to me." "Well," I said, "but He is able to save to the uttermost them that come unto God by Him." "That is the only text," he said, "I never can get over, for it says 'to the uttermost,' and I know I cannot have gone beyond that, and still it does not yield me comfort." I said, "But God asketh nothing of you but that you will believe Him; and you know if you have ever so feeble a faith you are like a child—the feeble hand of a child can receive; and that is the mark of a Christian,—'of His fulness have all we received'—and if you only receive with your hand, that is enough." "Aye, said he, "I have not the hand—I have not the hand of faith." "Very well," I said, "you have the mouth of desire; you can ask, if you cannot receive with the hand." "No," said he, "I have not; I do not pray, I cannot pray; I have not the mouth of desire." "Then," I said, "all that is wanted is an empty place, a vacuum, so that God can put it in." "Ah, Sir," said he, "you have got me there! I have a great deal of vacuum; I have an aching void—a vacuum. If ever there was an empty sinner in this world, I am one." "Well," I said, "Christ will fill that vacuum; there is a full Christ for empty sinners." Let me now say the same to you as I said to that poor man. All God wants is a vacuum. You have got a vacuum. This is not much to have; simply to be empty, to be pumped dry, to have nothing at all in you. But then, "He filleth the hungry with good things, and the rich He sendeth empty away." All that is wanted is to be down there on the ground. It is not hard work. It is not to sit up, nor to stand up, nor to kneel, but to lie there at His feet; and when He sees the soul flat on its face before Him, He will have mercy upon him.

Now, soul, for that shield of faith. Say to Satan, "In the name of God I dare believe." "Thou art a great sinner," says he. "Yes, but I believe He is a great Saviour." "But thou hast sinned beyond all hope." "No, there is forgiveness with Him, that He may be feared." But he says, "You are shut out." "No," say you, "though He slay me, yet will I trust Him." "But your disease is of long standing." Aye, but say you, "If I but touch the hem of His garment, I shall be clean." But saith Satan again, "How dare you? would you have the impudence?" "Well," say you, "if I perish I will trust Christ, and I will perish only there." Have it in your soul fixed, that in the teeth of everything you will trust Christ,—that be you such a sinner or no, still you will trust Christ,—that whether Satan's accusations be true or false, you mean to have done answering them and simply trust Christ. Ah, soul, then thou shalt have such joy and peace that nothing shall be like it. O that thou wouldst believe on Jesus now! Leave thy feelings, leave thy doings and thy willings, and trust Christ. "I dare not," saith one. Dare it, man, dare it! you cannot do wrong for He commands you. This is the commandment, that ye believe on Jesus Christ whom He hath sent. "Oh, but I may be lost even if I do." You will be lost if you do not, for "he that believeth not shall be damned." "But I am afraid of being condemned if I were to believe." "He that believeth not is condemned already." You are like the poor lepers at the gate; you are dying, and you say, "Let us fall to the Syrians: if they kill us we can but die, and if they save us alive we shall live." Say you, as Benhadad did concerning king Ahab, "We have heard that the kings of Israel are merciful kings, but let us put ropes upon our heads, and go out to the king of Israel: peradventure he will save thy life." So say thou to God, "I have heard that Thou art merciful; if there is a wretch out of hell that deserves to be in it, I am that sinner—if there is one that now feels that earth is provoked against him, and the ground says, swallow him up; and heaven is provoked against him, and cries, let the lightning flash destroy him; and the sea says, drown him; and the stars say, smite him with pestilence; and the sun says, scorch him; and the moon says, let him be blasted; and the mildew says, let me devour his crops; and fever says, let me cut off the thread of his life,—if there be such a wretch out of hell, I am he,"—yet, say, but to God, "I believe in Thy mercy, I believe in Thy promise, I believe in Thy Son Jesus. I believe in His precious blood, and here I am, do with me as seemeth good in Thy sight,"—say but this and thou shalt have mercy, and pardon, and peace. My dear hearers, shall I say this for myself and not for you? Nay, but may God grant that many a score of you this morning may be led to put your trust in Him who has said, "They that trust in Me shall never be confounded."

INCREASED FAITH THE STRENGTH OF PEACE PRINCIPLES

"The apostles said unto the Lord, Increase our faith,"—Luke xvii. 5.

The sermon of last Sabbath morning, in which I endeavoured earnestly to inculcate the doctrine of overcoming evil with good, and the frank and full forgiveness of all injuries for Christ's sake, has raised much discussion. I know that it startled a great many of you, and that you have held a great many questionings among yourselves as to whether such precepts are practicable by ordinary Christian men. At that I am not at all surprised, because when our Lord preached the same doctrine His disciples were so astonished that the apostles exclaimed in surprise, "Lord, increase our faith." It is most important in this case to see the connection of the text, or you will fail to see its drift and bearings. It was not for the sake of working miracles that the apostles sought increased faith; it was not in order to bear their present or future trials, neither was it to enable them to receive some mysterious article of faith, but their prayer referred to a common every-day duty enjoined by the gospel, the forgiving those who do us wrong; for the previous verses are to this effect: "Take heed to yourselves; if thy brother trespass against thee, rebuke him; and if he repent, forgive him. And if he trespass against thee seven times in a day, and seven times in a day turn again to thee, saying, I repent; thou shalt forgive him." And it was upon hearing this that the apostles cried, "Increase our faith." If you have been surprised, dear friends, at the high standard of Christian duty which my Lord has laid down for you, I only trust your surprise may drive you to the same resort as it did those first servants of the Lord, and compel you to appeal for help to Him who issued the command. Will He not help us in walking in His own ways? When we feel that His commandment is exceeding broad, to whom should we appeal for aid but to Him who is our leader in all holy conversation and godliness? He will not set you the task and refuse you His assistance in performing it.

Observe that these apostles did not, because of their having sinned against this precept in former times, conclude that they had no faith. They did not conclude because the precept was so much above them that therefore they were unbelievers altogether. Despair is no help to Christian duty; to doubt our discipleship will not help us to obey our Lord. If any of you have cut yourselves off from the household of faith because you fall short of the noblest forms of Christian love, I entreat you to begin again, and instead of doubting the existence of your faith ask to have it increased. There is a fountain opened for your past uncleannesses, and sanctifying power for your future lives; apply to Jesus at once for the double deliverance, and doubt not that he will deal graciously with you.

Neither did the disciples reject the precept as utterly impossible, nor excuse themselves from it on the ground that in their peculiar circumstances it must needs be modified. They did not complain that it was too much to expect of human nature, nor did they regard the command as only fit for dwellers in Utopia. No, they respected the precept which surprised them and admired the virtue which astonished them. As loyal followers of the Lord Jesus, they felt bound to follow where He led the way, for they believed that He was too wise to issue an impossible command, too good to teach an impracticable code of morals, and too honest to set up a standard to which no mortal could in any measure attain. They looked on His command and they felt such confidence in Him that instead of drawing back they resolved that it should be obeyed at all cost. Their resolve was to do His bidding, but feeling that they could not achieve it in their own strength they began to pray, and then prayer was for faith. They felt that only faith could work such a wonder of patient love; it was far out of the ordinary line of action; flesh and blood could not accomplish it, mere resolve would not achieve it, faith must do it, and even faith itself would need strengthening or it would fail in the attempt. They felt also that the kind of faith which could forgive to seventy times seven must be supernatural, and not such as they could grow in their own breasts without divine assistance, and therefore they said to the Lord, "Increase our faith." They needed such faith as He could give, in order that they might perform such duties as He enjoined. Beloved, imitate the example of these apostles: whenever you feel that you have something to do that is beyond you, stop a moment and breathe a prayer for more strength. If ever the leap is too wide, draw back, take breath, ask strength, and then, in the name of Him that will surely bear you over it, take your leap and succeed. He has not brought you into a condition in which you shall feel your infirmities so abjectly as to lie down and die, but He does intend you to feel your weakness so much that you may importunately pray for His aid, and then in the strength which you have gained by prayer may attain to heights of virtue which else had been far above and out of your sight. We are all the more likely to rise to holiness when we have seen our own incapacity for it. Those who at the first blush were somewhat staggered by the high and glorious precepts of Christian forgiveness, of non-resistance, and of returning good for evil, are none the less likely to become good practisers of this holy art, but all the more so if their astonishment drive them to pray, "Lord, increase our faith."

Let us then, this morning, in that connection, consider the prayer of the text; let us, secondly, see how it bears upon the duty of forgiveness, how the increase of faith can help us to forgive; and then, thirdly, let us note how our Lord Jesus answered this prayer. O divine Spirit, lead us into these truths while we meditate together, and afterwards help us to show in our lives the mind of Christ.

I. First, LET US CONSIDER THE PRAYER ITSELF. It may help us to see its meaning if we for a moment consider where the apostles learned to pray like this. Who suggested to them to say, "Lord, increase our faith"? Now, faith is the act of man: truly, it is the gift of God, but it is as surely the act of man. God does not believe for us, the Holy Spirit does not believe in our stead—the man himself believes. This would be clear enough to the apostles, but they might not so readily learn that Jesus had power to give and to increase faith. It is assuredly most proper to ask the Lord to increase our faith, but it was not very early in their Christian career that the apostles did so pray; in fact, it is a very singular fact that I think this is almost the only instance in which, as an apostolic company, they asked any spiritual thing of the Master. They did say, "Lord, teach us how to pray," but I am afraid they meant to learn a form of prayer rather than to be filled with the spirit of prayer. As to spiritual blessings, our Lord might well say to them, "Hitherto ye have asked nothing in my name." But they were at last so overwhelmed with a consciousness of their own weakness when they perceived the exceeding breadth and height of the law of Christian forgiveness, that they felt assured that there must be strength laid up for them somewhere or other, and where could it be but in their Lord, and so they prayed to the Lord, "increase our faith." It is not the only time in which a sense of their own personal emptiness has convinced men of the divine fulness, and driven them to it.

I think it was Jesus who had taught them so to pray. They must have caught the idea from that which is recorded in the eleventh of Mark, at the twenty-second verse, where you have much the same passage as the one before us, though expressed in different words. "Jesus answering saith unto them, Have faith in God. For verily I say unto you, that whosoever shall say unto this mountain, Be thou removed, and be thou cast into the sea; and shall not doubt in his heart, but shall believe that those things which He saith shall come to pass; he shall have whatsoever he saith. Therefore I say unto you, What things soever ye desire, when ye pray, believe that ye receive them, and ye shall have them. And when ye stand praying, forgive, if ye have ought against any: that your Father also which is in heaven may forgive you your trespasses. But if ye do not forgive, neither will your Father which is in heaven forgive your trespasses." Note that our Lord according to Mark commenced this exhortation concerning forgiveness by saying, "Have faith in God"; then showed the power of faith in working wonders, and especially in obtaining answers to prayer, and last of all commanded forgiveness of trespasses. Was not that sentence "Have faith in God" the mother of their prayer "Increase our faith"? Jesus had said "Have faith," and now when they fully understand what it is that He inculcates they take the word out of His mouth, and they say to their Lord, "add to our faith. We trust we have some of that precious grace, but add to it yet more and more, we beseech Thee." Our Master in His teaching was continually connecting the forgiveness of others with the exercise of faith. In the passage just referred to, and in that which surrounds my text, you have our Lord referring to the faith which moves mountains, or plucks up sycamore trees by the roots and coupling with it the forgiving of offences. Surely this may have led them so to pray.

Our Lord had also suggested this prayer for faith from the fact that as He had taught them that there must be faith in prayer, so He had also insisted upon it that prayer must always be connected with a forgiving spirit; in fact, in the model prayer, according to which we are always to shape our petitions, He has taught us to say, "Forgive us our debts, as we forgive our debtors," or, "Forgive us our trespasses as we forgive them that trespass against us." He has allowed us, as it were, to cut out for ourselves the measure of pardon that we wish to receive, and the measure is to be precisely that which we are prepared to give to others. God will pardon us in proportion as we are prepared to pardon. If you have a trespass which you cannot pardon, God also has an unpardonable sin written in His book against you: unpardonable, I mean, as long as you are unforgiving. If you will only pardon slowly, and after a niggardly fashion, you shall not for many a day enjoy the freeness and the bounty of the unlimited mercy of God. So you see as our Lord had connected success in prayer both with forgiveness and faith, He had suggested the increase of the one with the view of accomplishing the other. No man can pray successfully while he is in an unforgiving frame of mind, but a believing man always does pray successfully, therefore a believing man is ready to forgive. As faith increases we become more able to overlook the provocations we endure.

Do you know I think that the apostles had also learned this prayer, not only from the Master, but from one who was very much inferior to themselves, but who nevertheless had outrun them in the knowledge of the struggles of the heart,—I mean the father who had a lunatic child. That was a wonderful prayer of his, when Jesus came to him, "If thou canst believe, all things are possible to him that believeth." The poor man cried out, "Lord, I believe, help Thou my unbelief." This was a deeply experimental prayer. It showed how familiar he was to the workings of his own soul. He detected unbelief in his own heart, and yet he saw faith there too; whereas a great many Christians, if they discern some unbelief in their hearts, straightway imagine that there cannot be any faith, and if they possess a degree of faith, they fancy that there cannot be any unbelief surviving, whereas the two powers are in one man at the same time, and contend within his soul. The apostles appear to me to have learned a noble lesson from that tried father, and now they put his prayer into their own language, and use it on their own account. They do as good as confess their lingering unbelief, and yet they acknowledge that they do believe while they pray, "Lord, increase our faith." So what with the teaching of Jesus, and what with the example of that poor struggling soul, they had been taught to pray as they should. It is a grand thing when every day we learn to pray better, and both from the Master's lips and from the experience of all, His servants are being taught what to pray for as we ought. By the use of such means the Spirit helpeth our infirmity, and teaches us how to prevail with God.

Now let us come a little closer to prayer itself, and notice what it confesses. It confesses that they had faith, for they say, "Lord, increase our faith." He who asks for faith must have some faith, or he would not ask at all; indeed, it is with faith that we ask for faith. He who pleads, "Add to my faith," owns that he has some already, to which more is to be added. So that these apostles, notwithstanding that they were staggered by the duty before them, believed that Christ could help them through it, and believed also that He could at once give them the needful faith. When you ask for any blessing, always do so in such a way as to acknowledge what you have already received. Do not despise the little faith you have even though you feel bound to plead for more. They also confessed that while they had faith they had not enough of it. My brothers and sisters, must we not all make the same confession? Thou dost believe in Jesus Christ to the salvation of thy soul, but, brother, dost thou believe to the comfort of thy heart? Thou hast faith enough to bear the ordinary trials of life, but, dear brother, hast thou enough for the superior contests to which thou hast lately been called? If thou hast not, then here is the prayer for thee, "Lord, increase my faith." Certain it is that no one among us has too much faith, nor even enough should unusual storms arise. We have no faith to spare. God grants it to us always according to our day, and He giveth more grace and faith when He sendeth more trial. Often, when our faith is sorely tried, we are compelled to feel mere babes in faith's school, and need indeed to pray daily, "Lord, increase our faith."

But then by their prayer the apostles confessed that they could not increase their own faith. Faith is not a weed to grow upon every dunghill, without care or culture: it is a plant of heavenly growth, and requires divine watching and watering. He who is the author of faith and the finisher of it, is the only One who can increase it. As no man ever obtains his first faith apart from the Spirit of God, so no man ever getteth more faith except through the working of that selfsame divine power. The Spirit which rests upon

Jesus must anoint us also, or the measure of faith will not be enlarged. Breathe then the prayer to God, my brother, "Increase my faith": this will be a far wiser course than to resolve in your own strength, "I will believe more," for, perhaps, in rebuke of your pride you will fall into a decaying state, and even believe less. After having made so vainglorious a resolution, you may fall into grievous despondency: do not therefore say, "I will accumulate more faith," but pray "Lord, I believe, help thou mine unbelief." in is your wisdom.

The prayer also confesses that the Lord Jesus can increase faith. Dear brethren, the Lord Jesus Christ can increase your faith by the use of common means, through His Spirit. He is able to make all grace abound towards you. Not by any magical mode, nor by miracle, but even by such things as ye have, the Lord can make Little-faith grow into Greatheart, and turn Feeble-mind into Valiant-for-truth. He has the key of faith, and can open more of its chambers, and fill them with His treasures. He can reveal truth to you which shall cause you to believe more fully, or the truth already revealed He can set in clearer light and apply more powerfully to your heart, and so can add to your faith. Do not believe, brother, that you are condemned to lead an unbelieving life. No such necessity exists. Let no man among you sit down and say, "I have a withered arm of faith, and cannot stretch it out, or I have a weak eye, and shall never be able to see afar off." No, the name of our God is Jehovah Rophi, and He can heal us of all these ills. God can make thee strong, brother. Dost thou not know that He giveth power to the faint, and to them that have no might He increaseth strength. Present again and again the prayer "Lord increase our faith," with the full conviction that He can do so to any extent, and that He can lift even the most drooping soul among us into the full assurance of faith. May the Lord at this very hour work in you a childlike confidence in His love and faithfulness, and never may you be the victim of mistrust again.

I want you to observe who prayed this prayer. It is not often that the evangelists speak of "the apostles," separately, as asking anything. You will perceive in the first verse that our Lord spoke to the disciples. "Then said He to the disciples," but the persons who sought increased faith were the apostles. "The apostles said," How is this? Does it not show us that these men who were the leaders of the Christian church did not think themselves infallible? Fancy the successor of Peter saying, "Lord, increase our faith!" Surely, His Holiness wants no increase of faith! He who boasts that he is infallible cannot be unbelieving. Ah, brethren, the apostles knew nothing of such silly and wicked pretensions, none of them ever in their lives pretending to be the "Head of the Church" and "Vicar of Christ"; but they were ready to cry to their Master for increase of faith, just as soon as the rest of the disciples, ay, sooner, too, because they were the first to feel their need. They were the choice of the Lord's flock, and therefore they were the first to see and to confess their own failures. No man so soon knows and so much deplores his want of faith as the man who has most of it. It was not the little ones in the church who said, "Increase our faith,"—they might well say it; but it was the masters in Israel who had been best instructed by Christ, who had seen His miracles and preached His word; these were the very ones who cried to their Lord, "Increase our faith." The nearer you live to God, and the more full your soul is of faith, the less inclined will you be to be self-satisfied; and the more earnestly will you desire that your faith should be increased.

It is somewhat remarkable that the whole of the apostles thus prayed. They were unanimous in this prayer, though it did not often happen that they were so in anything. There were divisions among them, and strifes as to who among them should be the greatest; but this time they were all one in the petition to the Lord. A petition which commended itself to the entire college of the apostles is one which surely all of us may put up to our great Lord in the presence of that supreme duty, of which we have heard last Sabbath morning. In order that we may not resist evil, but overcome evil with good, be pleased, O Lord, to increase our faith.

While I am still explaining the prayer, let us notice once again why they asked for faith. They said unto the Lord, "increase our faith." Might they not more fitly have said,

"Lord, increase our meekness, Lord, increase our Christian love." Nay, but they went to the bottom of the thing, they looked to the mainspring of all Christian graces, they asked for faith. Sometimes, brethren, we are led to see that if a duty is to be performed at all it cannot be done in the strength of nature. Now the grace which deals with the supernatural is faith, hence we say, "Lord, increase our faith, for since this is a supernatural virtue which Thou dost ask of us, be pleased to give us the faculty which deals with supernatural power that we may be enabled to achieve this high and difficult duty." I know some of you think that faith was given to men of old, that they might work miracles, and you have admired the faith of Samson when he slew the Philistines with the jawbone of an ass, the faith which "quenched the violence of fire," the faith which "stopped the mouths of lions," and so on. Yes, but faith is meant for other matters besides miracles. The faith which enables a Christian man to live a holy life, especially the faith that will enable you not to be overcome of evil but to overcome evil with good, and to forgive your neighbour to seventy times seven is as great a faith as that which of old stopped the sun and divided the sea. It seems to be thought by some that faith now-a-days is only meant to raise money with, that we may support orphanages and colleges by obtaining answers to prayer. Well, these are noble deeds, and the faith which accomplishes them brings great glory to God. God give to His servants who are called to such work more and more success, for such works are a standing testimony to a sceptical world that God does hear prayer: but after all the feats which the most of you are to perform are neither miracles nor the maintenance of orphanages, but deeds of love in common life. You have not to stop the mouths of lions, but you have the equally difficult task of stopping your own mouth when you are in an angry temper; you are not called to quench the violence of fire, except as it burns in your own wrath; you have to smite no Philistine but your own sins, and cast down no walls but your own prejudices. Christian woman, your faith has to work its miracles in the drawing-room, in the parlour, in the kitchen, in the chamber. Man of business, your faith is to perform its marvels on the exchange, or in the shop, or in the commercial room. Working man, you are to achieve your wonders at the forge, or by the bench, or in the field, or in the mill. Here is your sphere of service, and you have need to lift to heaven the prayer of the apostles—"Lord, increase our faith," that you may live worthily, righteously, soberly, and after a Christian sort.

II. Secondly, I want to show HOW THE INCREASE OF FAITH BEARS UPON OUR POWER TO FORGIVE OTHERS. And I would answer first, that I think you already see that it does so, although you cannot explain the mode of its operation. If I were to bring before you a person of whom I might say, this man is strong in faith, you would feel certain that he would be a man who would readily forgive the injuries of others. Though you do not see the connection between the two, you are very conscious that there must be such a connection. Now, when I tell you of Abraham, how when the herdsmen of Abraham and Lot quarreled, Abraham did not quarrel with Lot, but, finding that they must separate, gave Lot, his junior, the choice as to which way he would go. It seems natural that Abraham should act in that gentle manner. That calm, quiet, believing man of God—you have only to look into his majestic face and feel quite certain that he will act with great gentleness and nobleness of soul. Joseph, the man so full of faith that he gave commandment concerning his bones,—when his brothers came before him and he made himself known to them, and wept over them and forgave them,—you feel that such conduct is just what you might expect from Joseph: the very fact that he was so true a believer in God makes you feel that he will not seek to avenge himself, though he had been shamefully treated by his unbrotherly brethren. Moses was so meek, so gentle, that you trace his meekness at once to his faith. And David, when you see him standing over sleeping Saul, and hear his companion say, "Let me smite him but this once"; when he will not allow the deed to be done, but leaves his enemy in the hands of God, you say to yourself, "I expected such conduct of David, for he is a truly believing man of God." Though you have not satisfactorily traced out the connection between the two, yet you know very well that if a man professes to be a believer in Christ you expect him to be gentle and forgiving; and you are right. But there is an actual connection between the two, which we shall, I doubt not, see directly.

When the apostles said "Lord, increase our faith," they meant, "Increase our confidence in Thee," and this is a very material help towards the performance of the duty. First, God must help us so to believe in Jesus that we may not suspect Him of setting us an impracticable task. The Lord has said, "Overcome evil with good," and has bidden us "Forgive seventy times seven": do you not feel ready to say, "This is a hard saying, who can bear it"? Do we not fancy that we shall never get through the world in that gentle fashion? It is our unbelief which tells us that we must sometimes bend our fists, or at least sometimes deliver our minds with great vigour of wrath or else we shall be trodden down like mire in the streets. We need to ask for grace that we may be helped to believe that Christ's way of forgiveness is after all the best way, the noblest way, the most truly manly and the most surely happy way.

Their prayer may be read as meaning "Lord, help us to believe that Thou canst enable us to do this." We cannot by our own unaided nature be always forgiving, lowly, gentle and loving in temper, but Thou hast said, "Take My yoke upon you and learn of Me; for I am meek and lowly in heart; and ye shall find rest unto your souls." Therefore, O Lord, give us more faith in Thee that we may believe that Thou canst make us meek and lowly, even as Thou art. We ought to believe that Jesus can turn our lion-like tempers into lambs, and our raven-like spirits into doves, and if we have not faith enough for that we must pray for it; for do you not see that if a man believes a duty to be impossible, or judges that grace itself cannot enable him to do it, then he never will do it; but when he obtains a confidence that the command is within his power, or that it can be obeyed by a force which is within his reach, then he has won half the battle already. In believing in the possibility of a high standard of holiness, a man is already on his way towards that holiness. I therefore earnestly exhort you to ask for more faith, that you may believe the duty of constant forgiveness to be possible of accomplishment through divine grace.

But, next, between faith and forgiveness a very close connection will be seen if we enquire what is the foundation of faith? Listen a moment. Faith believes that God for Christ's sake forgives us,—and how much? Seventy times seven? Beloved, God forgives us much more than that. And does the Lord forgive us seven times a day? If seven times a day we offend Him and repent, does He forgive? Ay, that He does. This is to be unfeignedly believed, and I do believe it: I believe that, often as I transgress, God is more ready to forgive me than I am ready to offend, though, alas, I am all too ready to transgress. Hast thou right thoughts of God, dear hearer? If so, then thou knowest that He is a tender father, willing to wipe the tear of penitence away, and press His offending child to His bosom, and kiss him with the kisses of His forgiving love. The mercy of God lies at the very foundation of our faith; and surely it wonderfully helps us to forgive. Dost not thou see at once, O forgiven one, that the natural inference is that if the Lord hath forgiven thee thy ten thousand talents of debt, thou darest not go and take thy brother by the throat for the hundred pence which he owes to thee, but thou must forgive him because God for Christ's sake has forgiven thee?

Notice again, that the joy of faith is a wonderful help to forgiveness. Do you recollect when you were first converted? I do remember well the first day in which I believed in Jesus Christ: do you not also remember your own spiritual birthday? Recall then the love of your espousals, the happy honeymoon of your spiritual life. Could you forgive your enemy then? Why, you thought nothing of injuries: you were so happy and joyful in the Lord that if anybody tried to irritate you they could not do it, or if you became a little annoyed for a minute, you soon came back to your moorings again. You were too full of holy joy to indulge in quarrelling. Dear brother, do you not know that you ought always to have retained that love and joy, and that the best thing you can do is to get them back if you have lost them! Therefore, pray to-day, "Lord, increase my faith, restore unto me once again the joy of Thy salvation." When you return from your backsliding and rejoice in the Lord with all your heart, you will find it easy enough to forgive your direst foe.

Again, it is quite certain that a spirit of rest is created by faith, which greatly aids the gentle spirit. The man who believes enters into rest and becomes calm of spirit, and this keeps him from seeking petty revenges. He knows that whatever happens all is right for ever; he knows whom he has believed, and he walks in the integrity of his heart, and therefore he is not a man that is likely to be irritated. It is wonderful when you are sure you are right what a deal you can put up with. Good Joseph Hughes, of Battersea, was of the founders of the Bible Society, and one of the most earnest workers for it. He was riding on a coach upon a dreadfully cold, bitter winter's day, and at his side sat a talkative person, who thought himself a gentleman. As the coach proceeded he began talking about religion in general, and denouncing Bible Societies in particular. With a sprinkling of swearing he went on to say that such societies were got up to keep lazy secretaries and other officials. "Those fellows," he said, "get fine salaries, and then they go travelling all about the country, enjoying themselves, and charging a pretty penny for their travelling expenses. I understand they always travel in the best style." Mr. Hughes quietly replied, "But what would you say, sir, if you were informed by one of the secretaries that he never received a farthing for his services; and that in order to save money to the Society he rode on the top of the coach on a cold day like this so that he might not pay so much as he would have to if he went inside?" "Now, sir," said he, "one of them is doing this before your eyes." Now you can understand how Mr. Hughes could be very cool, and allow the talkative man to proceed as long as he liked with his falsehoods, because he knew he had so crushing an answer for him; and so when faith gives perfect rest to the soul a man is not easily disturbed, for he knows that behind all there is a blessing which will compensate for present annoyances. Conscious strength removes us from the temptations which surround petty feebleness. May God gives you that increased faith which shall fix your heart in the sphere of perfect satisfaction in the Lord and patient waiting for His will, so shall you cease to fret yourself because of evil doers.

Again, faith when it is strong has a high expectancy about it, which helps it to bear with the assaults of men of the world. "What," saith she,—"what mattereth that which happens to me here, for I am on my journey, and I shall soon be in the glory-land, where I shall have a reward for all my travail by being for ever with the Lord." A man readily puts up with the little inconvenience of the present when he has great joys in store for the future. If you stay at an inn for a while when you are on a journey, it is only for a night, and though things may not be very comfortable, you say, "Well, I am not going to live here a week, I shall be gone in the morning: it does not matter, I am looking forward to my sweet home at my journey's end." So doth faith, by its blessed expectation of the future, make the troubles of the present to be very light, so that she bears them without fretfulness and anger. May the Holy Spirit cause faith thus to work in us.

III. But my time has gone sooner than I desired, and therefore I must close by noticing in the third place HOW THE LORD JESUS CHRIST ANSWERED THE PRAYER FOR INCREASED FAITH. He did it in two ways.

First, by assuring them that faith can do anything. The Lord said, "If ye had faith as a grain of mustard seed, ye might say unto this sycamore tree, be thou plucked up by the root and be thou planted in the sea, and it should obey you." I think He meant that to be understood as a proverbial expression, to signify that faith can accomplish anything. You say, "Ah, my bad temper is rooted in me: as a sycamore tree takes hold of the earth by its roots, so an ill temper has gone into the very depth of my nature. I am constitutionally quick tempered. From my very birth I have found it hard to forgive." If thou hast faith, my brother, thou canst say to that sycamore tree, or better still, to that tree within thee, "Be thou plucked up by the roots." But, saith one, "With such a nature as mine, such a changeable, exciteable, nervous disposition as mine, you cannot expect to plant in me the tree which bears the fruit of calm, quiet forgiveness." What says our Lord? "Ye shall say to that sycamore tree, be thou planted in the sea." A strange place for a tree to be planted! In the sea! Indeed, it is an impossible thing, because every wave would shake its roots out of their places; the substance is too insubstantial, the liquid of the sea is too movable for a single tree to grow therein. Our Lord says, "If ye had faith as a grain of mustard seed it should obey you." You can by faith plant a tree in the sea, and so can you plant this fruit-bearing glorious tree of love to God and love to man within your frail nature, if you have but faith enough. Brethren, we do not want to be moving mountains. If mountains required moving, I have no doubt faith would move them, but the mountains are in the best possible places they can be, and therefore why should we uproot them? We do not require to transplant sycamore trees by faith, for there are plenty of workmen to be had to lift them up, and carry them carefully to another place, and it would be a pity that we should use faith so as to deprive poor men of their means of livelihood; but I doubt not it would be done if it were necessary. Now, there is room enough in the moral and spiritual world for faith, and there she can work her miracles. We can say to our bad disposition, be plucked up by the roots, and it will be done; and if we have faith in God we can have the right disposition, the quiet, calm spirit implanted in us. Dost thou believe this? If thou dost not, then thou hast not the faith, and thou shalt not see it, but, if thou believest, it is possible to thee.

Once more, how did Christ answer the prayer? He answered it in a very remarkable manner, as I think, by teaching them humility. He said to them in effect, "You think that if you were to forgive to seventy times seven you would be doing a great deal. You fancy that if you were never to return evil for evil, but always to be gentle and loving, you would be somebody, and that God would almost be in debt to you"; but it is not so. And then He went on to tell them that the servant, when he is sent to plough or to attend to the cattle is not thanked. While he is doing his labour his master does not come to him and wonder at him as if he were doing some very extraordinary thing. The master does not hold up his hands in amazement and cry, "How well my servant can plough, how cleverly he fodders the oxen." And he does not go to him and say, "My dear, invaluable servant, I am sure I do not know what I could do without you, therefore come and sit down, and I will wait upon you." Oh, no, if he works well he only does his own work and nobody else's; he does what he is bound to do, and the master does not think of praising him, and feasting him. So says Christ, "So likewise ye, when ye shall have done all those things which are commanded you, say, We are unprofitable servants: we have done that which was our duty to do." This mode of increasing our faith reminds me of the hydropathic way of strengthening some people by pouring a douche of cold water upon the spine of their backs. The parable of the servant and his lord shows us our true place, and the small value which we may attach to our own services. It takes the man who thinks, "Oh, it is a great thing to forgive everybody, and if I were to do it I should be a great saint," and it pours a torrent of cold water upon his pride, by saying, "No, if you did it you would not be anything wonderful then, it is only what is your duty to do, you would have no reason to go about the world blowing your trumpet, and saying, 'What a wonderful martyr I am,' you would only then have fulfilled a common duty." Well now, it seems to me that this is a wonderful strengthener to my faith. I feel resolved within my spirit thus—my Lord and Master, I will no more say of anything Thou biddest me to do, "this is beyond my reach," but I will pray, "My Lord, increase my faith till I can do it, till I can live up to Thy standard; for even if I should do so by Thy grace, yet considering what Thou hast done for me, considering what I owe to Thee, considering the power of Thy blessed Spirit that dwells within me, considering the richness of the ultimate reward which Thou wilt surely give me, though it be of grace and not of debt, all I could do, if I could be zealous as a seraph, and perfect as the saints in heaven, would be too little, and I should have to confess that I am an unprofitable servant, I should have done no more than it was my duty to have done."

I pray God the Holy Spirit to let this sermon come on the back of the discourse of last Sabbath day, that you may not look upon the first as being impracticable, but may gather strength from the second to go and put into practice what you have learned. May God bless you for Christ's sake. Amen.

MATURE FAITH—ILLUSTRATED BY
ABRAHAM'S OFFERING UP ISAAC

"And He said, Take now thy son, thine only son Isaac, whom thou lovest, and get thee into the land of Moriah; and offer him there for a burnt offering upon one of the mountains which I will tell thee of."—Genesis xxii. 2.

I do not intend to enter into this narrative in its bearing upon our Lord, although we have here one of the most famous types of the Only-begotten, whom the Great Father offered up for the sins of His people. Peradventure that may be the subject this evening. But as I have, in the recollection of some of you, already given you three sermons upon the life of Abraham, illustrating his effectual calling, his justification, and his consecration to the Lord, we will now complete the series by dwelling upon the triumph of Abraham's faith when his spiritual life had come to the highest point of maturity.

Opening your Bibles at this chapter, you will please to observe the time when God tried Abraham with the severest of his many ordeals. It was "after these things," that is to say, after nine great trials, each of them most searching and remarkable. After he had passed through a great fight of affliction, and had through the process been strengthened and sanctified, he was called to endure a still sterner test. From which fact it is well to learn that God doth not put heavy burdens upon weak shoulders, and He doth not allot ordeals fit only for full-grown men to those who are but babes. He educates our faith, testing it by trials which increase little by little in proportion as our faith has increased. He only expects us to do man's work and to endure man's afflictions, when we have passed through the childhood state, and have arrived at the stature of men in Christ Jesus. Expect then, beloved, your trials to multiply as you proceed towards heaven. Do not that as you grow in grace the path will become smoother beneath your feet, and the heavens serener above your heads. On the contrary, reckon that as God gives you greater skill as a soldier, He will send you upon more arduous enterprises; and as He more fully fits your barque to brave the tempest and the storm, so will He send you out upon more boisterous seas, and upon longer voyages, that you may honour Him, and still further increase in holy confidence. You would have thought that Abraham had now come to the land Beulah, that in his old age, after the birth of Isaac, and especially after the expulsion of Ishmael, he would have had a time of perfect rest. Let this warn us that we are never to reckon upon rest from tribulation this side the grave. No, the clarion still sounds the note of war. Ye may not yet sit down and bind the chaplet of victory about your brow; for you no garlands of laurel and songs of victory as yet; ye have still to wear the helmet and bear the sword, and watch, and pray, and fight, expecting that, perhaps, your last battle will be the worst, and that the fiercest charge of the foe may be reserved for the end of the day.

Having thus observed the time when God was pleased to try the great pattern of believers, we shall next look at the trial itself; we shall next see Abraham's behaviour under it; and shall, in conclusion, spend a little time in noting the reward which came to him as the result of his endurance.

I. And first, **THE TRIAL ITSELF.**

Every syllable of the text is significant. If George Herbert were speaking of it, he would say the words are all a case of knives cutting at Abraham's soul. There is scarce a single syllable of God's address to him, in the opening of this trial, but seems intended to pierce the patriarch to the quick. Look. "Take now thy son." What! a father slay his son! Was there nothing in Abraham's tent that God would have but his son? He would cheerfully have given him hecatombs of bullocks, and flocks of sheep. All the silver and the gold he possessed he would have lavished from the bag with eager cheerfulness. Will nought content the Lord but Abraham's son? If one must be offered of human kind, why not Eliezer of Damascus, the steward of his house? Must it be his son? How this tugs at the father's heartstrings! His son, the offspring of his own loins, must be made a burnt offering? Will not God be content with any proof of his obedience but the surrender of the fruit of his body? The word *only* is made particularly emphatic by the fact that Ishmael had been exiled at the command of God. Very much to Abraham's grief Hagar's child had been driven out. "Cast out this bondwoman and her son: for the son of this bondwoman shall not be heir with my son, even with Isaac"; so said Sarah; and God bade the patriarch regard the voice of his wife, so that now Isaac was his only son. If Isaac shall die, there is no other descendant left, and no probabilities of any other to succeed him; the light of Abraham will be quenched, and his name forgotten. Sarah is very old, he himself is old also, no infant's cry will again gladden the tent; and Isaac is his only son, a lone star of the night, the only son, lamp of his father's old age. Nor is that all: "Thine only son, Isaac." What a multitude of memories that word "Isaac" awoke in Abraham's mind. This was the child of promise, of a promise graciously given, of a promise the fulfilment of which was anxiously expected, but long, long, long delayed. Isaac, who had made his parents' hearts to laugh, the child of the covenant, the child in whom the father's hopes all centred, for he had been assured, "In Isaac shall thy seed be called." What! after all must the gift of God be retracted? Must the covenant of God be nullified, and the channel of the promised blessings be dried up for ever. Oh, trial of trials! "Thy son," "thine only son," "thine only son, Isaac." Yet it was added, "whom thou lovest." Must he be reminded of his love to his heir at the very time when he is to lose him! Oh, stern word, that seemeth to have no bowels of compassion in it! Was it not enough to take away the loved one, without at the same instant awakening the affections which were so rudely to be shocked? Isaac was very rightly beloved of his father, for in addition to the ties of nature, and his being the gift of God's grace, Isaac's character was most lovely. His behaviour on the occasion of his sacrifice proves that in his spirit there was an abundance of humility, obedience, resignation, and gentleness, indeed of everything which can make up the beauty of holiness; and such a character was quite sure to have won the admiration of his father Abraham whose spiritual eye was well qualified to discern the excellences which shone in his beloved son. Ah, why must Isaac die? and die, too, by his father's hand! Oh, trial of trials! Contemplative imagination and sympathetic emotion can better depict the father's grief than any words which it is in my power to use. I cast a veil where I cannot paint a picture.

But note, not only was this tender father to lose the best of sons, but he was to lose him in the direct way. He must be sacrificed—he must be sacrificed by the father himself. If the Lord had said, "Speak thou with Eliezer, and charge him to offer up thy son," it would have softened the trial; but so far as Abraham could understand the command, it seemed to say, thou Abraham, thou must be the priest; thine own hand must grasp the sacrificial knife, and thou must stand there with breaking heart to drive the knife into the breast of thy son, and see him consumed, even to ashes upon the altar. All this appeared to him to be involved in God's word, although the Lord meant not so, but meant to accept the will for the deed. Everything was designed to make the trial severe. The friend of God was tried in such a way as probably never fell to the lot of man before or since. In addition to the sacrifice, Abraham was commanded to go to a mountain which God would show him. It is easy on the spur of the moment, and under the influence of sacred impulse, hastily to perform a heroic deed of self-sacrifice; but it is not so easy for men of passions, such as ours, to deliberate over the sacrifices demanded of us. But Abraham must have three days to chew this bitter pill, which was indeed hard enough merely to swallow, and all the more unpalatable when a man is made to learn in detail the wormwood and the gall: he must journey on with that dear son before his eyes all the day, listening to that voice so soon to be silent, and gazing into those bright eyes so soon to swim with tears, and to be dimmed in death; beholding in him his mother's joy and his own delight, and all the while meditating upon that fatal stroke which, so far as he knew, God required of him. Oh, this laying siege to us by long and careful barricade is that which tries us; a sharp assault we might far better bear. To be burnt quick to death upon the blazing fagot is comparatively an easy martyrdom, but to hang in chains roasting at a slow fire, to have the heart hour by hour pressed as in a vice, this it is that trieth faith: and this it was that Abraham endured through three long days. Only faith, mighty faith, could have assisted him to look in the fact the grim trial which now assailed him.

The patriarch was, no doubt, moved and tried, and exercised not merely by the words which God pronounced in his hearing, but by natural and painful suggestions which, however readily they may have been disposed of, were, it would appear to us, certain to arise. He might have said, "I am called upon to perform an act which violates every instinct of my nature. I am to offer up my child! Horrible! Murderous! I am to burn my slaughtered child as a religious act—terrible, barbarous, detestable! I am myself to offer him upon the altar deliberately. How can I do it? How can God ask me to do that which tears up by the roots every one of the affections which He Himself hath implanted, which runneth counter to the whole of my noblest humanity? How can I do this?"

Brethren and sisters, coming home to ourselves, and trying to make a personal application of this, we may be called by the word of God to acts of obedience which may seem to us to do violence to all our natural affections. Christians are sometimes commanded to come out from the world by decided acts, which provoke the hatred of those who are nearest and dearest. Now, if they love God, they will not love father nor mother, nor husband, nor brother, nor sister, in comparison with Him; and though Christians will ever be amongst the tenderest hearted of men, they will count their allegiance to God to be such that they must give up all for His sake, and deny every natural affection sooner than violate the divine law. Perhaps, to-day you are suffering under an affliction which is grieving all the powers of your nature; the Lord has been pleased to take away from you one dearer than life, for whom you could have been well content to die. Oh, learn with Abraham, to kiss the rod; let not Isaac stand before God. Let Isaac be dear, but let Isaac die sooner than God should be distrusted. Bow thine head and say, "Take what thou wilt, my God; slay me, or take all I have, but I will still bless Thy holy name." This was a main part of Abraham's trial, that it appeared to crush rudely all the tenderest outgrowths of the heart.

And it may have suggested itself to Abraham that he would in this way, by the slaughter of his son, be rendering all the promises of God futile. A very severe trial that, for in proportion as a man believes the promise and values it, will be his fear to do anything which might render it of no effect. Brethren, there are times with us when we are called to a course of action which looks as though it would jeopardise our highest hopes. A Christian man is sometimes bound by duty to perform an action which, to all appearance, will destroy his future usefulness. I have often heard men urge as a plea for remaining in a corrupt church, that they have obtained an influence in its midst, and by reason of their position, which they might lose if they followed their conscience and were true to God, they are bound to lose all their supposed influence and renounce their apparent vantage ground sooner than commit the least trespass upon their conscience; as much bound to do so as Abraham was bound to offer up Isaac, in whom all the promises of God were centred. It is neither your business nor mine to fulfil God's promise, nor to do the least wrong to produce the greatest good. To do evil that good may come is false morality, and wicked policy. For us is duty, for God is the fulfilment of His own promise, and the preservation of our usefulness. Though He dash my reputation into shivers, and cast my usefulness to the four winds, yet if duty calleth me, I must not hesitate a single second, for in that hesitation I shall be disobedient to my God. At the behest of God Isaac must be offered, though the heavens fall, and faith must answer all politic suggestions by the assurance that what God ordains can never, in its ultimate issue, produce anything but good; obedience can never endanger blessings, for commands are never in real conflict with promises, for God can raise up Isaac and fulfil His own decree.

Further, Abraham may have been—one would think must have been—the subject of the thought that the death of Isaac was the destruction of all his comfort. The tent shall be darkened for Sarah, and the plain of Mamre barren as a wilderness for her lamenting

78

heart. Alas! for the wretched parent who has lost the hope of his old age, and the stay of his decrepitude. The sun grows black at noon, and the moon is eclipsed in darkness if Isaac dies. Better that all calamities should have happened than this dear child be taken away! He must have felt thus, but it did not make him hesitate. Sometimes the course of duty may lie right over the dead body of our dearest comfort and our brightest hope. It may be our duty to do that which will involve a succession of sorrows all but endless. But you must do right come what may. If the Lord biddeth you, you must seek faith to do it, though from that moment never should another joy make glad your heart until you are fully compensated for the loss of all by entering into the joy of your Lord at the last.

It must also, I should think, have occurred to Abraham, though he did not let it weigh with him, that from that time forth he would make himself many enemies. Many would distrust his character, many would count him a perfect wretch: he would find wherever he went that he was shunned as a murderer of his own child. How should he bear to meet Sarah again? "Where is my son? Surely a bloody husband art thou to me," would she say, with far greater truth than Zipporah to Moses. How could he meet his servants again? How could he bear their looks which would say to him, "You have slain your son! Imbrued your hands in the blood of your own offspring!" How could he face Abimelech and the Philistines? How would the wandering tribes which roamed about his tent all hear of this strange massacre, and shudder at the thought of the monster who defiled the earth on which he trod. And yet observe the holy carelessness of this godlike man as to what might be thought or said of him? What mattered it to him? Let them count him a devil: let a universal hiss consign him to the lowest hell of hatred and contempt; he recks not of it. God's will must be done. God will take care of His servant's character, or if He do not, His servant must suffer the consequences for his Lord's sake. He must obey; no second course is open to him: he will not think of disobedience. He knows that God is right, and he must do God's will, come what may.

This, mark you, is one of the grandest points about the faith of the father of the faithful; and if you and I shall be called to exhibit it, may we never be found wanting, but brave calumny and reproach with cheerfulness, through the power of the Holy Ghost. How Luther's lips must at first have trembled when he ventured to say that the Pope was Antichrist. Why, man, how canst thou dare to say such a thing? The millions bow down before him; he is the vicar of God on earth. Do they not worship our Lord God the Pope? "Yet is he Antichrist, and a very devil," said Luther; and at first he must have felt his ears burn and his cheeks grow red, at such a piece of apparent wickedness. And when he found himself shunned by the ecclesiastics who once had courted Doctor Martin Luther's company, and heard the common howl that went up, even from the refuse of mankind, that the monk was a drunkard, and, inasmuch as he chose to marry a nun, was filled with lust and sold to Satan, and I know not what beside; it must have been a grand thing when Luther could feel, "They may call me what they will, but I know that God has spoken unto my soul the great truth that man is to be saved by faith in Jesus Christ, and not by ceremonies which the Pope ordains, nor the indulgences which he grants; and if my name be consigned to the limbo of the infernal, yet still will I speak out the truth which I know, and in God's name I will not hold my tongue." We must be brought to this, to be willing to put aside the verdict of our times, and of all times past or future, and to stand alone, if need be, in the midst of a howling and infuriated world, to do honour to the command of God, which is the only necessity to us, which it is imperative to us to obey, even though it should bring shame or death itself.

Here, then, was Abraham's faith made perfect, that, inasmuch as the outward circumstances were severe, and the suggestions arising out of the circumstances were peculiarly perplexing, he put aside both, dared the ills of all, in order that he might without delay or demur fulfil his Master's will to the full extent, firmly believing that no hurt would come of it, but that the rather he himself should be more blessed and God more glorified.

II. We shall now notice THE PATRIARCH UNDER THE TRIAL.

In Abraham's bearing during this test everything is delightful. In trying to mention each detail, I fear that I may mar the effect of the whole. His obedience is a picture of all the virtues in one, blended in marvellous harmony. It is not so much in one point that the great patriarch excels as in the whole of his sacred deed.

First notice the submission of Abraham under this temptation. His submission, I say, because you will observe that there is no record kept of any answer which Abraham gave to God, verbally, or in any other form. I suppose, therefore, that there was none. Strange and startling command, "Take thine only son, and offer him for a burnt sacrifice!" But Abraham does not argue the point. It is natural to expect that he should have said, "But, Lord, dost Thou really intend it? Can a human sacrifice ever be acceptable to Thee? I know it cannot. Thou art love and kindness: canst Thou take delight, therefore, in the blood of my dear son? It cannot be." But there is not a word of argument; not one solitary question that even looks like hesitation. "God is God," he seems to say, and it is not for me to ask Him why, or seek a reason for His bidding. He has said it: "I will do it." There does not appear to have been a word of entreaty or prayer. Prayer against so dread a trial might not have been sinful; if the man had been a less man it might have been not only natural, but right for him to say, "O my God, spare my child! Put me on some other trial, but not on this, so strange, so mysterious. My Lord, for Sarah's sake, and for Thy promise sake, test me not so." I say that such a prayer as that might not have been sinful from an ordinary man, it might have been, perhaps, even virtuous and commendable; but from this grand soul there is no such prayer. He does not ask to escape; he does not pray to be delivered when he once knows God's will. Much less is there the semblance of murmuring. The man goes about the whole business as if he had been only ordered to sacrifice a lamb ordinarily taken from the flock. There is a coolness of deliberation about it which does not prove that he was a Stoic, but which does prove that he was gigantic in his faith. "Not staggering," says the apostle; and that is just the word. You and I, if we had done right, would have done it in a staggering, hesitating manner; but he, not a nerve quivers, not a muscle is paralysed. He knows that God commands him, and with awful sternness, and yet with childlike simplicity, he sets about the sacrifice. The lesson I gather from this (and we may as well collect these lessons as we go, as gleaners who gather the ears as they walk down the furrows)—the lesson is this: when you know a duty, never pray to be excused, but go and do it in God's name in the power of faith. If ever you clearly see your Master's will, do not begin to argue it or wait for better opportunities, and so on; do it at once. I know not how much of joy and honour some of you may have missed by the evil habit of temporising with your consciences. It is a very terrible thing to begin to let conscience grow hard, for it soon sears as with a hot iron. It is like the freezing of a pond. The first film of ice is scarcely perceptible: keep the waters stirring, and you will prevent the ice from hardening it; but once let it film over and remain so, it thickens over the surface, and it thickens still, and at last it is so solid that a waggon might be drawn over the solid water. So with conscience, it films over gradually, and at last it becomes hard, unfeeling, and it can bear up with a weight of iniquity. Ah! it is not for us to delay obedience under the pretence of prayer, but to yield prompt service. I have been sometimes surprised and staggered with Christian people who have said in the matter of baptism, for instance, "I am persuaded that it is my duty as a believer to be baptised, but it has never been laid home to my conscience." Never laid home to your conscience! You know that God commands, and yet you dare confess your conscience has become so base that you do not feel it your duty to obey! "Oh, but I have not felt that it is impressed on me." Felt! And is feeling to be the measure of your allegiance to God, the clipper and the cutter of God's law? If you know it to be the right, I charge you on your fealty obey. O sirs, this world has come to a sad pass because of the tricks men play with their consciences. This is the cause of all those unnatural senses that people give to texts and creeds; this is the secret reason why the religion of this land which claims to be Protestant, is becoming Popish to its very core, because evangelical men have sworn to a Popish catechism, and given it another sense; and instead of coming out of a corrupt church, have dallied with their consciences, and so by their practice have nullified their preaching and taught men to lie. Small wonder is it that traders rob and cheat when men professing godliness use words in senses which they can never bear to unsophisticated minds. If professing men were but jealous for the glory of God, and exact and precise in all their walkings before the Most High, they would have more of the honour, more of the blessedness of Abraham, and their influence upon the world would be more like salt, and less like the evil leaven which corrupts the mass.

But we must pass on to notice next Abraham's prudence. Prudence, some of us heard this last week, may be a great virtue, but often becomes one of the meanest and most beggarly of vices. Prudence rightly considered is a notable handmaid to faith; and the prudence of Abraham was seen in this, that he did not consult Sarah as to what he was about to do. Naturally prudence, as we call it, would have said, "This is a strange command; you had better consult with the wise about it. You believe it comes from God, but you may be mistaken in your impression. At least, it is due to Sarah, having such an interest in her own child, to take her judgment in the case; moreover, there is that good man Eliezer, he has often helped and guided you in a dilemma; you had better have a talk with him." "Yes," but Abraham probably thought, "these beloved ones may weaken me, but cannot strengthen my resolution or alter my duty"; and, therefore, like Paul, he did not consult with flesh and blood. After all, my brethren, what is the good of consulting when we know the Lord's mind? If I go to the Bible and see very plainly there that such-and-such a thing is my duty, for me to consult with man as to whether I shall obey God or not is treason against the Majesty of heaven. It is vile for us to consult with men when we have the plain command of God. Fancy an inferior officer in an army, when ordered in the hour of battle to lead an attack, turning round to a fellow soldier to ask his opinion of the orders he has received from the commander-in-chief! Let the man be tried by court-martial, or shot down upon the field; he is utterly unloyal; it needs no overt act, the thought is mutiny, the words of enquiry a flat rebellion. When God commands we have nothing left but to obey; consultations with flesh and blood are sins of scarlet dye.

Notice, further, Abraham's alacrity. He rose up early in the morning. Oh, but the most of us would have taken a long sleep, or if we could not have slept, we would have lain till dinner time at least, tossing restlessly. "What, slay my son—my only son Isaac? The command does not specify the hour; there is no peremptory word as to the time of starting upon the awful journey. At least let us postpone it as long as we may, for the dear young man's sake; let him live as long as possible." But no. Delay was not in the patriarch's mind. Is it not grand? The holy man rises early; he will let his God see that he can trust Him, and that he will do His bidding without reluctance. O believers, always be prompt in doing what God commands you. Hesitate not. The very pith of your obedience will lie in your making haste and delaying not to keep the Lord's commandment. He showed his alacrity, again, by the fact that he prepared the wood himself. It is expressly said that he "clave the wood." He was a sheik and a mighty man in his camp, but he became a wood-splitter, thinking no work menial if done for God, and reckoning the work too sacred for other hands. With splitting heart he cleaves the wood. Wood for the burning of his heir! Wood for the sacrifice of his own dear child! Herein you see the alacrity of Abraham, and may it be ours to obey God with such a ready zeal, that in every little circumstance of our obedience it shall be seen that we are not unwilling slaves chained to the oar of duty, and flogged to service by the threatenings of the law, but loving children of a Father whom we count it our highest joy to serve, even though that service should involve the sacrifice of our dearest Isaacs.

Further, I must ask you to notice Abraham's forethought. He did not desire to break down in his deeds. Having cleft the wood, he took with him the fire, and everything else necessary to consummate the work. Some people take no forethought about serving God, and then if a little hitch occurs, they cry out that it is a providential circumstance, and make an excuse of it for escaping the unpleasant task. Oh, how easy it is when you do not want to involve yourselves in trouble, to think that you see some reason for not doing so! "You know," says one, "we must live." "Ah," says another, "why should I throw myself out of a situation merely because of a small point of conscience? And, indeed, there has just now happened a circumstance which almost compels me to act against my belief, at least for a time; indeed, providence clearly bids me remain as I am. I know that the Bible says I ought to act differently, but still you know we must take circumstances into consideration, and, if they do not quite alter the commandments, they may, you know, be an excuse for postponing obedience." Abraham the wise, thoughtful servant of God, takes care as far as possible to forestall all difficulties that might prevent his doing right. "No," saith he, "there is no compromise for me, my duty is clear. Doth God command it? I will provide all that is needful for the fulfilment of His will. I want no excuse for drawing back, for draw back I will not, come what may."

Observe, further, Abraham's perseverance. He continues three days in his journey, journeying towards the place where he was as much to sacrifice himself as to sacrifice his child. He bids his servants remain where they were, fearful perhaps lest they might be moved by pity to prevent the sacrifice. Now, you and I would have liked to provide ourselves with some friend who might have stepped in to prevent, and have taken the responsibility off our shoulders. But, no, the good man puts everything aside that may prevent him going to the end. Then he puts the wood on Isaac. Oh, what a load he placed on his own heart as he lay that burden on his dear son! He bare the fire himself in the censer at his side, but what a fire consumed his heart! How sharp was the trial when the son said artlessly, "My father, behold the fire and the wood, but where is the lamb?" Was there no tear for the patriarch to brush away? He made but a short reply. We have every reason to believe that other replies followed, which are not recorded, in which he explained to his son how the case stood, and what it was that God had commanded; for it is hard to suppose that Isaac would have blindly yielded, unless first an explanation had been given that such a command had come from the highest authority, and must be obeyed. Oh, the unhappiness of the father's mind, but let me rather say the majesty of the father's faith, that he puts down all his feelings, and though nature speaks, yet faith speaks louder still, and if the deep of his affliction calleth loud, yet the deeper faith in his God calleth louder still. Now see him! See the holy man as he gathers up the loose stones which lie on Mount Moriah! See him take them, and with the assistance of his son, place them one upon another, till the altar has been built. Do you see him next day lay the wood upon the altar in order? No signs of flurry or trepidation. See him bind his son with cords! Oh, what cords were those binding his poor, poor heart! He lays his son upon the altar as though he were a victim! Now he unsheaths the knife, and the deed is about to be done, but God is content; Abraham has truly sacrificed his son in his heart, and the command is fulfilled. Notice the obedience of this friend of God—it was no playing at giving up his son: it was really doing it. It was no talking about what he could do, and would do, perhaps, but his faith was practical and heroic. I call upon all believers to note this. We must not only love God so as to hope that we should be ready to give up all for Him, but we must be literally and actually ready to do it. We must ask for more faith, that when the trial comes, we shall not be proved to have been mere wind-bag pretenders, mere wordy talkers, but true to God in very deed. "Ah," said one the other night, "I thought I had great faith, but now I am racked with pain, I find I have scarcely any." "Oh," might some of us say, "my God, I thought I had faith in Thee, but now it comes to the endurance of this affliction which Thou puttest upon me, I am ready to kick against Thee, and cannot say, 'Thy will be done.'" Ah! How many professors love God until it comes to losing their pence and their pounds. They will obey God until it involves penury and poverty; they will be faithful to God till it comes to scoffing and shame, and then straightway they are offended, and thereby prove who is their God, for they turn away from the unseen and look for what they call the main chance, for the interest of time, and their own emolument, and their own pleasures. God is no God of theirs except to talk about. Let Christ's commands be pleasing, and men will accept them: let them grind a little too severely, and men turn aside; for, after all, most professors serve their God up to a certain point, but no further, and so show that they love not God at all.

I have but very feebly brought out into the light the obedience of Abraham. I must not, however, leave the picture till I have mentioned what was at the bottom of it all. Paul tells us in the eleventh chapter of the Hebrews, that *"by faith* Abraham offered up Isaac."* Now what was the faith that enabled Abraham to do this? Although many expositors think not, I adhere to the opinion that Abraham felt in his own mind that God could not lie, and God's word could not fail, and therefore hoped to see Isaac raised from the dead. "Now," he said to himself, "I have had an express promise that in Isaac shall be my seed; and if I be called to put him to death, that promise must still be kept, and peradventure God will raise him from the dead. Even if his body be consumed to ashes the Lord can yet restore my son to life." We are told in the New Testament that he believed in God that He could raise him from the dead, from which he also received him in a figure. Some have said, "But this lessons the trial." Granted, if you will, but it does not lessen the faith, and it is the faith which is most to be admired. He was sustained under the trial by the conviction that it was possible for God to raise his son from the dead, and so to fulfil His promise. But under that, and lower down, there was in Abraham's heart the conviction that by some means, if not by that means, God would justify him in doing what he was to do; that it could never be wrong to do what God commanded him; that God could not command him to do a wrong thing, and that therefore doing it he could not possibly suffer the loss of the promise made in regard to Isaac. In some way or other, God would take care of him if he did but faithfully keep to God. And I think the more indistinct Abraham's idea may have been of the way in which God could carry out the promise, the more glorious was the faith which still held to it that nothing could frustrate the promise and that he would do his duty, come what might. Brethren beloved in the Lord, believe that all things work together for your good, and that if you are commanded by conscience and God's word to do that which would beggar you or cast you into disrepute, it cannot be a real hurt to you; it must be all right. I have seen men cast out of work owing to their keeping the Lord's-day, or they have been for a little time out of a situation because they could not fall into the tricks of the trade, and they have suffered awhile; but, alas! some of them have lost heart after a time, and yielded to the evil. O for the faith which never will, under any persuasion or compulsion, fly from the field. If men had strength enough to say, "If I die and rot I will not sin; if they cast me out to the carrion crow, yet still nothing shall make me violate my conscience, or do what God commands me not to do, or fail to do what God commands me to perform!" This is the faith of Abraham. Would God we had it! We should have a glorious race of Christians if such were the case.

III. I have left myself only a few minutes for the last point, which was, let us OBSERVE THE BLESSING WHICH CAME TO ABRAHAM THROUGH THE TRIAL OF HIS FAITH. The blessing was sevenfold.

First, the trial was withdrawn: Isaac was unharmed. The nearest way to be at the end of tribulation is to be resigned to it. God will not try thee when thou canst fully bear any trial. Give up all, and thou shalt keep all. Give up thine Isaac, and Isaac shall not need to be given up; but if thou wilt save thy life thou shalt lose it.

Secondly, Abraham had the expressed approval of God: "Now I know that thou fearest God." The man whose conscience beareth witness with the Holy Ghost enjoys great peace, and that peace comes to him because under that trial he has proved himself a true and faithful servant. O brethren and sisters, if we cannot stand the trials of this life, what shall we do in the day of judgment? If in the common scales held in the hand of Providence we are found wanting, what shall we do before that great white throne, where every thought shall be brought into judgment before the Most High? How will you run with the horsemen at the last if you cannot run with the footmen now? If we are afraid of a little loss and a little scorn, what should we have done in the martyr days, when men counted not their lives dear to them that they might win Christ!

Abraham next had a clearer view of Christ than ever he had before—no small reward.

"Abraham saw My day," said Christ: "He saw it and was glad." In himself ready to sacrifice his son, he had a representation of Jehovah, who spared not His own Son. In the ram slaughtered instead of Isaac, he had a representation of the great Substitute who died that men might live.

More than that, to Abraham God's name was more fully revealed that day. He called him Jehovah-Jireh, a step in advance of anything that he had known before. "If any man will do His will, he shall know of the doctrine." The more you can stand the test of trial, the better instructed shall you be in the things of God. There is light beyond if thou hast grace to press through the difficulty.

To Abraham that day the covenant was confirmed by oath. The Lord swore by Himself. Brethren, you shall never get the grace of God so confirmed to you as when you have proved your fidelity to God by obeying Him at all risks; you shall then find how true are the promises, how faithful is God to the covenant of grace. The quickest road to full assurance is perfect obedience. While assurance will help you to obey, obedience will help you to be assured: "If ye keep My commandments, ye shall abide in My love; even as I have kept My Father's commandments, and abide in His love."

Then it was that Abraham had also a fuller promise with regard to the seed. Out of ten promises which Abraham received, the first are mainly about the land, but the last are concerning his seed only. We get to love Christ more, to value Him more, to see Him, and to understand Him better, the more we are consecrated to the Lord's will.

And last of all, God pronounced over Abraham's head a blessing, the like of which had never been given to man before; and what if I say that to no single individual in the whole lapse of time has there ever been given, distinctly and personally, such a blessing as was given to Abraham that day! First in trial, he is also first in blessing; first in faithfulness to his God, he becomes first in the sweet rewards which faithfulness is sure to obtain. Brethren and sisters, let us ask God to make us like Abraham, His true children, that we may gain such rewards as he obtained; may He help us to make a surrender this morning in our hearts of all that we have of the dearest objects of our affections. May we by faith take all to the altar to-day in our willingness to give all up, if so the Lord wills. This day may we feel the spirit of perfect faith, believing that God's promises must be kept though circumstances of outward providence, and even our own inward feelings, should seem to belie the sure word of God. Let us labour to know the reality of life by faith. May we believe God in the same literal way in which we believe our friends—but only after a higher and surer sort; let us from this day so believe in God, that we shall never ask a question about consequences, whenever we have a conviction of duty. May we never pause to ask whether this shall make us rich or poor, honourable, or despised, whether this will bring us peace or bring us anguish, but onward, right onward, as though God had shot us from the eternal bow, let us go right on, in the full conviction that if there be temporary darkness, it must end in everlasting light. If there be present loss, it must end in eternal gain. Let us set to our seal that God is true, that the rewards are to the righteous, and true peace to the obedient, and that in the end it must be our highest gain to serve God though that service should, for the present, bring with it direful loss. O that there may be trained in this house a race of much enduring believers, who can endure hardness, but cannot endure sin.

May you, my brethren, obey your convictions as constantly as matter obeys the laws of gravitation, and never may you sell your birthright for the world's wretched pottage. Could this house be filled with such men and women, London would shake beneath the tramp of our army, this whole state would perceive that a new power had arisen up in the land, truth and righteousness would exalt their horn on high, and then would deceitful trading, and greed for gold, and jesuitical faltering with words, this coquetry with the Popish harlot, be put an end to once and for all. O that the flag of truth and righteousness might be unfurled by a valiant band, for that banner shall wave in the day of the last triumph, when the bannerets of earth shall be rolled in blood. May our God thus bless us, and all the ends of the earth shall fear Him. The Lord make us true men like Abraham, true because believing, and may He help us to sacrifice our all, if need be, for Jesus' sake. Amen.

FAITH'S DAWN AND ITS CLOUD

"And straightway the father of the child cried out, and said with tears, Lord, I believe; help Thou mine unbelief."–Mark ix. 24.

Last Sabbath morning we treated upon the way by which faith comes to the soul. "Faith cometh by hearing." It is our joyful persuasion that on the past Sabbath faith actually came to many, and they were enabled to rest themselves upon the Lord Jesus Christ to their soul's salvation. Now, every good shepherd knows that he ought to look very carefully after the newborn lambs, and, therefore, it seemed to me that it would be most expedient this morning to search after those who have just believed in Christ, and to endeavour to strengthen and help them against the very serious trials which are incident to their present weak condition. When a man first lays hold upon Jesus he is very apt to be in distress, if his joy be not always at its full height; he is untrained in spiritual conflict, and easily dismayed; the tremor of his former conviction is upon him, and he is prone to relapse into it. The light which he has received fills him with intense delight, but it is not very clear and abiding; he sees men as trees walking, and is ready to conjure up a thousand fears. The weakness of newborn faith, therefore, calls for the compassion of all who love the souls of men. In addition to their own weakness they are liable to special dangers, for at such times Satan is frequently very active. No king will willingly lose his subjects, and the Prince of Darkness labours to bring back those who have just escaped over the confines of his dominion. If souls are never tried afterwards, they are pretty sure to be assailed on their outset from the City of Destruction to the Celestial City. Bunyan very wisely placed the Slough of Despond at the very commencement of the spiritual journey. The cowardly fiend of hell assails the weak, because he would put an end to them before they get strong enough to do mischief to his kingdom. Like Pharaoh, he would destroy the little ones. He seeks, if possible, to beat out of them every comfortable hope, so that their trembling faith may utterly perish. Perhaps, the text of this morning will be suitable to many here. I trust it may, and that the Spirit of God will give us reflections upon it which shall come home comfortably to all troubled souls. "Lord, I believe; help Thou mine unbelief."

In the text there are three things very clearly. Here is true faith; here is grievous unbelief; here is a battle between the two.

I. Very clearly in the text there is TRUE FAITH. "Lord, I believe," says the anxious father. When our Lord tells him that, if he can believe, all things are possible to him, he makes no demur, asks for no pause, wishes to hear no more evidence, but cries at once, "Lord, I believe." Now, observe we have called this faith true faith, and we will prove it to have been so. First, it was faith in the person of Christ. It is a great mistake to fancy that to endorse sound doctrine is the same thing as possessing saving faith, for while saving faith accepts the truth of God, it mainly concerns itself with the person and work of the Lord Jesus Christ, and its essence lies in reliance upon Jesus Himself. I am not saved because I believe the Scriptures, or because I believe the doctrines of grace, but I am saved if I believe Christ; or, in other words, trust in Him. Jesus is my creed. He is the truth. In the highest sense the Lord Jesus is the Word of God. To know Him is life eternal. By His knowledge He justifies many. I do not know that the father in the narrative before us had heard many sermons. I am not sure that he had very clear notions about everything that concerned the Saviour's kingdom: it was not essential that he should have in order to obtain a cure for his son. It was a very desirable thing that he should be an instructed disciple, but in the emergency before us the main thing was that

85

he should believe Christ to be both able and willing to cast the devil out of his son. Up to that point he did believe; and, though his faith may have been deficient as well in breadth as in depth, yet it enabled him to realise that the Messiah who stood before him was the Lord, and it led him to place all his reliance upon Him. He did not believe in the disciples; he had once trusted them and failed. He did not believe in himself; he knew his own impotence to drive out the evil spirit from his child. He believed no longer in any medicines or men, for doubtless he had spent much on physicians; but he believed the man of the shining countenance who had just come down from the mountain. When he heard Him say, "If thou canst believe, all things are possible to him that believeth," he at once said, "Lord, I believe." Beloved hearer, I hope that thou hast come, at some time or other—perhaps it is since last Sabbath day—to put thy trust in Jesus in the same way, believing Him to be able and willing to save thee. This is the faith that will effectually save thee. Dost thou rest in Him, in Him thy God, thy brother, thy Saviour; in Him as living among the sons of men; in Him as bleeding and suffering, as a substitutionary sacrifice, in thy stead; in Him as risen from the dead no more to die; in Him as sitting at the right hand of the Father, clothed with power to save? Dost thou trust Him? If not, whatever thou believest, and however orthodox thy creed, thou art short of eternal life; but, if all thy trust is stayed in Him, if thou bringest all thy help from Him, if His wounds are thine only shelter, His blood thine only plea, Himself thine only confidence, then art thou a saved man, thy transgressions are forgiven thee for His name's sake, thou art accepted in the Beloved. Rejoice with fulness of joy, for thou hast a right so to do, since every gladsome thing is thine.

The faith of this good man was true and saving for another reason. It was personal faith about the matter in hand, faith about the case which he was pleading. Have you never found it to be wonderfully easy to believe for other people? I know when I was seeking the Saviour, I had no doubt about His receiving any other penitent. I felt certain that if the vilest sinner out of hell had come to Him, He was able to save him: and though I had no faith in Him on my own account, yet had I met with another distressed soul in a similar condition to myself, I believe I should have encouraged him to put his trust in Jesus, though I was afraid to do so myself. To believe for others is an easy matter, but when it comes to your own case, to believe that sins like yours can be blotted out, that you, who have so badly played the prodigal, may be received by your loving Father, that your spiritual diseases can be cured, and that the devil can be cast out of you;—here is the labour, here is the difficulty. But, beloved, we must believe this or else we have not saving faith. O my Saviour, shall I trifle in faith by believing or pretending to believe that Thou canst heal a case parallel to mine, and yet cannot heal mine? Shall I draw a line and limit Thee, Thou Holy One of Israel, and say, "Thou canst save up to me, but not so far as I have gone"? Shall I dream that Thy precious blood has some power, but not power enough to blot out my sins? Shall I dare, in the arrogance of my despair, to set a boundary to the merits of Thy plea, and to the virtue of Thine atoning sacrifice? God forbid. Jesus is able to save to the uttermost them that come unto God by Him,—He is able to save me. Him that cometh unto Him He will in no wise cast out; I come to Him, and He will not, cannot cast me out. Hast thou a personal faith, a faith about thyself, about thine own sins, and thine own condition before God? Dost thou believe that Christ can save thee? Sink or swim, dost thou cast thyself upon Him, thine own proper self? He, His own self, bore our sins in His own body on the tree; and we, our own selves, must cast ourselves upon Him. If we have so done, then we, like the man in the narrative, have the real faith, the faith of God's elect.

Lest any, however, should think this a very small thing, let me go on to show you that this man's faith was real, because it was faith which triumphed over difficulties, difficulties which typify our own, and hence it was clearly the work of the Spirit of God, for no other will endure the trial. I shall ask thee, dear hearer, whether faith has triumphed over difficulties in thy case. For observe, his child was grievously tormented, and the malady was of long standing. When the Saviour said to him, "How long hath this happened unto him?" he said, "Of a child." Must it not have seemed, now that his son had grown older, a very unlikely thing that he should be recovered. We expect our children to outgrow some of their complaints; but here was one who, after many years, was none the better. Years had only increased but not diminished his pains. Yet in the teeth of that the man believed that Christ could cast that long-established demon out of his son. Dear friend, thy case of sin is similar. The sins of thy youth rise up before thee now: are they not in thy bones? The sins of thine early manhood, and the sins of thy riper years, and, mayhap, the sins of thy decaying years; all these come up before thee. Can the Ethiopian change his skin, or the leopard his spots? If so, then he that is accustomed to do evil may learn to do well. Can I, after lying asoak in the scarlet dye till it is ingrained in my very nature,—can I be washed and made whiter than snow? Crimes so long continued, evil habits so deeply rooted, can all these be overcome? O soul, if thou hast true faith, thou wilt say, "Yes," I believe that since Christ is God He can deliver me from all evil, and forgive me all sin. Even if I had lived as long as Methuselah, and had continued all that while in the vilest of transgression, yet Jesus is so mighty to save that He could deliver me in a moment. His word is, "All manner of sin and of blasphemy shall be forgiven unto men." Looking to those dear wounds, those founts of love and blood, I do believe, and will believe, that all my years of sin are gone as in a moment, and like thick clouds before a mighty wind are blown away never to return. Oh, this is faith, poor soul. I pray God enable thee to exercise it.

This man had for a long time considered his son's case to be hopeless. Well he might. In addition to the fact that the child was subject to attacks of epilepsy and to extreme fits of fury, he was deaf and dumb, so that no intelligent expression of feeling could come from him: if at any time he felt stronger and better, he could not give his father a word of hope, he could not utter his gratitude for the sympathetic care that watched over him, neither could he hear any word of consolation which his father addressed to him. The ear was closed and the tongue was bound. Painful affliction, exceedingly painful to the parent, and to be continued year after year! At last the father must have felt there was no use in making any further effort. The child must be controlled, but he could not be restored; he was a hopeless maniac. Peradventure there is one here, this morning, who had grown hopeless of salvation; he has felt as if his case was one out of the catalogue of mercy; he has written bitter things against himself, and supposed that God has sealed those bitter things and made them true; but you see the father in the presence of Christ believed over the head of his despair, "in hope believing against hope," and I pray that you may do the same. In the presence of Christ the man's confidence came back to him. Hast thou, my hearer, a hope that can do the same? I never could have believed it was possible for me to be delivered from my sins till now I see that He who came to save me is my Maker; He who came to redeem me is He who bears the earth's huge pillars on His shoulders and sustaineth all things by the word of His power. With Him nothing can be impossible. I see His pierced hands and feet, and feel that if He stooped to suffer in the sinner's stead, the merit of His sacrifice must be beyond conception great. In Jesus the hopeless one hath hope, he who had despaired else now bids his heart be of good cheer. Oh, that is true faith which will not suffer itself to be any longer the slave of doubt and despondency now that it sees Jesus the Lord drawing near. It is a mighty faith which refuses to sit any longer in the valley of the shadow of death, but arises and shakes itself from the dust, and puts on its beautiful garments.

The father had another trial for his faith in the fact that he had just then tried the disciples. He brought his child to Christ, and Christ being absent, he asked the apostles who were in the valley what they could do. They tried their best, but having lost their Master's power they utterly failed; and this must have been a very violent trial to the father's confidence. He knew that on other occasions Christ's power had passed through the apostles, and He had wrought His miracles by them; but here was a complete cessation of their healing energy. If Jesus did not choose to work by them on this occasion, the suggestion would arise in the man's heart, "Perhaps His own power also has become lessened." But he put the thought aside, and believed notwithstanding all. And, O soul, hast thou tried ministers and tried God's people, and hoped to get comfort, and hast thou found none? Hast thou gone to the ordinances and found them like dry wells? Hast thou resorted to the hearing of the gospel and found even it to be barrenness to thy spirit? Yes, yet suffer no shadow of suspicion to cross thy mind as to the Lord's ability or willingness to save thee. Come to the feet of Jesus and still believe in Him. Whatever reason may say in thy soul to excite thee to despondency on account of past defeats, believe thou firmly that His power is still invincible; His arm is not shortened that He cannot save, neither is His ear heavy that He cannot hear. It was meet that thou shouldst see the failure of man that thou mightest glorify the grace of God; it was meet that the servants should be unable that the Master's ability might be the more conspicuous. May the Lord help thee to believe that though no man can do thee good, though all the pastors and bishops of the church, and all the martyrs and confessors of past ages, and all the apostles, and all the prophets, are unable to find a balm in Gilead that can meet thy case, yet there is a hand, a pierced hand, which can heal thy wounds and bleed a balm into thy soul which shall effectually restore thee. Yes, true faith believes over even such a discouragement as this.

I would have you notice, also, once more, while we are upon this point, that this father believed in Christ and His power to save, though the child was at that very moment passing through a horrible stage of pain and misery. The spirit which possessed this poor child was accustomed to throw him sometimes into the fire, and sometimes into the water. Just our condition; for our spirit has sometimes been thrown into the very fire of presumption, and at another season into the floods of despair. We have alternated between the cold of melancholy and the heat of self-conceit. We have at one time cried, "I love pleasure, and after it I will go"; and at another time we have said, "My soul chooseth strangling rather than life; I would not live always." When Satan is in a man, and he is full of despair, he goes to all extremes, and resteth nowhere, walking like the unclean spirit himself through dry places, seeking rest and finding none. At the moment while the father was speaking, the poor boy was on the ground wallowing in dreadful paroxysms of his disorder, foaming at the mouth, and gnashing with his teeth. Satan had great wrath, because he knew that his time was short. When the Saviour spoke, and bade the devil come out of him, the fiercest struggle of all took place; for the unclean spirit rent the child, and the most terrible cries were heard. Still the father said, "Lord, I believe." Now, it may be, dear hearer, you are this morning yourself full of great trouble, vexed and tormented with innumerable fears of wrath to come; a little hell burns within your soul, anguish unutterable has taken hold upon you, your heart is like a battle field torn by contending hosts, which rush hither and thither, destroying on every side. You are yourself an embodied agony; you are like David when he said, "The pains of hell gat hold upon me, I found trouble and sorrow." Can you now believe? Will you now accept the word of the Most High? If thou canst, thou wilt greatly glorify God, and thou wilt bring to thyself much blessedness. Happy is that man who can not only believe when the waves softly ripple to the music of peace, but continues to trust in Him who is almighty to save when the hurricane is set loose in its fury, and the Atlantic breakers follow each other, eager to swallow up the barque of the mariner. Surely Christ Jesus is fit to be believed at all times, for, like the pole star, He abides in His faithfulness, let storms rage as they may. He is always divine, always omnipotent to succour, always overflowing with lovingkindness, ready and willing to receive sinners, even the very chief of them. Sorrowful one, do not add to thy sorrows by unbelief, that is a bitterness which is superfluous to mingle with thy cup. Better far is it to say, "Though He slay me yet will I trust in Him."

There must be power unbounded in Him who deigned to die upon the cross. Come ye to Calvary and see! Can you look to that head crowned with thorns, and mark the ruby drops standing on His brow, and yet be doubtful of His power to save? Can you mark that sacred face, more marred than that of any man—marred with our griefs and stained with our sins, can you gaze on it and remain an unbeliever? Survey that precious body tortured in every part for our transgressions, and can you yet distruct Him upon whom the chastisement of our peace was laid? Can you look upon that spectacle of woe, and know that Christ is divine, and yet harbour doubts as to His power to save you? As for myself, I am constrained to cry, "Lord, I believe, I must believe; Thou hast Thyself compelled my faith." Let all things reel beneath my feet, but the cross of my Lord stands fast. If the Son of God has died for sinners, it is certain that the believing sinner cannot die, but must be saved, since Jesus bled for him. May God grant to every one of us to stand just there where the poor father did as to his faith, and say as he did, "Lord, I believe."

I am forced to leave this head incomplete, for the hour commands me to hasten on. The faith before us was earnest, it led the man to tears of repentance, it taught him to pray, it led him to open confession; in all these points may your faith be of a like character.

II. But, now, we must turn to the second part of the subject, for HERE IS UNBELIEF. "Help Thou mine unbelief," said he. He had doubted the power of Christ, he had said, "If Thou canst do anything for us, have compassion on us and heal us"; but yet he had faith and he had avowed it; he had not kept it secret within himself as though he were ashamed of it; before the scoffing scribes he had confessed, "Lord, I believe." He avowed it, too, with remarkable earnestness, for he said it with tears, as though his heart saturated his confession, running over at his eyes to bedew the words, "Lord, I do believe; do not doubt it, I lie not; I do believe in Thee." But then, he went on to make the confession that at the same time there was an unbelief lingering in his soul. "Help Thou," said he, "mine unbelief." Albeit that his faith had triumphed over the considerations which I just now mentioned, which appeared enough to damp, if not to quench it, yet these considerations may have had some effect upon his mind: they did not prevent his believing, but they hampered his faith with many questions. Some unbelief lingered, though faith was supreme. Learn from this that a measure of doubt is consistent with saving faith; that weak faith is true faith, and a trembling faith will save the soul. If thou believest, even though thou be compelled to say, "Help Thou mine unbelief," yet that faith makes thee whole, and thou art justified before God.

I though I would, under this second head, mention some reflections which often cause unbelief to trouble the heart which, nevertheless, has been enabled by the Holy Spirit to believe.

First, there are many true believers who at the first are tried with unbelief, because they have now more than ever they had before, a sense of their past sins. Many a man receives a far deeper sense of sin after he is forgiven than he ever had before. The light of the law is but moonlight compared with the light of the gospel, which is the light of the sun. Love makes sin to become exceeding sinful.

"My sins, my sins, my Saviour!
  How sad on Thee they fall;
Seen through Thy gentle patience,
  I tenfold feel them all.

I know they are forgiven,
  But still their pain to me
Is all the grief and anguish
  They laid, my Lord, on Thee."

The light of the promise gleaming in the soul reveals the infinite abyss of horror which lies in indwelling sin. In the light of God's countenance we discover the filthiness, the abomination, the detestable ingratitude of our past conduct. We loathe ourselves in our own sight. While we bless God that sin is pardoned, we are staggered to think it should have been such sin as it is, and the natural feeling resulting from our discovery is a fear that we cannot be pardoned. We ask ourselves, can it be that such sins are forgiven? Possibly the memory of certain peculiarly heinous sins becomes very vivid to our conscience: we had half forgotten them, but they start up with dreadful energy, and cast suspicions into our mind as to whether forgiveness is possible. Oh, that we could blot out those evil days! We have said, "Cursed be the sun that it rose on such a day as that in which I so defiled myself with iniquity." Thus, under a sense of sin, though there is the belief that we are pardoned, there may also arise the unbelief against which we need the Lord to help us.

Some have been staggered at times by a consciousness of their present feebleness. "Yes," saith one, "I trust the past is blotted out, but then how can I hope that I am saved. What a poor creature I am, I try to pray, but it is not worth calling prayer. I go up to God's house vowing that I will praise His name, and I get talking on the way and forget all about it, and I am dull all through the service. Then I was tempted yesterday, and I spoke unadvisably with my lips, or I did not defend the cause of my Lord and Master against that sceptic as I ought to have done. Only, just lately, I hoped that I had found peace with God, and yet I am behaving like this. Why I must be a hypocrite, it cannot be that I am a saved soul. Surely if my sins were forgiven me I should act very differently from this." Now that is often the cause of unbelief. The soul still hopes in Jesus and rests in Him, and she has nowhere else to go; but for all that the old monster unbelief gives her a desperate twitch, and she trembles while she hopes.

Some others have been made to shiver with unbelief on account of fears for the future. "I am afraid I shall not hold on," says one. "Why, to be a Christian you must persevere to the end. With such a heart as mine, how can I hope to be steadfast: and in such a position as mine, surrounded by so many ungodly associates, how can I hope to persevere? I see so-and-so made a profession, and he is gone back; and I know such an one who said he was a Christian, and he is a worse man than he used to be. Suppose the last end of me should be worse than the first; suppose I should put my hand to the plough and should look back and prove unworthy of the kingdom." Poor heart, it forgets that word, "I will never leave thee nor forsake thee"; and remembers not that other word, "I give unto My sheep eternal life, and they shall never perish, neither shall any pluck them out of My hand." Rightly filled with a holy anxiety to hold on to the end, it gives way to improper unbelief, for it ought to rest confident that Jesus changeth not; and, where He has begun the good work, He will carry it on and perfect it unto the day of Christ.

I have known some, again, whose unbelief has been excited by a consideration of the freeness and greatness of the mercy bestowed. I recollect how this staggered me once. I had believed in Jesus, and rejoiced in His salvation, but in meditating upon divine grace I was overcome with fear. What, pardoned, justified, a child of God, an heir of heaven, a joint heir with Christ, one of God's elect, secure of heaven, with a crown waiting for me at the last, and power to win that crown daily secured to me,—why, it seemed altogether too good to be true. Unbelief whispered, "it cannot be." If such great grace had been shown to others I should not have marvelled. If men of great abilities, of high station, and of eminent character, had received such grace I could have believed it; or even if that holy woman, who had so long been a patient sufferer, had been so blessed, it would have appeared an ordinary circumstance; but for such a sinner as I was to be thus favoured appeared to be too strange a miracle of love. I do remember how the very grandeur of the divine mercy threatened to crush me down and bury me under its own mass of goodness. I could believe that the Lord would give me a little mercy, but that He should give me such mercy, such unexpected favour, almost exceeded belief. And yet, what folly is there in such ideas, for were we not told beforehand that "as high as the heavens are above the earth, so high are His ways above our ways, and His thoughts above our thoughts?" Do we not know that we are dealing with a great God, of whom the prophet asks, "Who is a

God like unto Thee, passing by iniquity, transgression, and sin?" Do we think that God will only give according to our stinted measure? Is God to take man for His model? Remember ye that word, "He is able to do exceeding abundantly above what we ask or even think." Instead of the greatness of the divine mercy staggering us, it ought to console us and assist us to believe, seeing that it is so congruous with His nature. Yet, ofttimes, on this sea of love poor leaky vessels have begun to sink.

I have known, too, not a few, whose unbelief has arisen through a sacred anxiety to be right—a most proper anxiety if not pushed beyond its sphere. The idea has been suggested to them: "Suppose I should be after all presumptuous, and should deceive myself, by thinking I am saved, whereas I am not? What if I should film the wound, when it ought to be lanced, before there can be effectual healing." How I wish that all hypocrites would be troubled with this sort of fear. It would be a great mercy for many boastful professors if they had grace enough to doubt. I think Cowper was right when he said—

"He that never doubted of his state,
He may, perhaps he may too late."

But yet, this anxiety may be carried too far, and the soul may slide into despondency through it. I ought to be afraid of presumption, but it cannot be presumptuous to believe God's word. I ought to be afraid of saying, "Peace, peace, where there is no peace"; but if peace comes to me through the word of Christ, I need never be suspicious of it, let it be as profound as it may. I may doubt myself; I may go further, I may despair of self, but I must not doubt the Lord. If He has said, "Trust in Me, believe in Me, and thou shalt be saved"; if I believe in Him, it is no presumption to know that I am saved. If He has declared that he that believeth in Him is justified from all things from which he could not be justified by the law of Moses; if I have believed in Him, I am justified from all my sins. There is far more presumption in doubting the Lord than there ever can be in trusting Him. Faith is no more than God's due, it ought never to be looked at as too daring. If I believe in Jesus I have no right to say, "I hope I am saved," for that implies a doubt of God's declaration that the believer is saved. I have no right to say, "I sometimes think I am safe." I am so undoubtedly if I believe in Jesus. It is no matter of opinion, but a matter of certainty. There is nothing in this world about which a man may be so sure as about his own salvation, because other things come to us by the evidence of our own fallible senses, or by the testimony of men who may be mistaken; but the fact that the believe in Jesus I have no right to say, "I hope I am saved," for that implies a doubt of the Scripture says plainly, "He that believeth and is baptised shall be saved," I, having believed, and having been baptised, ought not to question the divine declaration, but should be as sure that, if I have believed, I am saved, as I am sure that I exist. This assurance is attainable, and should be the common condition of the believer. Yet has it often happened, I say, that an anxiety, which was commendable in its outset, has ended in a censurable unbelief.

Once more, I have known unbelief arise in some souls through a most proper reverence for Christ, and a high esteem for all that belongs to Him. You remember our text a few Sabbath mornings ago told us of John, who when he saw his Master in all His glory fell at His feet as dead. Ah, when the soul gets near to Jesus it perceives His perfection, and becomes conscious of its own imperfection; it sees His glory, and becomes aware of its own nothingness; it sees His love, and blushes at its own unloveliness; and then it is very, very apt to be tortured with mistrust, though it ought not so to be.

And I have even known when children of God just converted have come into the church, they have had such a high esteem for their brethren and sisters, that they have feared to be numbered with them. When they have heard some earnest brother pray they have said, "Oh, what a prayer, I shall never be like that man"; and, perhaps, they have listened to the preachings of some servant of God and said, "Ah, I cannot come up to that standard; the very existence of such a man as that condemns me." It is beautiful to see the little children loving the elder sons of the family, and admiring what they see of the father in them; but even this holy modesty may be turned into unbelief, though it ought not so to be; for, O child of God, if Christ be so lovely, thou art on the way to be made like Him; and if there be anything beautiful in any of His people, that same shall be given unto thee, for they also are as thou art, men of like passions with thyself; and God who has done great things for them will do the like for thee, for He loves thee with the self-same love.

I have thus set before you the unbelief which often will exist side by side with faith.

III. Now, let us notice very briefly THE CONFLICT BETWEEN THE TWO.

It is observable that this poor man did not say, "Lord, I believe, but have some doubts," and mention it as if it were a mere matter of common intelligence which did not grieve him. Oh, no; he said it with tears; he made a sorrowful confession of it. It was not the mere statement of a fact, but it was the acknowledgment of a fault. With tears he said, "Lord, I believe," and then acknowledged his unbelief. Learn then, dear hearer, always to look at unbelief in Christ in the light of a fault. Never say, "This is my infirmity," but say, "This is my sin." There has been too much in the Church of God of regarding unbelief as though it were a calamity commanding sympathy, rather than a fault demanding censure as well. I am not to say to myself, "I am unbelieving, and therefore I am to be pitied." No, "I am unbelieving, and therefore I must blame myself for it." Why should I disbelieve my God? How dare I doubt Him who cannot lie? How can I mistrust the faithful Promiser who has added to His promise His oath, and over and above His promise and His oath has given His own blood as a seal, that by two immutable things, wherein it was impossible for God to lie, we might have strong consolation. Chide yourselves, ye doubters. Doubts are among the worst enemies of your souls. Do not entertain them. Do not treat them as though they were poor forlorn travellers to be hospitably entertained, but as rogues and vagabonds to be chased from thy door. Fight them, slay them, and pray God to help thee to kill them, and bury them, and not even to leave a bone or a piece of bone of a doubt above ground. Doubting and unbelief are to be abhorred, and to be confessed with tears as sins before God. We need pardon for doubting as much as for blasphemy. We ought no more to excuse doubting than lying, for doubting slanders God and makes Him a liar.

Then, again, having made a confession of his unbelief as you observe, the father, in the narrative, prayed against it, and an earnest prayer it was. It was, "Help Thou mine unbelief." It is very noticeable that he does not say, "Lord, I believe; help Thou my child." No, nor does he say, "Lord, I believe; now cast the devil out of my boy;" not at all; he perceives that his own unbelief was harder to overcome than the devil, and that to heal him of his spiritual disease was a more needful work, than even to heal his child of the sad malady under which he laboured. This is the point to arrive at, to feel that there is no deficiency in the merit of Christ; no lack of power in His precious blood; no unwillingness in Christ's heart to save me; but all the hindrance lies in my unbelief. There is the point. O God, bring Thy power to bear where it is wanted. It is not because the blood will not cleanse me, it is because I will not believe; it is not because Christ's plea is not heard, but because I do not trust that plea. If I am not in the possession of full salvation, it is not because Christ is not mighty to save, but because I do not lean on Him fully and entirely. O God, Thou seest this is the centre of the difficulty, bring Thy power to bear on that difficulty. I ask only this. No more do I cry, "Help me here, or help me there"; but, "Help mine unbelief." That is the Slough of Despond; I carry that in my heart; that is the weak point. "Lord, strengthen me just there." It is well when, in addition to confession, we bring up all the great guns of fervent prayer to bear upon that position which needs to be carried by storm.

And lastly, this man did well in looking for the help against his unbelief to the right quarter. He did not say, "Lord, I believe; and now I will try to overcome my unbelief." but "Lord help," as if he felt that the Lord alone could do it. No physician can cure unbelief but Christ. He is the physic for it, and He is the physician too. If thou hast any unbelief, take thou the blood of Christ to cure it with. Think of Him,—God in the glory of His person, tabernacling among men, working out a perfect righteousness, dying a felon's death upon the cross in the sinner's stead; think of Him as rising from the dead, no more to die; think of Him as ascending into heaven amidst the shouts of angels; think of Him as standing at the right hand of God with the keys of death and hell at His girdle; think of Him as always pleading the merit of His blood before the Father's throne; and, as thou considerest concerning Him, in the power of the Spirit, thine unbelief will die, for thou wilt say, "Lord, the thought of Thee has helped mine unbelief; while I have been studying Thee, and feeding my soul on Thee, and making Thee to be as bread and wine to my soul, my unbelief has gone. I do believe in Thee, and I will; for Thou hast helped mine unbelief." Go, any of you who are in trouble about this matter, go where you gained your first faith, go there to get more. If you first obtained your faith at the cross, foot, go there again to end your unbelief. View the flowing of His soul-redeeming blood, and continue viewing it till thou shalt by divine assurance know that He has made thy peace with God. God bless thee in Christ Jesus. Amen.

FAITH AND ITS ATTENDANT PRIVILEGES

"He came unto His own, and His own received Him not. But as many as received Him, to them gave He power to become the sons of God, even to them which believe on His name: which were born, not of blood, nor of the will of the flesh, nor of the will of man, but of God."—John i. 11-13.

According to this text, the principal matter in our salvation is faith. Faith is described as "receiving" Jesus. It is the empty cup placed under the flowing stream; the penniless hand held out for heavenly alms. It is also described in the text as "believing on His name." And this reception, this believing, is the main thing in real godliness. Faith is the simplest thing conceivable. When we hear people sing, "Only believe, and you shall be saved," they sing the truth, for we have the divine assurance that "whosoever believeth on Him is not condemned," and the gospel message is "Believe on the Lord Jesus Christ, and thou shalt be saved." The act of faith is the simplest in the world, it may be performed by a little child, it has often been performed by persons so short-witted that they have been almost incapable of any other intellectual act. And yet faith is as sublime as it is simple, as potent as it is plain. It is the connecting link between impotence and omnipotence, between necessity and all-sufficiency. He that by faith layeth hold on God has accomplished the simplest and yet the grandest act of the mind. Faith is apparently so small a matter that many who hear the gospel can hardly believe it possible that we can really mean to teach that it brings salvation to the soul. They have even misunderstood us, and imagined that we have meant to say that, if persons believed they were saved, they were saved. If that were the doctrine of justification by faith, it would be the most wicked of delusions. It is not so; faith in Jesus as our Saviour is a very different thing from persuading ourselves to believe that we are saved when we are not. We believe that men are saved by faith alone, but not by a faith which is alone, they are saved by faith without works, but not by a faith which is without works. The faith which saves is the most operative principle known to the human mind; for he that believes in Jesus for salvation, being saved, and knowing that he is saved, loves Him that saved him, and that love is the key of the whole matter. The loving believer ceases from everything which would displease Him whom he loves. He tries to abound in that which will please Him, his beloved Redeemer. So salvation becomes the great reason for gratitude, and changes the heart; and, the heart being turned, all the issues of life are changed. The man is like a watch which has a new mainspring, not a mere face and hands repaired, but new inward machinery, with freshly adjusted works, which act to a different time and tune; and

93

whereas he went wrong before, now he goes right, because he is right within. Faith is so simple, that the little child who believes becomes ere long strong in the Lord; it is a vital force which gets such mastery over men that it makes them other men than they ever were before, and as it grows it lifts them up from being mere men to be men of God, and then beyond that it leads them on till they become heroes, and they stop the mouths of lions, quench the violence of flames, obtain promises, and enter into rest. Faith the grain of mustard seed develops into faith that moves the mountain; faith the child increases into faith the giant. May we know by experience how true this is.

Our object is to show what faith does; and, oh, while I am trying to speak of this great gift of the Lord to men, by which they obtain every other gift, may many of you who have not believed come to believe in Jesus. If you do, there is nothing in this text but what shall certainly be yours.

I. We shall begin by saying, that FAITH MAKES THE GRANDEST OF DISTINCTIONS AMONG MEN.

This is clear from the text. Faith makes the grandest distinctions among men, for the text begins, "He came unto His own, and His own received Him not," that is one company;–"but as many as received Him," that is another company. Were an angel to come here with a drawn sword, and suddenly to separate the righteous from the wicked with one stroke, you would find that his sword had for its edge the question, "Believest thou in the Lord Jesus Christ?" This divides men into believers saved, and unbelievers with the wrath of God abiding on them. "He that believeth hath passed from death unto life, and shall never come into condemnation; but he that believeth not is condemned already, because he hath not believed on the Son of God." There are many distinctions among men, some proper and some improper, and there always will be such distinctions while this age lasts. There are rich and poor, and I fear there never will be a form of society in which there will be no poor; even in the kingdom of Christ when He comes it seems there will be poor, for He shall judge the poor and needy. There will be the governors and the governed; the wise and the foolish; teachers and taught. But, mark you, these distinctions pass away. The grave is an awful leveller. There in the sepulchre Caesar is no more than his vassal, Socrates is no greater than the slave who washed his feet. The great emperor who swayed the sceptre has in the tomb no higher rank than the bondwoman who toiled at the mill. Death recognises no caste, the sepulchre believes in equality. At the judgment-seat temporal distinctions will not be recognised, except so far as they involved responsibility: and so far as that point goes, some of the great and mighty men will then wish that they had been slaves, and regret that they cannot hide their heads amongst those whom they oppressed. The grand distinction which will outlast all time is that of faith or want of faith. Believest thou or doubtest thou? This makes the broad line of distinction. To the receivers of Christ, or the non-receivers–to which do you belong, dear friend?

I want you to observe that the faith which makes the distinction is described here as a receptive faith. Saving faith becomes a working faith by degrees, but at first it is a receptive faith, and in fact, work as it may afterwards, it must always be a receptive faith. We only work out our salvation as God worketh in us, and even the highest actions that are ever done for God are performed with the strength which God supplies. Working faith is merely receptive faith in action. A receiving faith is the vital point, and it is absolutely needful that the soul should receive Jesus to be its all in all. "To as many as received Him." Have you ever received Him, the Lord Jesus, the real Christ? Do you talk to Him? Do you know Him? Is He a companion? Is He a friend of yours? If you have received a personal Christ by confiding, trusting, and depending upon Him, you are on the safe side of the house.

The text further says, "Even to them that believe on His name." Now, what is it to believe on His name? It struck me it would be a fair and a right way of illustrating the text to notice what are the names which are used in the former verses of this chapter. Please to notice in the first chapter of John, where our text is, what name of Jesus is used. "In the beginning was the Word"; that is the first name. The Word. What is the meaning of that? Why is Jesus Christ called the Word? Why, because, brethren, if I want to communicate to you by writing or by speech, I use a word. My thought is here, and there is your mind. I could get the thought partly to your mind by a picture, that is what God has done in nature; but we cannot use pictures for a full communication of knowledge, we must employ words. So God, wanting to speak to man, spoke by sending Christ, and Christ is God's word. Have you ever received Christ as God's word to you? Will you just think of it, what a wonderful word He was? God said, "Men, stand no longer at a distance from Me; I will come and dwell among you": thirty-three years the Son of God dwelt amongst the sons of men. "Men," He said, "Men, I must punish your sins." There hung His Son bleeding on the tree for sin, God saying in a wonderful way, "I hate sin, and therefore Jesus must die." The Lord next cries, "Men, I can now be just, and yet can justify you. Come unto Me." There is Jesus risen from the dead, in newness of life, and He goes into heaven a man, and as man is received to the throne of God, and thus God says in a word to us, "I am willing to receive you up to My very throne." Actions speak louder than words, but Christ Himself is the word, the love-word, the tender word, the very heart-word of God, with acts attending and following which make His utterance the more convincing. God kept nothing back when He spoke to Christ. He spoke that word, and that word is the fulness of God's soul to sinners. Have you ever accepted Christ as the word between you and God? Have you ever spoken to God that word back again by pleading the name of Christ? Lord, there is no communication between me and Thee except this. Whenever thou speakest thou sayest "Christ," and my reply is "Christ." When I want Thee to pardon me, I say "Christ"; when I want Thee to bless me, indeed, and give me answers to my prayers, I plead, "Christ." That is the word from God to man, and back again from man to God. Now, to as many as believe on His name as the word, to them gives He power to become the sons of God. But many have never accepted Him as "the word," any more than if God had never spoken. They are deaf. At any rate, there is the word, and they have never received it.

Look down the chapter and you will find that Jesus is described as the life. "All things were made by Him, and without Him was not anything made that was made. In Him was life." Have you believed on His name as the life? Man is dead, by nature dead. When God said to Adam, "In the day thou eatest thereof thou shalt surely die," Adam did die that very day, and that is the keyword to what is meant by death in the Scriptures. Did he cease to exist? Nay, nor will you. But he ceased to live, and that is a very different thing. To exist is not to live, there is a wide distinction there. To die is not to cease to exist, no thoughtful man should fall into such an error. What is death? Practically it is the separation of a living being into its component elements. When the seed is put into the ground the apostle says it is not quickened except it die, or dissolve into its constituent elements. It dies in order more perfectly to live. When we die, neither body nor soul ceases to exist, but they cease to be united, and their separation is death. When a soul departs (and the life of the body is the soul) the life of the body is gone. When a soul dies it is separated from God, for union to God is the soul's true life. That is the death which Adam died, and which every impenitent sinner will have to die; nay, that is the death which every sinner is under now, for "he that believeth not shall not see life, but the wrath of God abideth on him." Mark well that "he that believeth not hath not life." He has an existence, and always will have, but he hath not life, but he abideth in death: but as for the man who believes in Jesus, he gets back his God, and that is his life; and Jesus says, "He that believeth in Me, though he were dead, yet shall he live; and he that liveth and believeth in Me shall never die." "I am the resurrection and the life." When we are brought back to God, God has made our soul alive. A soul without God is like a fair palace which has been deserted; you pace through all its halls and there is not a sound, but it is all death, decay and emptiness; but when the king comes back again to his palace, then the merry bells peal out their joyful notes, all is rejoicing, and there is life again throughout the house. God is the life of the soul, and as many as receive God in Christ receive the life.

Now see, Jesus is first the word, that is God speaking to men; secondly the life, that is God quickening man, and dwelling in him. Have we so received the Christ of God?

Note the third name here. "In Him was life, and the life was the light of men." Notice that this name of Jesus is repeated many times if you read through the chapter. "John came for a witness to bear witness of the light. He was not that light, but he was sent to bear witness of that light. That was the true light," and so on. So that the next name of Christ we have in this chapter is the Light. Have we received Christ as the light? What is it to have Christ to be your light? What is light? It is that by which we see. Everybody sees in a light. Take an illustration—only an illustration. A merchant comes to a city, town, village. He calculates whether it is a good place for business. "Bad place, this," says he; "A man cannot live here, it is a bad situation"; and he is not content unless he gets near the Bank or im Lombard Street, or some other business quarter. Now look at the artist. has another light. You take that artist into the city, and he says, "I could not live here in this dreary wilderness of brick, amid these fogs, let me get away to North Wales, or somewhere where the picturesque is to be seen," and he settles himself down in Bettws-y-coed, and he says, "This is beautiful." Take the rich man there, and say to him, "You are to live here for twenty years." "Twenty years?" says he, "I could not live here a month. It is preposterous. This is not a place where a man can live." Bring a man of gaiety into a religious circle, and he says, "Oh, I want a place where there is some life." I have been travelling sometimes where I thought the scenery very beautiful, and I have heard young men say, "This is a hateful place; there is no life here." Well, everybody sees according to the light he sees by. My dear hearer, have you ever seen things in the light of Christ? Did you ever feel, "this is the place where I can live, for here are Christians with whom I can commune, here is the gospel preached, and my soul will be fed here, I shall learn much of Christ. This is a sphere in which I can be useful." When you have life you will get light, and you will see things in that light. You will see yourself in the light of Christ. You will say, "O God be merciful to me a sinner." Everything looks according to your light. Yellow spectacles will make everything look yellow; but get the true light, the only light that can lighten any man that comes into the world, and things will be seen in truth. If you get Christ within you, you have light indeed. So the question comes back, have we believed on the name of Jesus as the Word, the life, and the light? If we have, it has made a distinction between us, and others, and there is a deep gulf fixed between us, across which, thank God, men may come to us by sovereign grace, but across which we shall never return; for he that hath received the word will find it an incorruptible seed; he that hath received the life hath received it with the assurance, "Because I live ye shall live also"; and he that hath received the light knows that it shineth more and more unto the perfect day.

This distinction, then, is a very grand one, and it is one which obliterates all others, for the text puts it, "As many as received Him": that is, if the chimney-sweep receives Christ, he is a child of God, and if the Czar of Russia receives Christ, he is a child of God, but not the one more than the other. If they receive Him—that is the point—they become the sons of God. It is a distinction, therefore, which is to be sought after abundantly by us, and which has to do with present things. "As many as received Him, to them gave He power to become the sons of God." Now I charge you, do not think of religion as a thing to be run after when you die, as your friends may see, after an undertaker to bury you. My bell sometimes sounds at dead of night or at three in the morning. "Would you come and pray for a dying person?" They even say, "Pray to some dying person." What do they send to me for? Why do not they think of sending for me when the man is in health? They send for me when the man has taken stupefying drugs, perhaps, to lull pain, or he is half asleep with coming death, or his sufferings are so intense that he cannot think, or if he can think he relies on my coming, and my visit rather ministers to his superstition than to his benefit. Religion is for life as well as death. It is for to-day. "*Now* are we the sons of God." Oh, have the gospel to-day, to-day, to-day, to-day! It is said that every man ought to repent on the last day of his life, and this day may be yours, "therefore to-day if ye will hear His voice harden not your hearts." I have many things to say unto you, but time flies, and I have much more behind. This is the first head, then. Faith makes the grandest of distinctions.

II. Secondly, FAITH OBTAINS THE GRANDEST OF ALL ENDOWMENTS. Read, "To as many as received Him to them gave He power to become the sons of God." The margin says the "privilege." The margin is right; but so is the common reading. The word *exousia* is a very great word in the Greek. It cannot be comprehended in the word "privilege" at all. It means power, privilege, and a great deal more. Everyone that has believed in Jesus has received the privilege, the power, and everything else that lies in being a son of God. This is described as being a privilege peculiar to believers, and yet there are some who are everlastingly talking about the "fatherhood" of God, because He made them. I suppose the man who made that table is the father of the table. They assert that the Creator is the Father of all His creatures. That is not the sense in which you believers say, "Our Father which art in heaven." If you are children of the devil and doing his works, why call God your Father? How dare you? If you have not believed on the Son of God He is not your Father in the sense of the text, and you have no right to think of yourself as His son. The privilege of the text is, "to as many as received Him," for "to them gave He the power" or "the privilege to become the sons of God." As for the unbeliever, what is written concerning him? "The wrath of God abideth on him."

Now, there is a distinction intended here in the use of this word, "son," rather than the old legal word servant. The most that they could attain to under the old dispensation was to be servants. "Moses was faithful in all his house as a servant." Yes, that is all. And what a blessed thing to be a servant of God! The poor prodigal would have been glad enough to have been one of the hired servants. But says our Master, "Henceforth I call you not servants, for the servant knoweth not what his Lord doeth, but I have called you friends"; and we know who hath said, "For this cause He is not ashamed to call them brethren," because they are sons in the same house. Oh, what a pleasure to rise from slavery to sonship, from the bondage of the law to the glorious liberty of the children of God! And that is where we all are who have believed; only sometimes, you know, we do not live up to this sonship privilege. Those who are under the law do not rise to sonship. They may be sons, but they are in their minority, and the child while he is yet in his nonage differeth little from a servant, though he be lord of all. He is under tutors until he is of age. Christ has come, and we are no longer under a schoolmaster, but now are we the sons of God, blessed be His name. Are we not His servants too? Oh, yes. Jesus Christ was first His Father's Son, and then His Father's servant; so we, being sons, have the joy of serving our Father; and I tell you it is a very different thing to serve your Father to what it is to serve a mere prince or ruler. We are sons then rather than servants. We are called sons of God, because of our new nature. We are the children of God by birth. We are also sons by likeness, for the Spirit of God dwelleth in us, and we are made like to God. The likeness between a son of God and God Himself is real and true. Have you never seen the likeness between yourself and your child? Yes. Yes, he is very like you. Some points of his character are caricatures of yours, you can see your image, distorted somewhat, and imperfect, but it is yourself. It is as near like yourself as a child can be like a man, but a child is not a man for all that. So God makes His children like Himself, but they are miniatures, they are little, childish, weak; there are many imperfections and shortcomings; but still mark that word, I often stagger as I read it—"He hath made us partakers of the divine nature." In moral qualities, and spiritual qualities, He has given us power to become the sons of God, that is, by making us like to God; showing us that as He is who was the chief Son, so are we also in this world. Oh, the privilege of this! I assure you I would enlarge upon it if I did not feel that I am quite incompetent. I can only stand as John did when he wanted to tell us about it, and could only cry "Behold," as much as to say,—"Look yourself, I cannot tell you," "Behold what manner of love the Father hath bestowed upon us that we should be called the children of God." We are such by prerogative, by nature, by growing like Him, and by privilege. We are now the sons of God. Some of you do not know what this means. Children, you know, take many liberties with their father; and are very familiar. I wonder what the little children of a judge think of him if they are ever taken into court to see him with his big wig on, sitting there trying prisoners. Well, I have no doubt they feel a great awe of him; but you should see him when he is at home. Why there he is down on the hearth-rug with the children on his back; he is the father, and the father somehow swallows up the judge, and the child does not seem to recollect that he is a judge, but only that he is his father. Oh, how many times has my soul, while prostrate with awe, in the presence of my God, laid hold on Him and said, "My Father, great as Thou art, Thou art not so great as to forget that Thou art my Father. Thou hast taught me to say it, Thou hast said, 'When ye pray, say our Father,' and I do say it, and I feel that 'Abba, Father,' is the natural cry of the spirit that is within me. Wilt Thou not answer to the cry?" He does answer us, and like as a father pitieth his children He pities us. He bows His omnipotence to help us in our little labours, and bows His mighty arm to help us in our little troubles. "He telleth the number of the stars, and calleth them all by their names. He healeth the broken in heart, and bindeth up their wounds." Is not that a grand stoop from rolling the orbs and wheeling the worlds along, to stoop down to bind broken hearts, and to strap their wounds with heaven's court plaster, lest they should bleed too much Blessed be His name!

"The God that rules on high,
And thunders when He please,
That rides upon the stormy sky,
And manages the seas:

This awful God is ours,
Our Father and our love;
He shall send down His heavenly powers
To carry us above."

But we must pass on. Faith makes the grandest of distinctions; and obtains the grandest of endowments.

III. Thirdly, FAITH IS THE EVIDENCE OF THE GRANDEST EXPERIENCE, for the text speaks of "them that believe on His name which were born, not of blood, nor of the will of man, but of God"; which teaches us that every man who believes in Jesus is a regenerate man. He has been born of God. What a wonderful thing it is to be born again! There are poor blind men about who say that persons are regenerated by the application of water, though they have no faith, and grow up without any. The Lord open their eyes! We will say no more; but wherever there is this regeneration there must be faith. Read the third chapter of John. See how faith and regeneration run together. Read this very passage: "To as many as believe on His name which were born, not of blood, nor of the will of man." Faith is the first, the unique token of being born again. Now, what is it to be born again; I saw a big man once, a strong, rough fellow, and he was evidently under conviction of sin, and he said, "Would God I had never been born." He thought again, and he said, "I remember when I used to pray at my mother's knee. I knew nothing then of the wickedness and vice through which I have gone. Would God I could begin life again like a little child!" I was pleased to hear him say that, for it enabled me to say, "That is exactly what you shall do, if you believe in Jesus. You shall be born again." Only if we could be born again as we were born at first, that is, of the will of the flesh, we should do as we did before; for that which is born of the flesh, if it could be born twice of flesh, would be still flesh. That which is born of the Spirit is spirit, and "ye must be born again from above": ye must be born of the Spirit of God. What the Spirit of God does for us is to give us a new life, to start us afresh with a new nature upon a new career. Whoever believes in Jesus is born again. Regeneration is a great mystery, but you have that mystery. Do not puzzle yourself about the new birth, you have experienced it if you really believe in the Lord Jesus. As I tried to explain it just now, you are born again: you are a new creature in Christ Jesus; you have begun life again. It is of little use to attempt to mend the old nature, it is too far gone. There was a certain prince who used to swear this oath, "God mend me!" but a good man said, "I think He had better make a new one." Some men think God will mend them, but they err. I like the drunkard to become sober, and the thief to become honest, and mend himself as much as he can; but what he really wants is making over again. I have heard of a man who brought his gun to the gunsmith's to be repaired. "You want it repaired," says the smith. "Well, what it wants is a new stock, lock, and barrel." That looked very like making a new one. You had better begin *de novo*. The old law had for its token the putting away of the filth of the flesh, but the distinguishing ordinance of the new covenant goes much further. What does Christ say to His people in the act of baptism? He says, "Ye are dead. Ye must be buried, and must rise into newness of life." Baptism cannot do this, but it sets forth our need of the death of the old nature and of resurrection into new life. We must be born again, not washed, not cleansed, not mended up, but made new creatures in Christ Jesus; and every man who believes in Jesus has undergone that wondrous change. He is not born of blood, that is, not born according to the natural way of birth, he is born in a new, celestial manner. He is not born of the will of the flesh—man's bad carnal will, nor of the will of man, man's best will; for the will of man, when it has done all it can, has done nothing at all savingly. If ye were born of the will of man, it would not answer the purpose—"born not of the will of the flesh, nor of the will of man, but of God." We need renewal by a supernatural power. God alone can create, and God alone can new-create. To make a new creature is a greater wonder than to make a world, because when God made a world there was nothing to stand in His way, but when He makes a new creature there is the old creature in conflict with Him. If I may be allowed to commit so palpable an error of speech I would say it takes double omnipotence to re-create. We must be born from above, but we are saved if we have believed in the Lord Jesus. God grant that if any here have not believed, the new birth may be given them, and faith in Christ Jesus.

IV. Now lastly, lest I weary you, FAITH RAISES THE BELIEVER TO THE NOBLEST CONCEIVABLE CONDITION.

The man who has received Christ has undergone a new birth, which fits him to be a child of God. Now, note, first the inconceivable honour of being a child of God. Ah, if all the degrees, dignities, honours, and titles that ever were conferred by men could be put into a heap, they would not make enough of real honour to be seen by a microscope, compared with the glory that belongs to the humblest, poorest, and most despised son of God. Son of God! "Unto which of the angels said He at any time, thou art My son, this day have I begotten thee?" I know the text applies to Christ, but it applies also to all His people. His angels are servants, they are not sons. It is their delight to keep watch and ward about us, as servants do over young princes of thy blood. "They shall bear thee up in their hands, lest thou dash thy foot against a stone." About the child of God there is even here a splendour which is none the less bright because carnal eyes cannot see it. It is like the splendour of God—invisible because too excessive for eye to see. I will picture a child of God, if you please—a daughter of Zion. She is a poor needle-girl. She has stitched a shroud as well as a shirt, and she lies upstairs dying. You would not like to fare as she does. She dwells in a wretched little room; it is scantily furnished, the bed is hard, and she lies there in agony. She can scarcely breathe; she gasps for life. She is very poor, and those upon whom she is depending have begun to feel her a burden, and sometimes say hard words to her. This is a gloomy place, is it not? Come here. I will touch your eyes with a salve for a moment, as the prophet did the eyes of His servant. And what do you see? You see one of the members of Christ's body struggling for the last time, and about to win the victory. Listen to her. She tells you that Christ is with her. Do you see Him? There He stands in the deepest sympathy, bending over His beloved, smiling upon a soul that He has chosen from before the foundations of the world, a daughter upon whom He has put a garment without spot, meet for royal wear. A king's daughter is she. Look about the room. Angels are here, they are waiting all around her, waiting to convoy her home. The Holy Ghost Himself is within her soul. See you the light of His consolations and revelations? If your eyes are open you can see it. Yea, the Father Himself is here, for He is never away from the death-beds of His children. "Precious in the sight of the Lord is the death of His saints." She has grown worse. Her eyes are dim. Her voice is feeble. Listen to her! I am picturing no fancy scene; I have heard it. She is just about to enter into life, and she cries,

> "And when you hear my heart-strings break,
>   How sweet my minutes roll!
> A mortal paleness on my cheek,
>   But glory in my soul."

If she has strength enough left, you will hear her sing,

> "'Midst darkest shades, if He appear,
>   My dawning is begun;
> He is my soul's bright morning star,
>   And He my rising sun."

Do not talk to me of Joan of Arc! This is the true heroine. She is battling with death, and singing while she dies. Fear? She has long forgotten what that means. Doubt? It is banished. Distress? Despondency? She has left them all behind. She is a believer; she has received Jesus, and she has power to be a child of God. Oh, the honour and dignity of being born from above!

Now, note again the safety of this birth. If you are a child of God, how safe you are. I am sure there is no father and mother here that would let any harm come by their children. None of us would if we could protect them. Do you think God will suffer His children to be harmed? He will cover them with His feathers, and under His wings shall they trust. His truth shall be their shield and buckler. There shall no evil befal them; neither shall any plague come nigh their dwelling. "I, the Lord, do keep it. I will water it every moment lest any hurt it, I will keep it night and day." "I give unto my sheep eternal life, and they shall never perish, neither shall any pluck them out of my hand. My Father which gave them Me is greater than all, and none is able to pluck them out of My Father's hand."

> "Safe in the arms of Jesus."

Well may you sing that, for so you are if you are the children of God.

And, last of all, though much more might be said, what happiness this brings to a man to know that he is a child of God. I recollect, some twenty-two years ago, being waited upon by a Mormonite who wanted to convince me of the divine mission of Joseph Smith, and after hearing some of his talk, I said, "Sir, would you kindly tell me what you have to offer me, and how I am to get it, and I will listen to you, if you will let me tell you afterwards what I have to offer you, and the way to it." I heard him with a great deal of patience. He listened to me not quite so patiently, but when I had done he saluted me thus, "If what you say be true, you ought to be the happiest man in the world": to which I replied, "Sir, you are correct; I ought to be, and, more, I am!" and so I left him. And so I am, and so is every child of God that lives up to his privilege. You are a child of God, forgiven, accepted, beloved, and what more do you want? In the name of goodness, what more do you want? If a man were to become an imperial prince, would he say, "I want more"? My dear man, what can you want more? If you are a son of God, what more can you ask? I recollect the time—perhaps you recollect it for yourself—when I was in bondage under sin, and I thought I should be sent to hell, and if the Lord had said to me, "I will forgive you, but you must live on bread and water till you die," I would have clapped my hands for joy. I would have said, "Lord, do but save me. If I can get rid of my sins, the very hardest lot will be a pleasure to me." Let us never complain, since we are possessors of salvation. The joy of the Lord is your strength. "Rejoice in the Lord alway: and again I say, rejoice."

Remember this as a practical word. There is an old French proverb which says that "Nobility obliges." There is an obligation upon nobles. You do not expect to see great princes sweeping the street crossing. You would not expect to hear of Her Majesty the Queen acting like a milkmaid. Well, now, if you are a son of God, you must act like it. If I hear of a man who says, "I am a child of God," and he gives short weight, and is hard in his bargains—I am ashamed of him. He is a son of God? He who must make money, and hold it, and keep it? He a son of God? He is not very like his Father. Son of God! And yet sharp, quick-tempered, angry, spiteful! He is not very like his Father. A child of God, and do a mean thing? My dear brethren, what are you at? A son of God, and tell a lie? A son of God, and be afraid of anybody? A son of God, and not look your fellow-man in the face without a blush? A son of God, and at home a tyrant? Such conduct will never bear a thought, and he who is guilty of it gravely offends. When the great Emperor Napoleon was in his power, if a member of his family married below his rank, he was made to know the emperor's anger, for members of the imperial house were under bonds of honour to keep up their dignity. You girls here, who are daughters of God, dare you marry out of the imperial family? Never do that. Take care that you are not unequally yoked. When a king was taken prisoner, Alexander asked him how he would be treated, and he said, "Like a king." Christian, act like a king. When a quarrelsome person offends us, we should say in our heart, "I would have quarrelled with you, but I could not stoop to it; I am a child of God." I read a bitter remark of Guizot's to his enemies the other day, which ran something like this, "Come up the steps, and mount as high as you can, and when you reach the top you will be beneath my contempt." So oftentimes may the child of God think of the world, and all the shams, and all the temptations which are in it, "I have a great work, and how can I come down to you. I am a son of God, my conversation is in heaven; I cannot leave my position to come down to you." Walk as children of light. "What manner of persons ought ye to be in all holy conversation and godliness?" Ye are "a peculiar people, a royal priesthood, a chosen generation, zealous for good works." Demean not yourselves.

Go your way, and may the Spirit of your Father rest upon you. Amen and amen.

THE NOBLEMAN'S FAITH

"There was a certain nobleman, whose son was sick at Capernaum. When he heard that Jesus was come out of Judea into Galilee, he went unto Him, and besought Him that He would come down, and heal his son: for he was at the point of death. Then said Jesus unto him, Except ye see signs and wonders, ye will not believe. The nobleman saith unto Him, Sir, come down ere my child die. Jesus saith unto him, Go thy way; thy son liveth. And the man believed the word that Jesus had spoken unto him, and he went his way. And as he was now going down, his servants met him, and told him, saying, Thy son liveth. Then enquired he of them the hour when he began to amend. And they said unto him, Yesterday at the seventh hour the fever left him. So the father knew that it was at the same hour, in the which Jesus said unto him, Thy son liveth: and himself believed, and his whole house."—John iv. 46-53.

This narrative illustrates the rise and progress of faith in the soul. While I try to speak of it, I pray that we may experimentally follow the track, desiring that such faith may have a rise in our hearts, may make progress in our spirits, and may become even stronger in us than it was in this nobleman. The point, my brethren, is not to hear about these

101

things only, but to have them repeated in your own soul. We want to come to real business, and to make the things of God matters of downright fact to ourselves: not only to hear about this nobleman from Capernaum, or anybody else, but to see in our own souls the same work of grace as was wrought in them. The same living Christ is here, and His help we as greatly need as ever did this nobleman. May we seek it as he sought it, and find it as he found it! Thus will the Holy Spirit, who inspired the narrative before us, be found writing it over again, not upon the pages of a book, but upon the fleshy tablets of our hearts.

Observe then, at the commencement, that trouble first of all led this courtly personage to Jesus. Had he been without trial, he might have lived forgetful of his God and Saviour; but sorrow came to his house, and it was God's angel in disguise. It may be, dear friend, that you are in trouble this morning; and, if so, I pray that affliction may be the black horse upon which mercy shall ride to your door. It is a sad, sad thing with some men that, the better the Lord deals with them in providence, the worse return they make. On the other hand, there are hearts that turn to the Lord when He smites them. When they drift into deep waters, when they can scarcely find bread to eat, when sickness attacks their bodies, and especially when their children are smitten, then they begin to think of God, and better things. Blessed is the discipline of the great Father in such a case. It is well for the troubled if their tribulation bruises their heart to repentance, and repentance leads them to seek and find pardon.

The particular form of trial which visited this nobleman was the sickness of his child. A little son he had, whom he dearly loved, and he was down with a deadly fever. The father appears to have been a naturally kind and affectionate person. His servants evidently took a great interest in him, and in the domestic affliction which grieved him; for you observe with what eagerness they came to meet him, to tell him of the recovery of his child. The father's heart was sadly wounded because his dear boy was at the point of death. No doubt he had tried all the remedies known to the times, had sent for every physician that could be found within miles of Capernaum; and now, having heard of one Jesus of Nazareth, who at Cana had turned water into wine, and at Jerusalem had done many mighty works, he resorts to Him with eager petition and desperate hope. He might never have thought of seeking Jesus if it had not been for that dear dying boy. How often does it happen that children, though they are not angels, yet are used to do better work than angels could accomplish; for they sweetly lead their parents to God and heaven! They twine themselves about our hearts, and then, if we see them sicken, and mark their pains, our sympathetic hearts are wrung with anguish, and we cry, "O God, spare my child! Lord, have mercy upon my little one!" The first prayers that come from many hearts are, under God, fetched forth by grief for little ones most dearly loved. Is it not written, "And a little child shall lead them"? It was so with this man; he was brought to Jesus by trouble; brought to Jesus by anxiety about a child. I have it strongly upon me at this moment that I am speaking to certain persons who are not converted, but they have come hither because they are in great sorrow: possibly a dear little one is pining away, and their hearts are crying to God that, if possible, the precious life may be spared. In the house of prayer they feel somewhat comforted; but their hearts are ready to break because of the loss they so much dread. How much I pray our Lord to make this trouble a means of grace!

Trial was the occasion, the preface to the work of divine grace. We will now proceed to look upon the saving part of it, namely, the faith which was born in this nobleman's heart. We will first spy out the spark of faith; then the smouldering fire of faith—much heaped over and damped, so as to be rather smoke than fire. Then, thirdly, we will look upon the flame of faith, or faith at length showing itself decidedly; and fourthly, the conflagration of faith, when faith at last blazed up in the man, fired his whole nature, and spread to his whole house—"And himself believed, and his whole house." Again, I say, let us try to follow in fact as well as in meditation.

I. I want you carefully to mark THE SPARK OF FAITH, all the while saying—I am going to look and see if I have such a spark of faith; and if I find it, I will prize it much, and pray the Holy Spirit to breathe softly upon it, that it may rise to something more permanent and powerful.

The faith of this nobleman rested, at the first, entirely upon the report of others. He lived at Capernaum, down there by the sea; and amongst the newsmongers it was common talk that there had arisen a great prophet who was working great wonders. He himself had never seen Jesus, nor heard Him speak; but he believed the report of others; and he was right in doing so, for they were credible persons. No doubt many are in the early stages of faith: they have heard friends say that the Lord Jesus receiveth sinners; that He puts away sin; that He calms the conscience; that He changes the nature; that He hears prayer; that He sustains His people under trouble: these things they have heard from persons of good repute, whom they esteem, and therefore they believe them. Friend, are you saying to yourself, "I have no doubt it is all true; I wonder whether it ever would be true to me. I am in trouble this morning: will the Lord Jesus help me? I have a present pressure upon my spirit: will prayer to Him relieve me?" You cannot say that you know, from anything you have ever seen of Him, that Jesus would thus bless you; but you infer that He will do so from what friends have told you. Well, faith often begins in that way. Men believe the report which is brought to them by well-known persons who have experienced the power of divine love, and thus at first, like the Samaritans, they believe because of the woman's report. In future time, they will come to believe because of having heard, and seen, and tasted, and handled, for themselves: but the beginning is good. This faith which comes of a report by others is a spark of true fire. Take care of it. May God grant you grace so to pray about it, that that spark may increase into a flame!

Observe that this faith was such a little faith that it only concerned the healing of the sick child. The nobleman did not know that he needed healing in his own heart; he did not perceive his own ignorance of Jesus, and his own blindness to the Messiah; he did not perhaps know that he needed to be born again; neither did he understand that the Saviour could give him spiritual life and light. He had little knowledge of the Saviour's spiritual power, and thus his faith had a very narrow range. What he did believe was that the Lord Jesus, if He would come to his house, could prevent his child from dying of the fever. He had reached as far as that; and such faith as he had, he turned to practical use at once. Friend, you do not as yet know how great my Lord is, and what wonderful things He doeth for those who put their trust in Him; but you are saying, "Surely He could help me this morning in my present trial, and deliver me out of my present difficulty." So far, so good. Use what faith you have. Bring before the Lord the trial of the hour. Let me encourage you to do so. If you cannot come to Him for heavenly things, you may, for the present, begin with the sorrows and trials of earth: if you cannot come to Him for an eternal blessing, you may come to Him for a passing favour, and He is ready to hear you. Though your prayer should only be about worldly things, and be nothing more than a merely natural prayer, yet pray it; for "He heareth the young ravens when they cry," and I am sure they do not pray spiritual prayers. All that ravens can ask for will be for worms and flies, and yet He hears them, and feeds them; and you, a man, though you may but pray at this time for a very commonplace mercy, one of the lighter blessings, yet you may pray with confidence if you have any faith in the gracious Lord. Though that faith will be only a spark, and nothing more, I would not blow it out; nor will the Lord Jesus do so, for He hath said that a smoking flax He will not quench. If you have any desire towards Him, and any degree of faith in Him, let it live, and lead you to the dear Master's feet.

The nobleman's faith was so feeble that he limited the power of Jesus to His local presence. Hence his prayer was, "Sir, come down ere my child die." If he could but induce the Lord Jesus to enter the room where the sick child lay, he believed that He would speak to the fever, and the fever would be allayed; but he had no idea that the Lord Jesus Christ could work at the distance of twenty-five miles: he had no notion that the word of the Lord could operate apart from His presence. Still, it was better to have that limited faith than to have none at all. You, children of God, when you get limiting the Holy One of Israel, are guilty of gross sin; but if those who are seeking the Lord, through ignorance and weakness of faith, are found limiting Him, it is far more excusable in them. The Lord Jesus treats it graciously, and removes it by a gentle rebuke. It is not the same thing for a beginner to be weak of faith as for you, who have enjoyed long experience of God's goodness, to fall into mistrust of Him. Therefore I say to you, in whom the Lord is beginning to work, if you have no more faith than just to say, "The Lord Jesus could heal me if He were here: the Lord would help me, and answer my cry, if He were here"—it is better to have such a faith than to be unbelieving. Your narrow faith limits Him exceedingly, and shuts Him up in a very close place; and therefore you may not expect Him to do many mighty works for you: and yet up to the measure of your faith He will go with you and bless you. As a matter of unpromised sovereign grace, He may even do exceeding abundantly above what you ask or even think. Therefore I would treat your faith like a little babe: I would nurse it until it can stand alone, and hold out my finger to help it till its tottering steps become firm. We will not blame the babe because it cannot run or leap, but we will cherish it, and urge it to greater strength; to which strength it will come in due time. Our Lord Jesus Christ deserves the largest faith from each one of us. Grieve Him not by suspicions of His ability. Give Him what faith you have, and ask for more.

His faith in the Lord Jesus Christ, though it was only a spark, yet influenced this nobleman. It led him to take a considerable journey to find our Lord. From Capernaum he went up the hills to Cana, that he might plead with Jesus. And he went personally. This is the more remarkable because he was a man of rank and position. I do not know whether he was Chuza, Herod's steward. I should not wonder if he was, because we do not hear of any other noble family being on the side of Christ; but we do hear of the wife of Chuza, Herod's steward, as amongst those that ministered to our Lord of their substance. We hear also of Manaen, foster-brother to Herod. It may have been one of these; we do not know: but noblemen were scarce birds in the church in those days; as, indeed, they are now. We naturally expect, therefore, to hear of such a person as this again; and as we have honourable mention of those two, we are not very rash in conjecturing that this nobleman may have been one of them. Now noblemen do not, as a rule, think of taking journeys themselves while they have so many servants at their disposal; but this nobleman came himself to Christ, and personally besought Him that He would come and heal his son. If your faith is weak in some respects, and yet strong enough in others to drive you personally to Christ, personally to pray to Him, it is faith of an acceptable order. If it leads you to pray to our Lord with all your heart, beseeching Him, then your faith is of the right sort. If it leads you to beseech Christ to have mercy upon you, it is the faith which saves the soul. It may be little as a grain of mustard-seed, but its importunity shows that there is pungency in it—it is true mustard. Dear sir, are you beginning to pray at this time because of sorrow? In the silence of your soul are you crying, "O God, save me to-day! I have come up to London to see other things, and I have dropped in here this morning: oh, that this may be the day in which I shall be helped out of my trouble, and myself be saved"? If your faith brings you to prayer, it is the acknowledged child of grace; for true-born faith always cries. If your faith helps you to lay hold of Jesus with a resolute grip, saying, "I will not let Thee go, except Thou bless me," it may be little faith, but it is true faith. It is wrought in your soul by the Spirit of God, and it will bring a blessing with it. You shall be saved by this faith, to our Lord's glory, and to your own comfort.

I notice that this man's faith taught him how to pray in the right style. Notice the argument he used: he besought Him that He would come down and heal his son, for he was at the point of death. He urged no merit, but pleaded the misery of the case. He did not plead that the boy was of noble birth—that would have been very bad pleading with Jesus; nor did he urge that he was a lovely child—that would have been a sorry argument; but he pleaded that he was at the point of death. His extremity was his reason for urgency: the child was at death's door; therefore his father begs that mercy's door may open. When you, my friend, are taught by grace to pray aright, you will urge those facts which reveal your own danger and distress, and not those which would make you appear rich and righteous. Remember how David prayed. "Lord," he said, "pardon mine iniquity; for it is great." That is evangelical pleading. Most men would have said, "Lord, pardon mine iniquity, for it was excusable, and by no means reached to the heinousness of my fellow-men." David knew better. His cry is, "Pardon mine iniquity; for it is great." Plead with God, poor sinner, the greatness of your necessity, the direness of your need; say that you are at the point of death, say that the matter about which you plead is a matter of life and death: this will be an argument calculated to move the heart of infinite compassion. Any tint of goodness that your pride would tempt you to throw into the picture would spoil it; lay on the black colours thick and threefold. Plead with God for His mercy's sake, for mercy is the only attribute which you can hopefully address while you are a sinner unforgiven. You cannot ask the Lord to bless you because of any desert or merit you have, for you hav eno trace of any such thing; but you will be wise to plead your necessities. Cry, "O God, have mercy upon me, for I need mercy!" State your child's case, and say, "For he is at the point of death." This is the key which opens the door of mercy.

Do you follow me, dear hearers, you that are not yet converted? Is there, at any rate, in you some desire to come to the Lord Jesus Christ, though it be only because a temporal trouble is pressing you sorely? A horse does not want a dozen spurs to make it run. The one which now wounds your flank is sharp enough, and it is plunged in so deep that you must feel it. Yield to it, lest there should be need of whip as well as spur to make you stir. If you are the Lord's chosen, you will have to come, and the more readily you do so the better will it be for you. Come at once. Be ye not as the horse or as the mule, which have no understanding; but come to Jesus while He gently draws. Though it be with such a feeble faith that you fear it is rather unbelief than faith, yet draw nigh to Him. Come just as you are, and look up to Jesus, and pray; for in that prayer shall lie the hope, nay, the certainty of relief. The great heart of Jesus will feel your prayer, and say, "Go in peace."

II. Thus have we seen faith in the spark: we will now look at THE FIRE OF FAITH, struggling to maintain itself, and gradually increasing. Let us see how the fire smoulders, and the heap begins to smoke, and thus betrays the inner fire.

This man's faith was true as far as it went. That is a great thing to say. He stood before the Saviour resolved not to go away from Him; his only hope for his child's life was in this great Prophet of Nazareth, and therefore he did not intend to leave Him till his request was granted. He does not at first get the answer that he wants, but he perseveres, and pleads on. This showed that his faith had heart and vitality in it. It was no whim, nor sudden impulse, but a real persuasion of the power of Jesus to heal. What a mercy to be delivered from all sham faith! Better to have little faith, and that faith real, than to possess a great creed, and give the Lord Jesus no hearty credit. Tell me, my hearer, have you any real practical faith in the Lord Jesus?

His faith was true as far as it went: but it was hindered by a desire for signs and wonders. Our Lord therefore gently chided him, saying, "Except ye see signs and wonders, ye will not believe." Now I know that many of you believe that the Lord Jesus can save, but you have fixed in your mind the way in which He must do it. You have been reading certain religious biographies, and you find that such a man was driven to despair, had horrible thoughts, and so on: therefore you settle it in your minds that you must have similar horrors, or you will be lost. You lay it down as a programme that you must be saved in that way, or not at all. Is this right? Is this wise? Do you mean to dictate to the Lord?

Perhaps you have read or heard that certain eminent persons were converted through singular dreams, or by remarkable movements of providence, and you say to yourself, "Something equally singular must happen to me, or I will not believe in the Lord Jesus."

In this you err like the nobleman. He expected the Saviour to come down to the house, and perform some act peculiar to His prophetic office. In fact, this nobleman is the New Testament reproduction of Naaman in the Old Testament. You remember how Naaman said, "Behold, I thought, he would surely come out to me, and stand, and call on the Lord his God, and strike his hand over the place, and recover the leper." Naaman had planned it all in his own mind, and had no doubt arranged a very proper and artistic performance; and, therefore, when the prophet simply said, "Go and wash in Jordan seven times," he could not receive so simple and bald a gospel: it was too commonplace, too free from ritual. Many persons, by their mental prejudices, would bind down the Lord of mercy to such and such a way of saving them; but our Lord will not be thus laid under constraint; why should He? He will save whom He wills, and He will save as He wills. His gospel is not, "Suffer so much horror and despair, and live"; but, "Believe on the Lord Jesus Christ, and thou shalt be saved." He comes to many, and calls them effectually by the soft whispers of His love: they do but trust Him, and they enter into immediate rest. With little striking feeling, either horrible, or ecstatic, they quietly exercise a childlike confidence in their crucified Lord, and they find eternal life. Why should it not be so with you? Why should you keep yourself out of comfort by laying down a programme, and demanding that the free Spirit should pay attention to it? Let Him save you as He wills. Away with foolish prejudices!

Yet this is to be said of the nobleman's faith: it could endure a rebuff. Think of the Master only saying to this poor anguished father, "Except ye see signs and wonders, ye will not believe." It was sadly true, but it sounded honestly sharp. Oh, the dear lips of Jesus; they are always like lilies, dropping sweet-smelling myrrh! Myrrh, you know, is bitter to the taste, and there was a seeming bitterness about this speech to the nobleman; yet the father did not give up his suit, and turn on his heel, and say, "He treats me hardly." He said within himself, "to whom should I go?" and therefore he went not away. He was like that woman for whom the Lord's lips dropped a far more pungent morsel of myrrh, as He said, "It is not meet to take the children's bread, and to cast it to dogs." Yet she found a sweet smell in that myrrh, and perfumed her prayer with it as she said, "Truth, Lord: yet the dogs eat of the crumbs which fall from their masters' table." This man answered our Lord by still greater importunity. He would not go away; not he. Oh, dear heart, may you have such faith in Christ that, though He should rebuke you, you will not leave Him! Jesus is your only hope; therefore do not turn away from Him. Imitate Bunyan when he spake words to this effect:—"I was driven to such straits that I must of necessity go to Jesus; and if He had met me with a drawn sword in His hand, I would sooner have thrown myself upon the edge of His sword than have gone away from Him; for I knew Him to be my last hope." O soul, cling to thy Lord, come what may!

Then see how passionately this man pleaded. He cried, "Sir, come down ere my child die"; as much as if he had said, "Lord do not question me just now about my faith. O my Lord, I pray Thee do not think of me at all, but heal my dear child, or he will be dead! He was at the point of death when I left him: do hasten down and save him." Limited was that faith, for he still asks Christ to come down, and seems to think it essential that our Lord should make a journey to Capernaum to work the cure; but note how intense, how eager, how persevering was his pleading. If his faith failed in breadth, it excelled in force. Dear anxious friend, keep close to the example now before us. Pray, and pray again; hold on, and hold out; cry on, and cry out; never cease till the Lord of love grants you an answer of peace.

III. We come to a higher stage, and watch THE FLAME OF FAITH. The spark increased as a smouldering fire, and now the fire reveals itself in flame. Observe that Jesus said to the petitioner, "Go thy way; thy son liveth." And the man truly believed, and went his way.

Here note that he believed the word of Jesus over the head of all his former prejudices. He had thought only that Christ could heal if He came down to Capernaum; but now he believes, though Jesus remains where He is, and only speaks the word. Friend, wilt thou at this moment, believe the Lord Jesus Christ on His bare word? Without laying down any rules as to how He will save thee, wilt thou trust Him? Thou hast prescribed dark convictions, or vivid dreams, or strange sensations; wilt thou cease from such folly? Wilt thou believe in Jesus Christ as He is revealed in the Scriptures? Wilt thou believe that He can and will save thee now upon thy simple trust? Hast thou not heard of His passion, and death upon the cross for the guilty? Hast thou not heard it said that all manner of sin and of iniquity shall be forgiven unto men if they believe in Him? Dost thou not know that he that believeth in Him hath everlasting life? Wilt thou have done with thy nonsense about "Come down, and save me," or "Make me feel this, and I will believe Thee"? Wilt thou believe in Him now, despite all thy former thoughts, and pretensions, and desires, and just say, "I will trust my soul with Christ, believing that He can save me"? Thou shalt be saved as surely as thou dost thus trust.

The next thing this man did to prove the sincerity of his faith was that he at once obeyed Christ. Jesus said to him, "Go thy way"; that is, "Go home"–"thy son liveth." If the man had not believed the word he would have lingered there, and kept on pleading, and looking for favourable signs; but as he has believed, he is satisfied with the word of the Lord, and goes his way without another word. "Thy son liveth" is enough for him. Many of you have said, when you have heard the gospel preached, "You tell us to believe in Christ; but we will continue in prayer." That is not what the gospel commands you. Do I hear you say, "I shall continue to read my Bible, and attend the means of grace"? That is not the precept of the Saviour. Are you not satisfied with His word? Will you not take that word, and go your way? If you believe in Him, you will go your way in peace: you will believe that He has saved you, and act as if you knew it to be true. You will joy and rejoice in the fact that you are saved. You will not stop to cavil, and to question, and to follow after all kinds of religious experiences and feelings; but you will exclaim, "He tells me to believe Him, and I believe Him. He says, 'He that believeth on Me hath everlasting life'; and I do believe in Him, and therefore I have everlasting life. I may not feel any peculiar emotion, but I have eternal life. Whether I see my salvation or not, I am saved. It is written, 'Look unto Me, and be ye saved, all ye ends of the earth.' Lord, I have looked, and I am saved. My reason for believing it is that Thou hast said it. I have done as Thou hast bidden me, and Thou wilt keep Thy promise." This mode of reasoning is due to the Lord Jesus. He deserves to be taken at His word, and trusted in real earnest.

Now, the nobleman's faith has flamed up indeed. He believes not upon mere report, but upon the word of Jesus. He does not wait for a sign, but he hears the word, and on that word he hangs his confidence. Jesus said, "Thy son liveth; go thy way": and he goes his way, that he may find his son alive. O seeking soul, may God, the Holy Spirit, bring you to this state at once, that you may now say, "O Lord, I will wait no longer for any sort of feeling, or evidence, or sign, but on the word Thy blood hath sealed I will trust my everlasting all, for I do now accept Thy promise, and since I believe it, I will go my way in peace."

Still, I am bound to say concerning this man's faith at this stage, that it still fell somewhat short of what it might have been. It was a great thing for him to have come so far; but he had farther yet to go. He expected less than he might have expected, and therefore, when he saw his servants, he asked them when the dear child began to amend. He was overjoyed when they virtually said, "He never did begin to amend; the fever left him all at once; at the seventh hour he recovered." You see he expected a gradual restoration. He looked for the ordinary course of nature; but here was a miraculous work. He received far more than he reckoned on. How little we know of Christ, and how little we believe in Him even when we do trust Him. We measure His boundless treasure by our scanty purses. Yet the faith that saves is not always full-grown: there is room for us to believe more, and to expect more, of our blessed Lord. Oh, that we would do so!

But one thing I want to mention here, though I do not quite understand it; perhaps you can make it out. The father travelled with the leisure of confidence. It was about twenty-five or thirty miles to Capernaum, and I have no doubt the good man started off directly the Master said, "Go thy way." No doubt he would go at once in obedience to such a command, and make progress on the road home. But we read that the servants met him. Did they start as soon as the child was cured? If so, they might meet him half-way, or thereabouts. It was uphill: say, therefore, that they came ten miles; and that fifteen, or even twenty, remained for the nobleman to travel. The servants said, "Yesterday at the seventh hour the fever left him." The seventh hour was about one o'clock in the day, and that day was "yesterday." I know that the day closed at set of sun, yet one would hardly talk of "yesterday" without a night between. Did he take fifteen or sixteen hours for that part journey? If so, he did not travel with any excessive speed. It is true that twenty-five miles was a good day's journey for a camel, for in the East the roads are execrable; but still it does seem to me that the happy father moved with the ease of a believer rather than with the hurry of an anxious parent. A nobleman's usual progress through the villages was slow, and he did not alter the usual pace, because he would not even seem to hurry now that his mind was believingly at rest. He felt quite sure that his son was all right, and therefore the fever of anxiety left the father, even as the fever had left his child. Anxious minds, even when they believe, are in a hurry to see; but this good man was so sure that he would not allow parental love to make him act as if the shadow of a doubt remained. It is written, "He that believeth shall not make haste"; and in him it was literally fulfilled. He journeyed on in such style as a member of the royal household would be expected to travel if accompanied by a fitting retinue, and thus all saw that his mind was at ease about his son. I like this consecrated restfulness; it befits a solid faith. I want you all, when you believe in Jesus Christ, to believe right up to the hilt. Give Him not a half faith, but a whole faith; whether about a child, or about yourself, believe in earnest. Say, "Let God be true, but every man a liar.' On His bare word my soul reposes. I will 'rest in the Lord, and wait patiently for Him.' What though no amazing joys flash through my spirit? God hath said, 'He that believeth on Me hath everlasting life'; and therefore I have everlasting life. What if I do not rise up, and dance for joy? yet will I sit still, and sing within my soul, because God has visited His believing servant. I will wait until high joys shall come to me, but meanwhile I will trust, and not be afraid."

Dear hearer, are you accompanying me in all this? Are you ready in this manner to exercise a substantial, restful confidence in Jesus?

IV. So far the nobleman's faith has grown, but now we shall see it become THE CONFLAGRATION OF FAITH. As he went home, his servants met him with good news. In the quietude of his faith he was exceedingly delighted when they said, "Thy son liveth." The message came upon him like the echo of the word of Jesus. "I heard that," said he, "yesterday, at the seventh hour; for then Jesus said, 'Thy son liveth.' Another day has come, and, behold, my servants salute me with the same word, 'Thy son liveth.' " The repetition must have astonished him. I often notice about the preaching of the word, how the sentences strike you as to their very words when God blesses them. People say to me, "You said, sir, the selfsame thing that we were talking of when we were on the road: you described our cases even to our thoughts, and you mentioned certain expressions which had been used in our conversation; surely God was speaking through you." Yes, it is often so; Christ's own word finds many echoes from the mouths of His commissioned servants. The Lord's providence rules words as well as deeds, and makes men say the right words without their knowing why they say them. God is so graciously omnipresent that all things reveal Him when they are bidden to do so.

Now the nobleman's faith is confirmed by the answer to his prayers. His experience has come in to the aid of his faith. He believes in a more assured sense than he did before. He has proved the truth of the Lord's word, and therefore he knows and is persuaded that He is Lord and God. The faith of a sinner coming to Christ is one thing; the faith of a man who has come to Christ, and has obtained the blessing, is another and stronger matter. The first faith, the simpler faith, is that which saves; but the further faith is that which brings comfort, and joy, and strength into the spirit.

"My prayer is heard," said he; and then he spoke to the servants, and after enquiry his faith was sustained by each detail. He cried, "Tell me all about it: when was it?" When they replied, "At the seventh hour the fever left him," he remembered that at that very moment, when over there above the hills at Cana, the Lord Jesus Christ had said, "Go thy way; thy son liveth." The more he studied the case the more wonderful it became. The details were singularly confirmatory of his confidence, and by their means he rose to a clearer and firmer faith. Brethren, how many such confirmations some of us have had! Doubters attempt to argue with us about the simplicities of the gospel; and they want to fight with us upon their own ground of mere speculative reasoning. Dear sir, this is hardly fair to us. Our own ground is of quite another kind. We are not strangers to the business of faith, but adepts in it; and you ought to allow something for our personal experience of the faithfulness of the Lord our God. We have a thousand treasured memories of happy details which we cannot tell you. We do not call you swine, but at the same time we dare not throw our pearls before you. We have a host of things laid by; but we cannot repeat them, for to us they are too sacred; thus we are not able to use those reasons which to our own hearts are the most convincing. We have other arguments than we choose to bandy in open court. Be not surprised if we seem obstinate; you do not know how intensely sure we are. You cannot argue us out of our secret consciousness; you might as well try to argue our eyes out of their sockets. We know, and are sure; for we have seen, and heard, and tasted, and handled of the good Word of the Lord. Certain things are so intertwisted with our lives that we are anchored by them. "Coincidences," you say. Ah well! say what you please; to us they are other than to you! Our soul has cried out, time after time, "This is the finger of God." A man who has been helped out of a very severe trouble cannot forget his deliverer. Do you reply, "You were fortunate to get out of it"? O sir; this seems a very cold-blooded remark!

If you had been where I have been, and experienced what I have experienced, you would own that the Lord stretched out His hand, and saved His servant: you would have the same solemn conviction as I have that God was there, working out salvation. I know that I cannot create those convictions in you by telling you my story. If you are determined not to believe, you will not accept my testimony, but will think me a deluded person, though I am no more apt to be deluded than you are. However, whether you are inclined to believe or to disbelieve, I am in no such hesitation. I am forced to believe, for the more carefully I examine my life, the more I am convinced that God must have been at work with me and for me.

At the same moment that Christ said, "Thy son liveth," the nobleman's son did live; the same word that Jesus used to the father was used also by the servants who had been thirty miles away; and, therefore, the father felt that something more than human had crossed his path. Do you wonder at it? Besides, that dear boy, whom he found sound and well, was a potent argument. You could not argue the happy father out of a faith which had brought him such joy. The child was at the point of death till faith received the word of the Lord Jesus, and then the fever fled. The father must believe: would you have him doubt?

Strengthened in his faith by his experience, after having believed the bare word of Jesus, the good man now sees that word fulfilled, and he believes in Jesus in the fullest sense; believes for everything; for his body, and for his soul; for all that he is, and for all that he has. From that day forth he becomes a disciple of the Lord Jesus. He follows Him, not as a Healer only, nor as a Prophet only, nor as a Saviour only, but as his Lord and his God. His hope, his trust, and his confidence are fixed upon Jesus as the true Messiah.

What follows is so natural, and yet so joyous, that I pray it may be true to all of you: his family also believe. When he gets home, his wife meets him. Oh, the delight that sparkles in that woman's eyes! "The dear boy is well," she said, "he is as well as ever he was in his life. He did not need to lie in bed for weeks to recover his strength after the weakening influence of the fever; but the fever is all gone, and the boy is well. Oh, my dear husband, what a wonderful Being this must be who has heard your prayers, and at all that distance has spoken our child into health! I believe in Him, husband; I believe in Him." I am sure she would speak in that fashion. The same processes which had been working in her husband had been working in her. Now, think of the little boy. Here he comes, so happy and cheerful; and his father tells him all about his fever, and his going to see that wonderful Prophet at Cana, and how He said, "Thy son liveth." The little boy cries, "Father, I believe in Jesus. He is the Son of God." Nobody doubts the dear child's faith: he was not too young to be healed, and he is not too young to believe. He had enjoyed a special experience, more personal than even that of his father and mother. He had felt the power of Jesus; and it was no marvel that he believed. Meanwhile, the father is rejoicing to find that he will not be a solitary believer, for there are his wife and boy also confessing their faith. But we are not at the end of the matter, for the servants standing around exclaim, "Master, we cannot help believing in Jesus, also; for we watched the dear child, and saw him recover, and the power which healed him must have been divine." One and all, they emulate their master's faith in Jesus. "I sat up with the dear boy," says the old nurse; "I would not go to sleep, for I felt that if I did sleep I might find him dead when I awoke. I watched him, and just at the seventh hour I saw a delightful change come over him, and the fever left him." "Glory be to Jesus!" shouted the old woman, "I never saw or heard of such a thing; it is the finger of God." All the other servants were of the same mind. Happy household! There was a grand baptism soon after, when they all went to confess their faith in Jesus. Not only was the child cured, but the whole household was cured. The father did not know, when he went pleading about his boy, that he himself needed to be saved; the mother, also, probably thought only of her son; but now salvation has come to the whole family, and the fever of sin and unbelief is gone away with the other fever. May the Lord work such a wonder as that in all our houses! If any of you are groaning under a burden of grief, I trust you will be so relieved that, when you tell your wife of it, she will believe in Jesus too. May the dear child of your care believe in Jesus while yet a child; and may all who belong to your domestic circle also belong to the divine Lord! Grant, at this time, thy servants desire O Lord Jesus, for Thy glory's sake! Amen.

www.ingramcontent.com/pod-product-compliance
Lightning Source LLC
Chambersburg PA
CBHW030110070426
42448CB00036B/593